W9-BLK-677

FLYING CADETS OF WWII

They delivered the bullets and bombs
that ultimately spelled—Victory!

ROBERT N. MAUPIN

McGraw-Hill

New York San Francisco Washington, D.C. Auckland Bogotá
Caracas Lisbon London Madrid Mexico City Milan
Montreal New Delhi San Juan Singapore
Sydney Tokyo Toronto

Library of Congress Cataloging-in-Publication Data

Maupin, Robert N.
    Flying cadets of World War II / Robert Maupin.
       p. cm.
    Includes index.
    ISBN 0-07-134843-3
       1. World War, 1939–1945—Aerial operations, American. I. Title.
    II. Title: Flying cadets of World War Two. III. Title: Flying
    cadets of World War 2.
    D790.M388   1999
    940.54'4973—dc21   99-33029
                                                  CIP

McGraw-Hill

A Division of The McGraw·Hill Companies

1 2 3 4 5 6 7 8 9 0 DOC/DOC 9 0 9 8 7 6 5 4 3 2 1 0 9

ISBN 0-07-134843-3

*The sponsoring editor for this book was Shelley Carr, the editing supervisor
was Charles F. Spence, and the production supervisor was Pamela Pelton. It
was set in Hiroshige Book by Jana Fisher through the services of Barry E.
Brown (Broker—Editing, Design and Production)*

Printed and bound by R.R. Donnelley & Sons Company.

McGraw-Hill books are available at special quantity discounts to use as
premiums and sales promotions, or for use in corporate training programs.
For more information, please write to the Director of Special Sales,
McGraw-Hill, 11 West 19th Street, New York, NY 10011. Or contact your
local bookstore.

With honor and respect to
Wilbur and Orville Wright and
Gen. H.H. Arnold
Who had Visions of Flight

Contents

Foreword

FROM WORLD WAR I came the concepts that would one day create an organization designed to develop air power and the methods to utilize it. The road would be risky and dangerous with air accidents, loss of life, professional jealousy, and hostility from senior army brass. A lack of aviation technology and a preponderance of negative opinion worked against the use of public funds for its development. It was a task befitting *Don Quixote* who struggled mightily against his windmills, determined that right should prevail. Supporting the effort to develop air power was the human determination to conquer gravity. With it, as with so many great inventions, the participants were willing to sacrifice their lives. It took courage and patience.

This is a story of how early air power believers fought the battle to defy the laws of gravity in heavier-than-air machines. By their diligence and patience they overcame the dictates of a strict, entrenched military hierarchy supported politically at the nation's highest level of government. Out of those efforts evolved the method to expand into what eventually would become the United States Air Force. Vital among these efforts was the recruitment and training of Flying Cadets. Because of the inhibited growth of personnel during the years leading up to December 7, 1941 when the United States was plunged into World War II, the need for experienced officers in the squadrons, groups, and support organizations was imperative. The solution fell squarely on those Flying Cadets who graduated from Randolph Field and Kelly Field during the 1930s. The total number for the 23 classes, according to class rosters, reached a maximum of 1700 cadets to be graduated from the Training Center. Before the start of WWII, most held the rank of Lieutenant. Only a few had advanced to Captains. Some pilots had already been lost to air accidents. Those remaining would have to jump-start the expansion.

Each new squadron required a commander, operations, engineer, and supply officers. Likewise, new groups required a commander and staff. In addition to the Flying Cadets, a small number of West Pointers, who had taken flight training, were available to shoulder the growing demands. In 1939, total pilot strength stood at 3000[1], of which 1700[2] were former Flying Cadets from classes of 1931 through 1939, minus 98 from accidental deaths and transfers. A dramatic change in training methods during 1940 eventually provided more military pilots, but it would take time, training, and experience before they could become competent command and staff officers. By the end of 1940, pilot and airmen strength reached 51,165. It grew to 2,372,292 by the end of 1944[3].

On the eve of WWII, when the security of free people was threatened, former Flying Cadets were on duty. Whether in Europe, Pearl Harbor, Alaska, the South Pacific, or the Philippines, when the enemy threw down the gauntlet of war, it was picked up and returned a hundredfold. Bombers attacked the heartland of the enemy and fighters destroyed their adversaries until air superiority was established and the attackers vanquished—*they were the very best, the cream of America's youth.*

Lt. Gen. James V. Edmundson USAF-Ret.

Author's note: Jim Edmundson, Flying Cadet class of 1938A, saw the end of WWII from the pilot's seat on a B-29. His boss was General Curtis LeMay. Jim continued his career under LeMay, flying B-36s during the "Cold War." The B-36 had been designed to fly nonstop a long way, and the Russians knew that. Jim's assigned targets—if necessary—would be in Asiatic Russia. To get there the route would be to fly across Alaska, near the North Pole, approach Siberia from across the ice cap, and destroy these targets. Refueling locations for return were assigned. Following the end of the "Cold War," Jim wrote: *I watched the Soviet Union peeled, layer by layer, like a big onion. First, it failed in Africa, then Ethiopia, Mozambique, Angola, Panama, Nicaragua and Granada. Only impoverished North Korea and Cuba remained as relics of the Soviet dreams of a worldwide empire.*

[1] Pg. 136, *The United States Air Force, a Turbulent History*
[2] Graduating Class Rosters
[3] Appendix A Herbert Molloy Mason, Jr.

Preface

THE SHAPING AND destination of human lives may be dramatically altered by events over which they exercise no control. One such event took place in the United States between the years of 1930 and 1941. It was styled as the Great Depression. Unfortunately, politicians of the day failed to establish safety regulations for investments and the country went broke. Subsequent government social experimenting during that period provided little improvement. The condition was solved December 7, 1941 when the Japanese attacked Pearl Harbor and the United States became a participant in a worldwide war. The government offered war bonds for sale to raise the money for arms. A generous and patriotic public responded with its hoarded nickels, dimes, and quarters and the country went back to work—building airplanes and tanks.

During the depression years, a group of 1700 men altered the direction of their lives to become a part of Uncle Sam's Air Corps. They weren't gamblers or high rollers, just normal, college-trained lads who found the prospects of military flying to be exciting, tough, and risky—their cup of tea. In response to air corps offers, the first group arrived in 1931, and attached themselves to the umbilical cord of learning and flying at the training center, Randolph Field and Kelly Field. Subsequently, three classes per year were selected and assigned until 1939. Upon successful completion of their training under strict supervision, each received the coveted silver wings, signifying military pilot, and a commission as Second Lieutenant. They were specialists, trained to fly, shoot, and destroy in defense of their country. There was a fundamental difference in their outlook and that of most other men: they flew military planes for their country during peace or war! They were volunteers!

Thus was created the method of producing military pilots, a virtual part of the planning for development of the Air Corps envisioned by the early military aviation pioneers. It was not easy. In excess of 4000 applied through the years. More than half were rejected. The reasons were many. Qualifying to be a Flying Cadet was difficult. Physically, there was no set pattern to their makeup. Some were tall and lanky, others short and stocky, of medium build. They were the normal American types. However, there were unusual things they could do, like see airplanes miles away, hear a pin drop in the next room, react to harm as quickly as a cobra strikes, and run their minds like computers. They had stout hearts, good circulation, and strong lungs and could race a deer over a measured mile. That they were gifted men would be an understatement. Enemy pilots, unfortunate enough to face them, would belatedly agree.

With great attention to detail, Robert N. Maupin spotlights the historic early battles to build the air corps, leading to development of the Flight Training Center and its volunteer Flying Cadets. The early great men of the Air Corps, following World War One, have been named *Legends* by him in appreciation of their effort to create air power. They were accomplishing two goals: the development of aviation and the military air mission to protect the United States. These two were of equal importance, as war would prove.

Through the early years these Legends held one important goal: train military pilots. As a father looks upon his son for relief from burdens one day, the Legends looked to the Flying Cadets for their combat readiness in defense of the United States. These Legends passed the torch to the younger generation military pilots on 7 December, 1941. The volunteer Flying Cadets, mostly Lieutenants, accepted their challenge, starting the process of building squadrons, groups, and wings. Even as the Legends had struggled with the pressures of top army staff to dominate in policy and structure during peacetime, this struggle manifested itself once more on the battlefield of North Africa. Gen. George Marshall, then Chief of Army GHQ, determined that air superiority belonged to the air command. Air support of army troops on the battlefield would be a negated matter between air and ground commanders. It freed the control of air power, permitting the young squadron and group commanders to engage the enemy air forces as their primary mission. It was a victory of sorts for the air force units in battle.

To add participation in the work, Maupin invited the former Flying Cadets to provide personal military experiences. These accounts are in the *Reflections* section. The volunteer Flying Cadets of the 23 classes during the 1930s met the enemies of their country and destroyed them. They forfeited the young years of their lives in preparation for battle and then went beyond that to duty in service to their nation. They served with distinction and honor. Are they heroes? If they served as volunteers, accomplished missions for their country in war, and were prepared to die in the effort—the answer would be yes.

Ray Toliver

Acknowledgments

The purest contribution to history comes from those who made that history. Although history as recorded by others is essential for research and must be a reference for support or data or happenings, the heart of this historical research is in the *Personal Reflections* section. The historical contributions to development of the United States Air Force by Generals William "Billy" Mitchell; Henry H. "Hap" Arnold; Benjamin "Benny" Foulois; Frank M. "Andy" Andrews; Carl L. "Tooey" Spaatz; and Ira C. Eaker are well known. They are the *Legends* of this work. For the following who have made written contributions about their war and peace experiences—all former Flying Cadets—with gratitude and respect, thanks to each of you.

Gen. Horace Wade; Col. Marvin Zipp; Maj. Gen. Marvin Demler; Brig. Gen. Dorr Newton, Jr; Maj. Gen. Winston Close; Col. Jack Randolph; Lt. Gen. Joe Moore; Col. Don Dunlap; Col. Robert Emmens; Maj. Gen. David "Davy" Jones; Col. Vic Anderson; Col. Wayne Thurman; Col. Joe Schneider; Maj. Gen. H. "Dude" Hanes; Col. Ancil Baker; Brig. Gen. Paul Tibbets, from his book: *The Tibbets Story*; Maj. Gen. George "Benji" Greene, Jr; Lt. Gen. James Edmundson; Col. John Weltman; Col. John Kane; Lt. Col. Jesse Tobler; Brig. Gen. William Yancey; Col. William Feallock; Col. Kenneth Martin with special thanks for use of *Target Luftwaffe* by Bill Ong; Lt. Gen. Marvin McNickle; Col. William Stewart; Maj. Gen. Walter Putnam; Col. Ray Toliver; Maj. Gen. Charles "Chuck" Sweeney, all USAF Retired. Capt. Paul Wooley, Sr. Airline Chief Pilot-ret; Olin K. Haley, Chief Aeronautic Inspector, CAA; Capt. Peter Wiltjer, UAL-Ret; Capt. John Templeton, AAL-ret.

A special thanks to Mrs. Annie Laurie Culbertson (wife of Brig. Gen. Allman T. Culbertson, USAF Ret-dec., who dug into her trunk and located information about "Cubby "during and after Flying Cadet days. Thanks to others too numerous to mention, who provided class photos, rosters, and helpful information for this project. Credits for pictures are mentioned with the photo. Others not listed are from USAF and Air Force Association files.

A special thanks to Col. Ray Toliver for his ever-ready assistance in proofing and editing, technical assistance, and use of his personal library of USAF material, planes, and photos.

Thanks and credit to The Air Force Association for permission to reprint article by Lt. Gen. James Edmundson, USAF Ret. Reference material: American Heritage (World War II Chronicles); Forbes, Inc. C 1995; *A Few Great Captains*, DeWitt S. Copp, the USAF Historical Foundation; and the USAF Air Education and Training Command, Randolph Field.

Appreciation to PARADE Publications for permission to reprint "I want Americans to Know The Facts" by Maj. Gen. Chuck Sweeney, USAF Ret. and to the author—*former Secretary of Navy*—James Webb, Jr.

Editor's Note: This book recounts events of a past era and reveals the personal experiences of some individuals that participated in those events. These are persons whose actions were responsible for the deaths and injuries of then-enemies of the United States. They carried that burden then and now. Many also sustained physical injuries, suffered in prisoner of war camps, and saw their closest friends die. Where possible throughout the book the text has been made bias-free. However, to more accurately portray the times, in some instances the vernacular of the period is retained.

Introduction

ORVILLE AND WILBUR WRIGHT—determined that humans should fly—successfully flew a heavier-than-air machine in 1903 off the windblown sands of Kitty Hawk, North Carolina. It was not just a hit or miss accomplishment. The brothers had designed a small wind tunnel for measuring and testing airfoils to determine wing camber and the required aspect ratio. In the final analysis, they applied what was needed for flight by persons: persistence, imagination, and careful experimentation. Thus, they were able to provide flight controls over the three axis of flight: pitch, roll, and yaw. Lift, drag, and wing area could be computed to provide the necessary engine power, eliminating any need for guesswork. This put them well ahead of others who were attempting to emulate their efforts.

From the day the Wrights made their first flight, humanity's vision of flying became the dominant desire in the hearts and minds of many Americans. As interest grew with the military enthusiasts, it was also growing in the thoughts of men conscious of the dramatic effect for air transportation. The romantic idea of flying captured the excitement and interest of all America, indeed the world. The Wrights realized their primitive engine-powered glider must be refined with power to launch it from takeoff to flight, control it during flight, and bring it safely to a landing. Indeed, that would signal the beginning of an industry that would change the world's concepts of transportation.

By 1907, through intense efforts, the Wrights had built the first heavier-than-air machine for sale. It represented long years of work marked by many disappointing setbacks before finally achieving their goal. Persons of lesser determination would have given up. Eventually, by correcting each failure, they successfully flew the Flyer and offered it for sale to the United States Army.

The reluctant military

This led to a meeting of army personnel with Orville and Wilbur, and on December 23, 1907, Specification No. 486 was issued for purchase of a "Heavier-than-Air" Flying Machine. Shortly, thereafter, on February 10, 1908, the Signal Corps, then in charge of army flying, and the Wrights signed the contract. Upon completion, according to the contract, it was offered to the army. By that time the populace, unaware of the improvements made by the Wrights, had lost some of its enthusiasm for flying. While flying appeared to be glamorous and exciting, the dangers of falling out of the sky negated interest in spending public money on such a contraption. With money not forthcoming from the army, the Wrights could sell their plane elsewhere. Sensing the possibility of losing this first airplane, President Roosevelt—later to become the first President to fly— stepped in and issued the funds from his personal presidential account. In this manner, the army acquired its first airplane.

Orville Wright discusses his invention with two MP guards wearing white leggings. This is a later model of the Wright airplane, about five years after the first flight at Kitty Hawk.

Soon, thereafter, in October 1909, Lts. Frederick Humphreys and Frank P. Lahm became the army's first pilots. It was a risky business and death or injury could be but moments away when flight activity was in progress. Knowledge of aeronautics and problems facing aircraft in flight were virtually unknown. For example, it would take years to learn why the deadly spin occurred, causing airplanes to crash. Until then, many hapless military pilots perished. Only time, effort and much danger would eventually prove the military airplane as a reliable weapon of war.

Flying in space once reserved for birds, free of earthly confinement, found persons of daring and vision rushing to join in this magnificent adventure. This rapid growth extracted a cost in crashed airplanes and dead pilots. Between 1909, when the army's brave and daring volunteered to fly, and the end of 1913, twenty-four applicants qualified for flight training. Eleven were killed during training and seven others were subsequently killed in crashes. Still, they persisted, reinforced by mechanical improvements as well as more knowledge about the art of flying. Much had to be learned about the theory of fight: why stalling a plane related to its speed; improved control during flight; and more efficient engines and propellers.

Air power enters the war

By 1917, several companies were building airplanes and improvement was evident. Abroad, the British, French, and Germans were creating combat aircraft for war operations. The United States entered the war in 1917 and promised to furnish combat aircraft and pilots. Although many attempts were made to build combat aircraft and engines by American companies, none succeeded. The only military airplane built was the DH-4, a British designed two-place biplane. The planes arrived in August 1917. One, powered with an untested Liberty engine, was shipped to France during the following winter. It never arrived. A German U-boat sank the ship on which it was being transported. More were shipped, but pilots avoided flying them because the plane was very poor in maneuvering and the engine was not reliable. The American effort to produce military aircraft was severely criticized after the war, but this failed to take into account that those responsible were struggling with inexperience to create a new industry quickly in the midst of a war.

Probably the greatest gain came from production efforts that went into better planes for the military after the war. A few types were the Martin GMB, a twin-engine bomber, the Packard-Lepere observation plane, which was considered superior to the DH-4, and the Thomas-Morse MB-3, which became a standard fighter plane. These were all superior planes of the day resulting directly from wartime efforts. Flying Cadets were first introduced at the French base at Issoudon. Initially, 100 cadets were sent to France each month. This number grew to 1060 by January 1, 1918. The first cadets found themselves in the middle of an immense mud field, living in the worst of primitive conditions. They were given shovels instead of airplanes. The French lacked the capability to provide shelter or aircraft for training, and conditions were deplorable. Eventually, the program got underway, training a total of 10,000 pilots, none of which reached combat before Armistice.

Many American pilots volunteered to fly with the British and French air units. For instance, highly-decorated Eddie Rickenbacher managed training from French pilots and flew the French Spad XIII fighter in combat. He had 26 victories and was awarded the *Medal of Honor*.

Military officers assigned included Billy Mitchell, Carl "Tooey" Spaatz, "Monk" Hunter, Benny Foulois, and George Kenney. All became involved in operations and training. Mitchell, Spaatz, Hunter, and Kenney returned as decorated combat pilots. World War I combat pilots were fortunate to survive since they received limited combat training in French and British planes. "Hap" Arnold, destined to become Commanding General of the largest air force ever known, arrived for duty but was hospitalized by the flu, and the war ended before he saw action.

Emergence of the fighter airplane, offensive and defensive fighter doctrine, plus the trained fighter pilot all trace their roots to World War I. Development of fighter aircraft became an engineering and design function. Fighter doctrine would develop in tactical research schools with the training of pilots accomplished under select instructors and the very best training facilities. Although use of aircraft for bombing was limited, little doubt was left concerning its future use in strategic warfare.

The bold speak out and are punished

Immediately following the return of air personnel and units from the aerial war fields of France, it became obvious that the Army GHQ considered air officers a liability. Those holding senior rank and positions were reduced in prestige to assignments as mail orderly and clerical functions. Air personnel experienced great difficulty relating the changes essential to development of air power. Higher authorities within the military establishment of the War Department weren't interested. Army officials sensed that a rise in air priorities would act to decrease their own importance and advancement, positions they had enjoyed prior to the war. It was a consensus that aviation would be confined to army's needs and army control. In

Henry H. "Hap" Arnold learned to fly at the Wright's flying school. Arnold, together with the Wrights, represented the beginnings of aviation throughout the world. In later years, he would meet the outspoken champion of military air power, Billy Mitchell. Together they would forge the beginnings of the United States Air Force. On December 7, 1941, when the Japanese attacked Pearl Harbor, the need for air power became painfully clear.

addition, a conflict with the navy loomed over defense policy. Navy admirals wanted to keep control of the seas and the air over the seas.

Cost of the war placed a damper on defense funds during the early 1920s. Consequently, squabbles by the army and navy over available funds were vicious. The navy was determined to keep the battleship as the protector against sea invasion, and the army was determined that the infantry and artillery would protect the land. The fledgling Air Service, subservient within the military hierarchy, had to fight tooth and toenail just to remain alive.

Supporters of air power, like Billy Mitchell, "Hap" Arnold, Frank Andrews, "Tooey" Spaatz, Benny Foulois, and Ira Eaker, were determined that air power would take its rightful place in America's defense. These men were military pilots who had learned to fly when little was known about the theory of flight or the science of aeronautics. They flew crude products of a new industry not yet proficient in building either the airplane or its engine. Yet, enthusiasm was so great by all of the pioneer pilots that difficult flights were made ordinary with new records for speed, altitude, and even aerial refueling accomplished in rapid order. Their relentless energy to develop airplanes that could create air power for war, and keep the public abreast of their success, never abated. They were challenged each step of the way. Blocking funds, preventing promotion to higher rank for qualified officers, holding up vital orders, and spreading misinformation were routine.

During the early 1920s, the Army GHQ ruled with an iron glove, having short shrift for air power advocates wearing the army uniform. The army considered the use of the airplane merely an extension to field artillery and battlefield intelligence. It determined to control air activity through development of the IX Corps Area system. Geographically located throughout the United States, these army commanders were given authority over the air bases in matters of supply and certain training exercises. Corps Area commanders held General rank, which made it difficult for junior-ranked air officers to disagree when conflicts in training arose. Many times plans made by air officers for intensive training, requiring participation from other bases, had to be scrapped for some unknown army plan. Training plans submitted for approval were often left unattended because the army required corps area commanders to participate in other matters.

Distrust and disgust of air power resulted in tragedies. Capt. Robert Olds, air officer, documented one example during the court-martial trial of Billy Mitchell, an outspoken advocate of air power. Olds testified: "My CO in Hawaii had been Maj. Sheldon Wheeler. Because his squadron had numerous forced landings in the DH-4 airplane, the non-flying commanding General issued an order that pilots would be required to pay for damages resulting from forced landings away from home. The next day Major Wheeler took off and the engine quit. Instead of landing straight ahead, he attempted to make a 180-degree turn at low altitude and land on the home field. He lost control and the plane spun in killing him. Without that order, Major Wheeler would be alive today."

Interference by army brass also occurred in the recognition for heroism and risk of life. As an example, "Hap" Arnold led a flight of bombers to Alaska during the early 1930s. It was a mission to establish a United States military presence in that far-north country, and to demonstrate the strategic ability to fly great distances outside the contiguous boundary of the U.S. It was a dangerous undertaking with few places for landing and almost a total lack of weather reporting. The mountainous nature of the terrain and the lack of any organized search assistance if one of the bombers was forced down added to difficulties. The mission accomplished its purpose and also provided the first aerial mapping of the territory. The successfully completed mission for the world to witness added great prestige to our country. Despite these achievements, the army denied a proper and well-earned recognition for the airmen, the recommendation for award of the *Distinguished Flying Cross*.

Later, during WWII, Capt. Wayne Thornbrough, Air Corps, and a graduate Flying Cadet of the class of February 1939, took off from Cold Bay near Dutch Harbor in a B-26 to drop a torpedo on the attacking Japanese Carrier Task Force. He located the ship in poor weather conditions and dropped the torpedo amidships, only to see it malfunction and drop into the sea. He wheeled the big bomber around and gave full throttle back for another torpedo. By now the weather had become marginal, but he determinedly took off to destroy the carrier. Unable to locate it in a thickening fog, he set course back to the base. However, the weather forced him to climb to a higher altitude. Unable to land, he eventually ran out of fuel and crashed into the sea. Parts of the bomber washed up on the beach a few days later. Captain Thornbrough met all the requirements for the *Medal of Honor*, having given his life in pursuit of the enemy. The Army GHQ in Alaska denied it.

Between public apathy toward the military and a chronic shortage of funds, a realistic count in 1926 revealed only 913 air officers, 8725 enlisted personnel and 142 Flying Cadets on duty. It resulted in public indignation that reached the floor of Congress. One action taken was to create an Assistant Secretary for Air, and the appointment of F. Trubee Davison to that position. His prudent and personal political contacts assured the passage of the Air Corps Act of 1926 by Congress. It provided for a new Air Corps with a five-year expansion program to reach strength of 1518 officers, 106,000 enlisted airmen, 500 Flying Cadets, and 1800 first-line aircraft. Shortly thereafter the Air Corps Training Center was established near San Antonio. It included the primary and basic flight programs at a new Randolph Field, plus a school of aviation medicine. Advanced flight training continued at Kelly Field.

Acquisition of the necessary land for Randolph Field was difficult. Farmers owned the 2300 acres finally approved. Money to purchase was raised by the Chamber of Commerce and a corporation named the San Antonio Airport Company. The city approved a tax plan. Abstracts for the land were given to the Adjutant General of the army and work commenced. It was destined to become the finest military training base in the world. San Antonio's all around good weather and relatively flat land made it ideal as a prime location for flight training. At the dedication ceremonies, Texas Governor Moody made a profound and prognostic comment: *It occurs to me that the future of our whole country may depend on a well-trained Air Corps. All that we are to become may well depend on the men who are trained at this field.* Within a relatively short time, his comment would become a visionary's statement of truth.

In 1934, a political plan developed around the airmail contracts awarded to certain airlines. Those not awarded contracts accused the winners of using political favor. This was adroitly brought to the attention of the new President (Franklin Roosevelt) who agreed to look into the matter. It was really a plan to deprive certain airline companies of their just contracts. Before anything could be done, some arrangement would have to be made to deliver the airmail. Through a bit of chicanery, the Air Corps Chief was trapped into making a statement that he and others would regret. General Foulois answered an off-hand question from an assistant in the post office department: Could the Air Corps carry airmail? Being proud of his service, and believing it to be a hypothetical question, he replied in the affirmative. Of course he was thinking in terms of having equipment and organization similar to the airlines that could fly during bad weather and at night. However, the President accepted his offer and canceled the airmail contracts. Foulois was bewildered. His comment concerning flying the mail had been only conjecture, and he hadn't discussed it with the Army GHQ Chief, Gen. Douglas MacArthur. When he did get around to that obvious problem, MacArthur told him he was on his own.

In one way if MacArthur's remark was complimentary; the Air Corps, for the first time, would be totally free from army interference. However, the Air Corps had no airplanes equipped for cargo, winter weather, or night flying. Even its best pilots were not seasoned for night flying in the fiercely-cold, open-cockpit airplanes. Unfortunately, General Foulois had taken on the task during the worse winter weather of icy snowstorms, gusting winds, and airports covered with snow and ice. Nevertheless, when the pilots and men heard about the mission, they responded with determination. Some would lose their lives in storms that suddenly engulfed them or froze their engines at night causing a loss of control and crash. When these accidents occurred, the press condemned the Air Corps. No one condemned the airlines for refusal to assist the Air Corps. When funds promised by General MacArthur didn't materialize, the pilots borrowed money and chipped in for their enlisted airmen to eat and have someplace to sleep. The Air Corps moved the mail.

As winter weather abated, flights were more on time and more mail was delivered. In the end, the airmail was moved with no help from the army. It was no surprise that the airlines failed to help. Congress and the President were aware of the money problems enlisted personnel encounter when away from their base, but they made no effort to help. General Foulois received unjust criticism; he was not trained or skilled to move airmail.

Courage of their convictions

As the Great Depression years passed and the Air Corps slowly grew, the believers who supported Billy Mitchell's air power theories displayed great courage to garner public recognition of the Air Corps and its purpose. Prior to the massive order of military aircraft in 1939, Maj. Gen. Frank M. Andrews, in command of the GHQ Air Force, appeared before the National Aeronautic Association Convention and stated: *The United States is a fifth- or sixth-rate power. The air force must be built up around the long-range bomber. That means equipping our air force with enough airplanes of sufficient range and bomb-carrying capacity to enable them, from available bases, to reach any locality where an enemy might attempt to establish air bases, either land or water.*

This position was not favored by the Army GHQ or President Roosevelt. Neither approved of the statement. On February 16, 1939, this most qualified military pilot and General officer of the GHQ Air Force was ignominiously reduced to Colonel and transferred to the VIII Corps Area in San Antonio. He was to serve as air officer to army commanders, the same indignity accorded earlier to General Mitchell for publicly speaking the truth. This castigation of a senior air officer was indicative of the abusive and malignant treatment of air supporters by the high army command at that time. Fortunately, the new Army GHQ Chief, Gen. George Marshall, would act to quickly correct the injustice. That such punitive action would be taken against a highly qualified air officer barely 23 months before the Japanese Navy attacked Pearl Harbor is indicative of the closed-mind attitude at the highest military level in government of that day. Fortunately, because of the direct insistence by General Andrews—over army heads— more strategic B-17 bombers were on order.

23 Classes of heroes

Despite the restraints from political and army leaders, groups of men volunteered to fly and fight for their country. A hero is defined by the action taken when comrades are in the line of fire. No person is a hero by plan, but only when faced with the impromptu of saving another placed in harm's way, or in the act of supreme sacrifice for his country. All Flying Cadets of this group volunteered to undergo training to become military pilots. As such, the purpose of a military pilot in wartime is to eliminate the enemy with bullets, bombs, and missiles. In peacetime, the pilot practices to do it. Doing so might subject the person to harm at anytime while flying in the machine. Malfunctions or mechanical failures are to be expected in high performance aircraft. Some might be corrected in time—some might not. It was a privilege to train, live, and fly with many of these men whose accomplishment in wartime became legendary.

From 1931 through 1939, a total of 23 classes of Flying Cadets entered training at Randolph Field. They passed strict entrance qualifications: single men of good repute, college level education, and excellent health. Pay was $75 per month, including uniforms and mess. They would find military life austere and demanding. The maintenance of honor and morals is essential in the operation of military aircraft. A pilot's word must be truthful and reliable. Failure to report a malfunction in an airplane can result in injury or death. Creating doubt in the minds of peers can cause havoc in any military unit. It is a pathway of demanding consequences. Failure to abide by the rules through neglect, a careless act, or mistake unreported, cannot be tolerated. In addition, the chain of command must be followed. Failure to do so, whether flying or handling the myriad of ground duties, destroys the cohesion and adherence essential to unit performance.

More than 4000 applicants brought their dreams of becoming military pilots to San Antonio, but only 1700 Flying Cadets graduated from Randolph Field and Kelly Field. Graduation culminated their training and they received the silver wings of military pilots, and appointments in the Army Air Corps Reserves, as Second Lieutenants. The first year of active duty was the most dangerous for new pilots. Combat aircraft were much more of a challenge than trainers. Regardless of the steps taken by squadron commanders to urge new pilots to restrain themselves, show-off new pilots treating the family or girl friend to a roll at low altitude over the hometown was not to be denied. These men did not deliberately violate the rules, they bent them a little out of pride to demonstrate skill, and they miscalculated. But it cost the air force a highly-skilled member of a trained unit. Over the years, such losses added up, leaving vacancies at roll call on December 7, 1941.

During those years from 1931 through 1939, the economic depression cut deeply into the military funds for training regular air units. The ideal arrangement for the air corps was to train a potential military pilot, then send him to active duty for at least one year to receive valuable training in a flying unit. That was the very minimum to expect in creating a combat pilot. The economy did not concern itself with such problems and funds were allocated carefully for basic training needs only. Thus, many pilots were unable to serve on active duty or continue flying. Fortunately, the airlines were just being organized and needed pilots. The two needs— job and pilot—were thusly mated. This worked well for the military and the airlines. When war was declared, those military-trained pilots flew essential military cargo to war zones throughout the world. Thus, dividends were received for the military expense of training those pilots and the airlines harvested the benefits during their early development.

The legacy of the Flying Cadets rests in their imprint on military air power. These men in the prime of life volunteered to serve their country. They did so to train themselves in the art of military flying and to support the air corps during a difficult time of its formation. It certainly wasn't the pay of $75 per month as a Flying Cadet, or the $125 as Second Lieutenant that intrigued them. Many become outstanding fighter, bomber, or specialty pilots, rising through the ranks to become ranking officers in high command positions. The road was dangerous and treacherous as other countries—Germany, Japan, and Italy—were training their pilots in actual combat over Spain and China. Also, those nations were developing combat aircraft years before the United States became involved. In face of this air superiority and the knowledge that one day there would be a reckoning, determined Flying Cadets worked diligently to learn skills and improve abilities in preparation for that day. First, they did combat with what they had: A-20 light bombers, P-39s, P-40s, borrowed Spitfires and Hurricanes, and a precious few B-17s. Then came the P-47s, B-25s, B-24s and B-26 with a newer model of the B-17, and the daddy of them all—the B-29s. Finally in 1943, Ken Martin took his 354th Fighter Group to England and the P-51 Mustangs had arrived. As production grew with more pilots and planes arriving daily, the enemy was soon backed to the wall. Finally, air superiority was claimed and the battle was over in Europe when the enemy, from sheer exhaustion, realized it was out-gunned, out-matched, and tired.

The Pacific theater was different. Jimmy Edmundson with his group of B-29s was running daily trips to Japan from the small island of Tinian. Still, these offensive moves were a far advance from his introduction to hostilities.

Finally, the long and arduous quest for air power had ended. The early pioneers' visions that air power was the urgent need for the nation's defense finally came true when, in 1947, Congress approved complete autonomy for the United States Air Force, marred only by the continued objection of the Army GHQ.

Book One

1

The Legends of Air Power

THE 23 CLASSES of cadets that trained in frail airplanes at Kelly Field in Texas during the depression days of the 1930s were not aware of their significant place in history. Most were there because it was a job, and jobs outside the military were scarce. Their role in World War II and the aviation legacy that the victory of the Allies left for future generations were far from their minds as they strove to meet the challenges of flight. Some might have envisioned the future importance of air power but few could foresee their own places in the shaping of it and world events. They struggled not only to master the art of flying but also to overcome constraints of a civilian government and a military blind to the value of the aircraft. They became part of the legends of air power.

These civilian volunteers were the first wave of airmen who flew in the breach while their country caught up and assembled what became the strongest air power the world had ever seen. Some became famous; some remain identified only as records in military files. They were the bridge between the few in the past who recognized and risked careers for their beliefs in air power and those in more recent years who have benefited from the building of air power to capture the wonders of the skies and beyond. Early events shaped their circumstances just as their actions influenced what has come after.

Fortunately for the cadets—and for the United States—there were a few persons who had stood tall in the defense of air power against an indifferent civilian government and often the wrath of their superior officers. They became the first in the legends of air power. It was the determination of these early legends that molded the major advances in military aviation, starting with the reluctance of the military to accept flight.

Legends are often elders whose deeds and times are remembered and handed down through stories and tales. There is greatness attached to legends; some true, some from memories of those who were around when they lived. There is a reverence attached to the thoughts of these people that, while not god-like, is treated with dignity and pride. The legends of early military aviation were men of vision and passion, vitally concerned for their country's well-being in a future when air power would dominate and rule the skies and beyond.

To name all the legends in military aviation is not possible. Some are identified here. There are many more. Some were quiet persons who worked in the shadows, devoted to mastering the job at hand and happy to apply all their resources to that task. Some were enlisted and others were civilians, but they were all of one mind: create an air force that surpassed all others.

From the first flights by Orville and Wilbur Wright, through the years that they flew their invention of a heavier-than-air machine, all flights were considered to be test flights. After the Wright Flyer was delivered to the army, a training school was established with Wilbur Wright as its instructor. Unfortunately, the Flyer, being a first in almost everything, had several features not conducive to safe flight. Probably, the worst was the location of the engine directly behind the pilots. Whenever a crash occurred, the engine broke loose and ended up on the backs of the unfortunate occupants. Although the Wrights made drastic changes in the Flyer and reconfigured an entirely new plane, they were unable to meet the advent of newer designs. The JN-2, followed by the JN-3 and 4, and the Curtiss R-2s were used to assist Gen. John Pershing during the Mexican action against Pancho Villa. These aircraft had little success. The airplanes were either unable to attain sufficient altitude to visually see the area to report activity, or were out of service for lack of parts. The attempted use of aircraft had the effect, however, of letting the Congress and public know how poorly the military aviation section was equipped. It also demonstrated the dangers that pilots were subjected to.

The lives and careers of the legends intertwined throughout the years of struggle for strong air power. They were often parts of the same programs and participants in the same events, but from different approaches. Instead of lumping all into a chronological recount of the times, a better understanding can be achieved by looking at the happenings from the perspective of each individual Legend of air power.

Gen. Benjamin D. Foulois

Benjamin D. Foulois

One of the first early legends of air power was Lt. Benjamin Dalahauf Foulois, who had received his commission while serving under Captain Pershing in the Philipines. When Foulois returned to the States, he was assigned to the Signal Corps and ended up in the aviation section. The army contract to purchase an airplane from the Wrights included a clause that two army officers would be taught to be pilots. Lieutenant Foulois was disappointed that he was not one of the chosen. Virtually without help he risked his life to learn to fly. A strong believer in the future of military aviation, he espoused that air power would one day determine the outcome of warfare. This earned him the reputation of eccentric in military and naval circles.

After acquiring the Wright Flyer, Foulois flew it for his first solo. He had brought the plane to San Antonio with him in boxes and assembled it with the help of anyone willing. He had corresponded with the Wright brothers concerning landing instructions. He received a reply to the effect that "landing was the most critical" part of the flight. He probably already knew that. Although his solo landing was actually a controlled crash, he survived. He flew it for eight months, logging just nine hours of flight time. Maintenance and the shortage of parts kept the plane grounded.

In 1915, Foulois commanded the First Aero Squadron. Although the squadron by this time was equipped with JN-3s and Curtiss R-2s, little improvement was noted in either the flying capabilities of the planes or of the pilots. The death rate from spins and stalls close to the ground kept rising. Regardless of efforts by Foulois to improve operations, nothing worked.

The fact that General Pershing had made his foray deep into Mexico with no aerial surveillance assistance helped to bring the aviation problems to a head. Secretary of War Newton Baker indicated his intention to reorganize the aviation section and asked Congress to authorize $13 million to expand and equip it. The money was granted without question. Three weeks after the Secretary made his views known, war was declared against Germany on April 6, 1917. Foulois was transferred to Washington and the First Aero Squadron was ordered to England. Later in the year, Charles D. Walcott, head of the Aeronautics Committee of the Council for National Defense, made the following statement: *"No amount of money will buy time. Even the most generous preparations would not open up the years we have passed and enable us to lay carefully the foundations of a great industry and a great aero army through the education of engineers, manufacturers, teachers and the wide variety of personnel required. In aviation, we have hardly made a beginning."*

Since the statement came from the top, its ramifications were enormous. One could hardly rule out, however, that what had been accomplished was the result of Lieutenant Foulois and his ardent little band of military aviation supporters who had risked their lives each time they flew. On May 21, 1918, the Aviation Section was removed from the Signal

Corps and renamed the Air Service. Foulois was elevated to Major and in short order promoted to Brigadier General.

General Foulois arrived in France in 1917 with a staff of 112 officers and 300 enlisted men. He immediately found himself embroiled with Lt. Col. Billy Mitchell over numerous details on which Mitchell had taken action. Mitchell was an "action" type, Foulois a stickler for the methodical "army way." As a result, they often locked horns. Foulois was named Chief of the Air Service, A.E.F. and shortly thereafter moved to Chaumont on June 3, 1918. Because of the row, General Pershing appointed General Mason Patrick to be Chief of Air Service and Foulois became Chief of Operations. It was his job to supply men, aircraft, and material to Mitchell.

Foulois and his staff had little time to contribute to the war effort. On November 11, 1918 the shooting war ended and he was ordered back to Washington. On his return, he was stunned to find himself reduced in rank to Major and given a duty assignment liquidating contracts for airplanes and engines. It soon appeared obvious to Foulois that military aviation was being consigned to the rock pile. He noted that the aviation branch was under command of an infantry General and no funds were being made available to provide for the purchase of airplanes or the training of pilots. He made direct attacks on the General Staff, the navy, and the Assistant Secretary of the Navy Franklin D. Roosevelt for the strident objections Roosevelt made to creation of a separate Department of Aeronautics. In the spring, Foulois applied for duty as military attaché and was ordered to Berlin, Germany. There, he obtained a variety of secrets pertaining to German aviation improvements and plans. When he returned to Washington, he turned the documents over to Army Intelligence. They were stored and then dumped into the trash pile. He had, however, sent numerous written reports concerning the intelligence information collected, which, he claimed, obviously indicated the future desire of the Germans to rebuild the Luftwaffe and their aircraft factories.

During the years following his return from France, Foulois tenaciously forged his way up the unstable command ladder of the Air Corps. While stationed in Germany he was promoted to Lieutenant Colonel and subsequently ordered to the Command and General Staff School. The Air Reorganization Act of 1926 greatly brightened the hopes and prospects of many Air Corps supporters. Foulois was assigned to command Mitchel Field for a tour and upon conclusion, he became Assistant to the Chief of Air Corps. He was jumped two grades to again hold the rank of Brigadier General.

Considerable speculation surrounded who would be the next Chief of Air Corps since General Fechet planned to retire at the end of his term in

1931. Many assumed that as assistant chief, Foulois would be nominated. However, there were rumors that Fechet might not support him. Lt. Col. Frank Andrews, Air Corps Chief of Training and Operations, indicated that General Foulois was the logical and probable successor. Andrews was about to release plans for a huge training exercise that would last ten days. The organization and operation of the exercise had been assigned to General Foulois with the approval of Secretary of War and the General Staff.

The program was scheduled to take place in May 1931. It was designed to be the largest aerial demonstration ever seen. It called for 659 planes and 720 pilots to operate a bomber wing, pursuit wing, two observation wings, an attack group, and transport group. Flying Cadets, for the first time, would be included. At that time cadets were graduated as military pilots, commissioned in the reserve, but could fly only on active duty status as cadets. It was a matter of funds: a 2nd lieutenant was paid $125 per month, a cadet received $75 per month. This was not a helpful situation to attract applicants for flight training but reflected problems of the Depression and budget.

The flight schedule for the training mission called for aircraft to assemble at Dayton, fly to Chicago, New England, and New York, arriving at Washington, DC, on Memorial Day for a huge 20-mile aerial parade fly-over. The flight assembled and departed Dayton on time. At its conclusion, more than 30,000 hours had been flown without a single crack-up, and not one pilot injured. Much praise was received from military and public sources, including the President. As a result, General Foulois was recommended to become the next Chief of the Air Corps.

In 1933, an abstract of air-warfare doctrines by Gen. Guilio Douhet of the Italian government was published. The article was widely read by Air Corps personnel and it came to the attention of General Foulois. The purpose of the article was to support the independent air concept. Foulois had copies made and mailed them to influential contacts. The election of Franklin D. Roosevelt to be President caused some alarm for Foulois. The Assistant Secretary of Air, Trubee Davison, would soon be leaving and no word had been received as to a successor. The concern related to a statement Roosevelt had made concerning the independent status of the Air Corps. The new President had strong reservations about the arrangement and voiced them. Foulois and others believed it was because of his close ties to the navy. Also, another problem existed with the Senate Appropriations Committee. General MacArthur testified the Air Corps had operated almost entirely on its own with only minimal involvement by the army.

The discussion concerned the Air Corps failure to meet its five-year plan. Foulois made notes that MacArthur was wrong and knew it. His real purpose was to eliminate the office of Assistant Secretary of Air. The army had exercised continuous control over Air Corps training through its command structure, the only method for the Air Corps to obtain supplies for training. Foulois further added that programs sent to the General Staff for approval had been rejected one after another. The basic problem with the Corps concept was the inability of Corps commanders, usually of General rank with little or no experience in air matters, to hamstring and otherwise interfere with Air Corps operations and training. Without inquiry, they would often call operations for a plane standby that was scheduled for a different mission. It was a plan devised by GHQ to control air activities in the field. At best it was awkward, inept, and of no value to the Air Corps.

Not long after the budget hearing, another problem came to Foulois' attention. Frank Andrews, new commanding officer at Selfridge Field, was very perturbed that his pilots were unable to practice instrument flights. The training realistically required two cockpits; one for the pilot, who would fly by reference to instruments in the aircraft, and one for the instructor. The matter reached the desk of Foulois and he was receptive, having tried before to establish an instrument program for all pilots. It was not only the airplane that was needed, but better radio equipment and some method to remove ice from the wings and propellers during flight. The airlines were ahead in the field, already using boots on their wings and de-icing on the propellers. Again, those most interested scratched their heads over funds. A serious problem existed concerning the ability to fly by instruments and Foulois was well aware of it: the Air Corps lived on its mission of Coastal Defense, without it there would be no reason for the Air Corps to exist.

Not long after the election of Roosevelt, a question arose regarding the method used in buying military aircraft. The procedure followed was for Wright Field to issue certain specifications for aircraft to be purchased. These specifications would be given to companies who built airplanes to examine and report their estimates. The winner would then develop a prototype that would fulfill the required specifications. From there, steps would be taken toward purchasing a certain number of the planes. The basis for this type of buying was to insure quality. The other type of bidding was to open up the requirements to all interested parties, regardless of qualifications. It was believed this would lead to inferior equipment because of the lowered specifications. Foulois strongly objected to this type of bidding but was now being pressured to utilize it as a method of saving money.

This was a typical time for political changes when a new party takes over, and as this development unfolded Foulois received a request to meet with a Post Office official over some minor change in procedures. The Chief of Air Corps was unaware of a developing fight over airmail contracts. He was asked point blank if the Air Corps could carry mail. Without knowing the purpose he acknowledged that probably military airplanes could do that. Unknowingly, he had committed the Air Corps to fly the mail. Roosevelt had bought on to the idea that the big airlines were keeping small bidders out and costing too much. Without checking the problems involved in flying during bad weather and at night over mountain areas, he maneuvered the Air Corps into the job. Immediately after the announcement was made from the President's office that the mail contracts with the airlines would be canceled in ten days, Foulois was seated in General MacArthur's office explaining what had happened. Although he had little of the resources needed to carry the mail, Foulois' basic nature had always been to get the job done. While it was admirable, the consequences could be disastrous. The Air Corps had no planes equipped for instrument or night flying that could carry mail. It was woefully short on experienced pilots. It had no commercial radio net set up to communicate with pilots or advise them of schedules and weather.

The airlines were weighing in with their complaints and that included such men as Charles Lindbergh and Eddie Rickenbacker, both heavyweights in commercial airline operations. Rickenbacker commented, "Either they are going to pile up ships all the way across the continent, or they are not going to be able to fly the mail on schedule." At the time, the airlines were flying 200,000 miles a day using planes designed to carry cargo, and instrumented for the job.

General Foulois and his staff were busy finding airplanes and pilots and getting them into position to start carrying the mail within ten days. Reserve pilots were recalled and among them were several airline pilots. That would be the only assistance the Air Corps would receive. None would be offered by the airlines. The position of the airlines was understandable. Instead of helping, the airlines chose to bad mouth the Air Corps and subject its pilots and efforts to ridicule.

In the first few days of the army flying mail, six pilots were killed. The public became alarmed and Foulois spoke on the radio advising that his pilots were not babies and could do the job. The media reaction was not good. They charged Foulois was too tough and uncaring for his pilots. In addition to these problems, the Air Corps was hard up for funds. Money promised Foulois was not delivered. The result was that pilots and enlisted personnel were paying for room and board themselves. The army was notorious for not getting due pay to personnel on duty under unusual circumstances. Since General MacArthur had washed his hands of the mail program, the army was even slower. Regardless, the mail was being delivered and the morale of the Air Corps was high.

Following one very bad week of accidents, Foulois was commanded to meet with the President at the White House to explain. Roosevelt demanded to know when the dying would stop. Foulois calmly answered that would happen when the planes stopped flying. He then received a bawling out for the next ten minutes. Foulois ordered a ten-day shut down in the operations, and his men took the time to reorganize and get the planes back in tip-top condition. Shortly afterwards, the new B-10s started arriving and were immediately put into operation. It changed the entire picture and within days the tonnage of airmail delivered began to rise. The Air Corps flew its last mail mission in May 1934. The mail program resulted in 66 accidents that claimed the lives of 12 pilots. Six more were killed while ferrying aircraft to positions.

Considering all the difficulties encountered and doing a job for which its personnel and equipment were not trained, the job done by the Air Corps was very creditable. It had become well-known that the eruption over the airmail contracts was political. However, there was a desire to pin the fiasco on someone by the Administration and Congress. The Air Corps itself has scored such high marks for its performance that the only one left for the sacrifice was General Foulois. Investigations were demanded from military and civilian sources. When the frenzy cooled, General Foulois had taken all the arrows. Not being a political person he had no one to battle for him on that front. And, although the Inspector General cleared him of all charges, Foulois was condemned for being too vociferous in his defense. Trumped up charges by a Congressman that Foulois accepted funds in contract arrangements were thrown out, but Foulois was concerned that the following year's budget might be held up in the political machinations. He decided to retire. At his request, he was given accrued leave and on December 31, 1935, General Foulois departed the Washington scene, confusing in its politics and unforgiving in its treatment of a military man whose devotion to duty and fealty were unquestioned. Regardless of blame, he had perhaps unknowingly, demonstrated that the Air Corps could function on its own.

The New York Times reported: *The proponents of a separate air force see for the first time an opportunity to obtain their objective.*

Maj. Gen. Benjamin D. Foulois, Army Air Corps
who served beyond duty and honor is recognized as a
Legend of Air Power

Gen. William Mitchell

William Mitchell

William "Billy" Mitchell was the son of Sen. John L. Mitchell from Milwaukee. He did not attend West Point, but enlisted in the army as a private. He was later commissioned through a direct appointment. Mitchell was energetic and headstrong in his views, blunt in his position and not inclined to compromise. His fervent and determined belief that air power would eventually save the nation did not rest well with the Army GHQ. In 1914, Congress passed an act that organized the Aviation Section, Signal Corps. It provided that officers, under the age of 30 and unmarried, could apply for flight training. The language had been provided by Captain Mitchell, who was 33 at the time and a career officer. He had not yet taken his first flight.

Three weeks before war was declared, Mitchell left for France with other officers to observe the French conduct of the air war. He learned to fly in Nieuport type trainers and fighters, qualifying for the title of Junior Military Aviator. He was fluent in French and established excellent relations with the French and British aviation authorities. After arriving in France he represented the American Air Service with rank of Major. Later, in a reorganization by General Pershing, he was assigned as Chief of Air Service, 1st. Army, and promoted to rank of Colonel. He introduced a new concept of air strategy that organized all tactical air units consisting of 1500 allied planes into a single strike force. He utilized it to carry out concentrated air strikes against German positions. Its first action was in support of allied troops attacking the St. Mihiel salient. The troops went over the top on the morning of September 12, 1918, in drizzly weather. Despite the lack of visibility, Mitchell's air units supported the troops by attacking German positions in front of the advancing infantry and tanks. The battle was won after the first day by American infantry in what was then considered a walkover. Mitchell's use of Allied air units at St. Mihiel was commended by General Pershing: *The organization and control of the tremendous concentration of air forces, including American, British, French and Italian units, which has enabled the Air Service of the First Army to carry out so successfully its dangerous and important mission, is a fine tribute to you personally as is the courage and nerve shown by your officers a signal proof of the high morale which permeates the service under your command . . . . I am proud of you all.*

Americans launched a second offensive less than two weeks after the St. Mihiel salient was secured. The U.S. infantry attacked the Argonne Forest where the French had made no headway in four years. The battle would be long and difficult. Mitchell's airmen had no breather from one offensive to the next; flying twice a day, seven days a week. Only the incessant rain permitted a day of rest.

Mitchell remained in Germany for six months following Armistice as chief of air units in the Army of Occupation. He returned to the United States to assume his position as Director of Military Aeronautics. To his chagrin, the new Chief of Air Service, an infantry Major General, had abolished the position. Mitchell was assigned to a staff job. The army demobilized all but 10,000 men and officers out of 200,000 Air Corps personnel at war's end. No money was made available for the purchase of new aircraft. In Mitchell's mind, however, he was convinced that air power would one day become a method to end wars.

Billy Mitchell began his campaign for a modern air service by writing memos to the General Staff requesting varying types of aircraft and numbers. Each day he sent a new memo via the message center to a different member of the GHQ. The messages were ignored and, later Mitchell's memos were automatically filed in the basement in *The flying trash file.* Undaunted, he began stumping the country explaining the need of an air force separate from the army. Proponents were able to include in the 1920 Army Reorganization Act, a 20,000-man air force under the separate command of air force personnel. However, when the act was finally passed, the Air Service remained attached to the army, with less strength than originally requested. Even though 25,000 trainee pilots were authored, funds were available to graduate only 190 flying cadets by 1921. Airplanes were old and in 1921 there were 330 crashes killing 69 men.

Mitchell was distressed and complained long and loud to everyone to no avail. Finally, in desperateness he made the decision to take on the navy. Mitchell appeared before Congress and argued that the days of the battleship ruling the seas were over. He illustrated how the cost of one battleship would equal a thousand modern bombers. He cited the failure of the navy to realize that coming technology would eliminate the security of America's shores under its antiquated policy. Mitchell stated he could use old bombers and sink any ship the navy had. A money-saving Congress could not resist the temptation and ordered the navy to provide old ships for the tests. Mitchell had to consider what was available to carry bombs. He found very little. Neither were bombs in stock that could do the job. He decided to organize the First Provisional Brigade at Langley Field, Virginia. By raiding every air unit, he managed to assemble 1000 men and 250 airplanes. Ordnance shops constructed 2000- and 4000-pound bombs, considered large enough to sink a battleship. It was the first of a kind. In test runs on old targets, the 2000-pound bomb with a dummy charge penetrated a concrete barrier 6 feet with ease, making Mitchell feel more positive.

Having decided there was little advantage in trying to change the thinking of the army about air power, Mitchell decided he needed the public on his side of the struggle. It was a tricky and dangerous business as the wrong statement or slip of the tongue could quickly cause bad reprisals. In his usual manner, he ignored possible problems. First, he utilized any opportunity to speak out on the need for a separate air arm. That might cause irritation among the brass, but not much more. But when he started downplaying the army, calling its general staff hidebound and behind times for not providing the best defenses for the country, it caused a lot of fist pounding. Then, his book *Our Air Force* was published and became popular reading. Mitchell was getting the public support he wanted. More was to come.

An unfortunate incident provided the next move. A Curtiss Eagle plane crashed in stormy weather killing seven air corps men. Billy hopped on the incident claiming the lack of weather stations and failure to provide better information to pilots was gross incompetence by those in charge of research and development. Major General Menoher, the infantry officer placed in charge of the air service by GHQ, reacted violently and attempted to remove Mitchell as Assistant Chief of the Air Service. Secretary of War John Weeks called in Menoher and Mitchell and told them to cool their passions, adding that Mitchell would remain with the test run on schedule.

As the time grew near, Franklin D. Roosevelt commented: *It is highly unlikely that an airplane or a fleet of them could ever successfully attack a fleet of navy vessels under battle conditions.* The time would come when Roosevelt regretted he had ever uttered such a statement. On June 20, the tests started in the morning with a strike against a captured German submarine by flights of navy planes dropping 165-pound bombs. It required only 16 minutes to sink it. On June 29, a search operation was carried out over 25,000 square miles of open sea looking for the USS *Iowa*. Mitchell's airmen found it, demonstrating the ability to locate a ship by air. It was considered a victory for Mitchell. The next test on July 29 was against the German ship G-102, a destroyer. It was a Krupp-built vessel measuring 312 feet in length. The first attack was by fighters carrying 25-pound bombs and machine guns. Then Mitchell sent the new Martin bombers from 1500 feet dropping 300-pounders. That broke the back of the ship and sent her plunging to the bottom within 19 minutes. A victory celebration was held that night at Langley Field. No Admirals attended.

Five days later a test was scheduled against the German light cruiser *Frankfurt*, a graceful, 5100-ton warship only six years old. Army, Navy and Marine Corps planes made attacks in ten waves. The first run was on August 18 and the cruiser withstood the first wave of 100-, 200-, and 300-pound bombs. Afterwards, the navy inspection team went aboard and found the ship still intact, much to the pleasure of the navy. Then Mitchell sent in the big Martin MB-2s loaded with 600-pound bombs. Eleven hits put the cruiser beneath the waves in 35 minutes.

The ultimate challenge would be the German battleship *Ostfriesland*, a well built 27,000-ton vessel, multi-skinned and honey-combed with watertight compartments. Naval ship builders considered her to be unsinkable. Due to rough seas, the attack was put off until the afternoon of August 20. Tension was running high. First, Navy and Marines made runs with 250-pound bombs but that caused damage only to the ship's superstructure. Then, five Martin bombers appeared and dropped 600-pound bombs; two struck portside forward, and three exploded underwater on both sides of the battleship. Because of an approaching storm the planes were returned to base. The *Ostfriesland* appeared to be riding normally at anchor. However, the following morning she had settled ten feet by the stern. The day was clear and calm. The next run would carry 1000-pound bombs. The first bomb hit the battleship squarely near the bow. Then two more strikes were made and the navy called for a halt to allow the inspection teams to examine the ship. The damage was severe; water was flooding the fourth deck, but in their opinion the ship could still make it to port under its own steam. The Admirals agreed that Mitchell had failed.

That afternoon eight bombers were loaded up with 2000-pound bombs. One of the planes ditched but the other seven continued on the mission. The first bomb missed; the second bomb landed in the water amidships and blasted the battleship out of the water; the third struck a direct hit forward splitting the decks; the next bomb landed in the water by the fantail and the stricken ship rolled over exposing her bottom. She started sinking. A final bomb sent her plunging to the bottom of the sea. It had taken only 22 minutes to sink her.

Regardless, the navy insisted the battleship would continue as the backbone of the fleet. Mitchell received adulation and praise from the public and the infantry Major General retired as Chief of the Air Service. Mitchell did not get the assignment, however, he was not yet through. On September 23, his planes flew out over Chesapeake Bay, headed for the tethered *Alabama*. The planes first made a smokescreen around the ship, then more planes flew over its deck and dropped phosphorous bombs causing flames to sweep the ship. They returned to base, loaded more bombs and flew back at nightfall. A giant magnesium flare was dropped and lit up the battleship for 300-pound bombs to shower it. She blazed up after the attack and was still smoking a few days later. She was then hit with a 2000-pound bomb causing her to roll over and sink within 30 seconds.

Mitchell was not satisfied that the tests had been fully accepted by the navy. He continued to badger the Admirals until in the summer of 1923 they agreed to furnish the *Virginia* and the *New Jersey*. They were towed to a point 20 miles off Cape Hatteras. On September 3, Mitchell's bombers, equipped with a new bombsight supplied by Alexander de Seversky, made their attack on the ships from 10,000 feet. A variety of 600-, 1000- and 2000-pound bombs were used. There were several direct hits on the superstructure and near hits that ripped the seams underwater. The *New Jersey* wallowed and sank first, followed in a few minutes by the *Virginia*. This time the entire event was censored by the navy and Mitchell's own report of the incident remained classified as secret by the army.

After the tests Mitchell was ordered on an intelligence-collecting mission to the Pacific. He spent nine months in Hawaii, the Marianas, the Philippines, and Japan. He was amazed to find no plans for protection, and no coordination between the navy and army. Pearl Harbor functioned almost as a civilian recreational spot in the sea. It troubled him to

*In July 1921, Billy Mitchell proved aerial bombs could sink a navy battleship.
After much discussion, the Secretary of War ordered a test. The picture depicts
results of a phosphorous bomb shower over the Alabama to dispose of the ship's
antiaircraft guns. She was sunk with a 2000-pound bomb. Mitchell's purpose was
to alert the country to a need for air power.*

find the Japanese aviation industry busy increasing its resources for
building aircraft. He went on record to predict that Oahu would eventually be attacked by Japanese. No one took him seriously. He returned to
the United States in late 1924 and provided a detailed 75,000-word report
pointing out the deficiencies of American strengths in the area, and called
for long range aircraft capable of attacking any enemy ships approaching
America's shores or its territories. Ships could not attack if their bases
could be destroyed. The recommendation went unheeded.

General Mitchell was unbelieving in finding the Air Corps disorganized
and in such low morale. General Patrick has asked for new planes and in-
tensified pilot training, but instead, planes and pilots had been reduced.

Half of the aircraft inventory was grounded for parts or maintenance, and the remaining were old planes from WWI production runs. After the long years of campaigning for America to wake up and understand the critical situation she faced, it seemed that few understood, or cared. He once more began his speeches to congressional committees, warning of the threat in the Pacific. He charged that air officers were muzzled and would not speak out. He complained that the ability to destroy navy capital ships placed the nation at risk, and demanded to know why the results had been kept secret. His warnings were printed almost daily, but had no effect on congress and the GHQ.

General Patrick, realizing what Mitchell was attempting to do and that no other qualified officer would speak out, recommended him for a second term as Assistant Chief of the Air Service, but he was turned down. He simply had stepped on too many brass toes. Secretary of War Weeks ordered him reduced to grade of Colonel and posted for duty at Fort Sam Houston. He was silenced vocally, but he kept writing.

On September 2, 1925, the navy ordered the dirigible *Shenandoah* to make a public relations tour of state fairs in the Midwest. The ship's commander recommended against it because the weather was already stormy, but the navy instructed him to go. The airship flew into a storm area over Ohio and was violently torn apart. It killed the skipper and 12 of the crew. Mitchell wrote a press release and gave it to the local reporters. It was a bombshell. Mitchell charged incompetence, criminal negligence, and virtual treason by the navy and army. After it was printed, Mitchell called reporters and stated: "Let every American know that we are going to better our national defense. We are on the warpath and we are going to stay there until these conditions are remedied." Two weeks later, President Coolidge ordered Mitchell court-martialed.

The trial was held in an old warehouse. Mitchell's judges included six major generals and six brigadier generals. There were no aviators among them. The charges were breach-of-conduct citing Mitchell with behavior, prejudicial to good order and discipline, insubordination, contempt and disrespect. Wartime flier Fiorello La Guardia, a congressman from New York and later mayor of New York City, was among the witnesses. He was questioned by the prosecutor concerning remarks he made to the newspapers: "Mr. La Guardia, the newspapers quoted you as saying that Billy Mitchell isn't being tried by a jury of his peers, but by nine beribboned dog-robbers of the General Staff. Were your correctly quoted?"

"I didn't say beribboned," La Guardia replied.

Mitchell was found guilty and reduced in rank to Colonel. He resigned effective February 1, 1926. He had his day in court and expected no favors. In his and the public's eyes, he could walk away with his principles and beliefs intact. The banishment could not still the warnings and forecasts related to the urgency and need of a strong, separate air force.

Brig. Gen. William "Billy" Mitchell, Army Air Service
who served beyond duty and honor is recognized as a *Legend of Air Power*

Henry "Hap" Arnold

The first congressional hearings on an army air force, separate from the Signal Corps, were held in 1913. Henry H. Arnold testified against the separation. Later, he made a dramatic turn around as aeronautical devel-

Gen. H.H. "Hap" Arnold, commander U.S. air forces in WWII.

opments improved rapidly. The thinking of the GHQ held that aviation was merely an adjunct to assist the army in carrying out its mission. Regardless of air operations in combat, which army reluctantly agreed might occur, control would remain in the army. The doctrinal argument was that unity of command could not be retained with two separate forces in time of war. The argument was specious and had been refuted before, but air clout at those high levels was minimal and even some in aviation agreed with the army point of view. The basic fact was that army had the clout and had no intention of parting with control of one of its branches.

Arnold entered aviation two years earlier, when in 1911, the War Department inquired if he would volunteer for flight training with the Wright Brothers at Dayton, Ohio. Not being a daredevil, but always interested in new quests and eager for a promotion to first lieutenant, he accepted. The course consisted of 11 days studying the airplane itself. Following that, he received 4 hours of flying instruction. Next, Arnold was ordered to the army's first flying school at College Park, Maryland. The mission for the Air Service was to develop the airplanes into a military weapon. Beyond that, the army seemed reluctant to speculate. It was as though the army leaders admitted military air service existed, but what it might do would be left for others to determine under the army's watchful eye. Arnold reasoned that attitude gave him a free reign to explore the realm of flight without regulations.

On March 11, 1913, the first aviation appropriation provided $125,000 to purchase several Wright-Burgess and Curtiss airplanes for training. These aircraft gave Arnold the opportunity to study and test what he learned at his leisure. The only instrument was a piece of string that indicated whether the plane was flying straight or in a skid. Later, a tachometer was added for reading the speed of the propeller in revolutions per minute. Bugs hitting the eyes made the use of goggles imperative, and a strong helmet was added to the flight gear after one crash victim suffered lacerations as his head was dragged along the ground. One other item—the seat belt—was added to prevent occupants catapulting from the seat when the plane encountered down drafts.

After making several flights, the spirit of adventure entered Arnold's thinking. He decided to see how high the plane would go. The effort resulted in setting a new record of more than 4000 feet. Another effort earned him the first Mackay Trophy for setting a 42-mile endurance record on a reconnaissance mission. In September, 1911, after participating in a meet sponsored by the Aero Club of America, he was asked to double for the lead actor as a stunt man. His attitude, happy eyes, and smiling grin tagged him with the nickname of "Happy." Later, it was shortened to "Hap. "

Arnold's position placed him in contact with numerous notables in military and civilian capacity. None was more important than a 32-year old nonflying captain named Billy Mitchell who was assigned to the GHQ. Having just returned from Alaska and the Orient, Mitchell had written a paper noting the growth and size of the Japanese Air Force. During a visit with Arnold at College Park, he pointed out the capability of the airplane's use as a bomber and fighter in addition to spotting for field artillery. Mitchell was preparing a paper to be delivered to the Army War College on the future of military aviation. He wanted Arnold's opinion as a flying officer. Mitchell had impressed Arnold with his grasp of military aviation. During the next 18 months Arnold would fly constantly, accruing more than 120 flight hours. He flew 638 flights in 357 days. Considering the crashes and near crashes inherent in the flying of pusher-type planes, whose propellers would tear off, or the engine chains snap under pressure, Arnold's flying was quite a record.

On one flight during a field artillery exercise, information had been relayed via a crude radio for correcting the artillery fire. All had gone well and Arnold was preparing to land. As he made a gentle descending turn, the plane suddenly would not respond to control movement and continued to tighten the turn picking up speed. The plane snapped into a dive, which became vertical, rushing toward the ground. Arnold checked behind to see if a propeller chain had snapped, but it was normal. Then, suddenly, the plane reacted to the elevator control and resumed normal flight. Arnold landed, feeling as though he had left his stomach high in the air. His nerves were shot and he had suffered the fear that all pilots feel when controls are useless. In a letter to his commanding officer, Arnold stated he had no interest in flying as a passenger or pilot for some time to come. He had, effectively, grounded himself the day of his last flight.

Orville Wright wrote in a letter that most of the accidents in the Flyer were caused by loss of flying speed. He explained in aeronautical terms the occurrence of losing control when gliding and gradually slowing speed. That's why it's called a heavier-than-air machine. It's very possible that when Arnold slowed to a glide he simply lost flying speed. No airplane will continue to fly without it. Later, in a hearing before the House Military Affairs Committee, Arnold restated his desire not to fly. Following his marriage on September 10, 1913, Arnold was transferred to the Far East. He served in the Philippines for two years and was then ordered back to stateside duty.

Following his return he was offered a promotion to Captain if he would accept assignment to duty with the Signal Corps, assuming he would continue his flying career. He lost no time in accepting, admitting to himself how much he had missed flying. It's quite likely he detected the fine hand of Billy Mitchell in the arrangements. A short time later he got out his goggles and helmet and met with a friend, Bert Dargue. The two of them took off in a Jenny and after 20 minutes Arnold knew he was back. The controls of the Jenny were much easier to handle and the OX5 engine provided power and response. At year's end he had been up 28 times, 14 as pilot.

During Arnold's early career he found difficulty working through channels in the traditional army way. When something needed to be done just do it, the heck with paperwork. Sometimes this caused trouble. While at the Rockwell Aviation School one of the instructor pilots made a weekend training flight to Yuma. He didn't arrive and it soon was apparent that the plane was down somewhere in the rugged terrain. The pilots got together and proposed a voluntary search. The commanding officer, who was in his sixties and a balloonist, turned down the plan, suggesting the pilot might have flown over the border. The commander was concerned about relations with Mexico. The missing pilot had been gone four days when messages began to arrive from Washington asking for the status. The CO then had a truck loaded with fuel and arranged with the Mexican government to send it to the Calexico area. There a search would be initiated. That was too slow for Arnold, he and two other pilots got together and decided to make an aerial search of the area. It was to no avail and those participating were called in and reprimanded for disobeying orders. Following nine days of search, the pilot and passenger were found alive. The entire affair had caused deep problems for Rockwell Field over the delayed search process, and the press made the incident a national issue.

During the fiasco, Arnold received orders to proceed to the Canal Zone and look for a site to build a base. He would then be given three squadrons and be assigned as the Panama Department Aviation Officer. Arnold, now promoted to Major, proceeded as instructed. He learned two things on his arrival: his boss at Rockwell Field had given him a very negative efficiency report, and the location of a suitable aviation base was not available. He reported his findings to the GHQ and returned for further duty assignment. On his way home he learned of the declaration of war against Germany.

Arnold was assigned as assistant to the Director of the Aeronautical Division and promoted to the temporary rank of Colonel. After his boss, Brigadier General Foulois departed for France, Arnold found himself in the vortex of the vast changes being implemented by the expansion of war production in military aircraft. In his eyes, any job not being done required immediate action, much to the displeasure of the Washington crowd not known for hurried response. Arnold disliked Washington and its habit of backbiting and political gossiping. He accomplished all that was possible and important to the war effort through the chaotic months that followed. After the war, Arnold would always remember the lessons of the failure of aircraft production; some 20 years later they would serve him at a crucial time for his country.

General Pershing had heard of a pilotless bomb being tested and was eager to learn about it first hand. Arnold had worked on the device and wrangled permission to take it overseas. Unfortunately, he encountered the flu bug and was consigned to his bed in England. By the time he was well enough to journey on to France, the war had ended. Hap Arnold went home from his brief and unrewarding visit to France. He was hopeful that Mitchell would soon become the peacetime Chief of the Air Service. It was not to be. In the meager days that followed, Arnold served in a number of commands, struggling to keep his dreams of the Air Service alive and growing. It was not easy. Perhaps without knowing, he was meeting the people who would be most helpful in forming up his view of the air force to come.

Arnold became commander of Crissy Field at the Presidio, San Francisco, and his assistant was red-haired combat veteran Maj. Carl Spaatz, who had the unusual nickname of "Tooey." It had been given to him at West Point after a so-named upperclassman. He and Arnold worked well together and both enjoyed the same vision of air power. They centered their efforts on flying and public relations. In one event, Arnold organized the first aerial forest-fire patrols over California, Washington, and Oregon. In another he offered to prove his plane could beat a flock of homing pigeons from Portland to San Francisco. Even delayed when cold weather caused difficulties starting the engine of the DH-4, he finally got the engine started and won. The pair constantly thought up odd or zany funny ideas that would keep army aviation in the limelight without incurring the wrath of the public or Washington. It was a time when the two men would become close friends but more important, reliable and dependable for the job ahead.

In 1922, Arnold was reassigned to Rockwell Field as commanding officer. His duties included patrolling the Mexican border. The DH-4B was used for the patrol. Arnold decided the patrol could be improved with more time in the air, but his engineering officer advised that fuel tanks could not be enlarged without adversely affecting the plane's stability. In his daily confabs with the engineering officer, he came up with an idea entirely new to the field of aeronautics. The way to increase range of flight was to keep the patrolling plane in the air by midair refueling. Arnold acknowledged he had no basis to assume success and no precedents to follow. Modifications of the aircraft were necessary so that needed supplies could be transferred. A 40-foot metal-lined steam hose provided the connecting link. After making dry runs two planes took off one August morning and did not land until the next day; they had been in the air for 37 hours and covered more than 3200 miles. The flight broke all records for distance and speed. Arnold kept moving things along with the forest-fire patrols, the Mexican-border patrols, making drops of food and fodder to snowbound Indians, and midair refueling. He constantly strove to exhibit the Air Service at work in peacetime ventures for the public to see or read about.

Despite the National Defense Act of 1920, which had authorized 1500 officers, 16,000 enlisted personnel, and 2500 cadets, in the summer of 1923 only 880 officers and 8300 enlisted men were on duty, including 91 cadets. Maj. Gen. Mason Patrick, Air Service Chief, stated before a congressional committee that the Air Service was practically demobilized and totally unable to meet its mission requirements. This condition was dangerous to the defense of the nation and needed to be known by the public-at-large. This was one reason why Arnold's Air Service superiors supported his efforts in public relations work. In the summer of 1924, Arnold received orders to attend the Army Industrial College in Washington. These schools were considered important to the advancement of middle-rank permanent officers, and a prerequisite to serving on the prestigious General Headquarters Staff. At the conclusion of the course at the Army Industrial College, Arnold was assigned as Chief of Information for the Air Service. It was not a particularly easy task. The public could not be convinced a military threat existed. He saw this lack of public support as a threat to Billy Mitchell's demands for a separate air force. Another problem arose when the navy refused to agree with the Lassiter Board that recommended a single appropriation for aviation. The army and navy steadfastly opposed separation, in any form, regardless of national defense needs.

Even as Mitchell's position with the public was eroding, Arnold continued to stand with him in support of a separate air position. When Mitchell was refused for a second term as Assistant Chief of Air Service, Arnold arranged for the get-together with his supporters before leaving Washington. Later, after Mitchell's outburst over the crash of the Shenandoah and a court-martial was ordered, Arnold met Mitchell when he arrived in Washington for the trial, treating him with the same support as before.

The treatment of Mitchell and failure to gain congressional approval in support of the Service discouraged Arnold. During this period, General

Patrick's legislative bill, which called for the Air Service to be a unit under the army much the same as the Marine Corps was in the navy, was under consideration. Arnold decided it would take pressure from the public to have any chance of passage. He and close friend Bert Dargue arranged for a message to be printed asking voters to call on their elected officials in Washington to support the Patrick bill. It was sent to all officers on duty and in reserves. This prompted an investigation to determine who was responsible. Arnold was called in and told he had a choice: he could resign or face a court-martial. Crestfallen, Arnold went home thinking he might as well write out his resignation. After discussing it at home, he told his boss he would take the court-martial. It was an embarrassing situation for General Patrick since he had urged Arnold to take similar action in other situations. The punishment was a transfer to Fort Riley, Kansas. For Arnold, leaving Washington was not the greatest of punishments.

Arnold packed his family on a train and headed for Kansas. It was a long trip and, with children, an exhausting one. On arrival he felt great trepidation in making his official duty call on the CO, Maj. Gen. Ewing E. Booth. To add to his concerns, a party was in progress when he arrived. Arnold and his wife were led into the living room filled with officers and their wives. General Booth walked swiftly to meet them and graciously welcomed them to the post. He loudly stated his pleasure at having Arnold assigned to his command, and told him he could write anything he liked, only inform him in advance.

Arnold's two years on the plains of Kansas were relatively calm and quiet. He kept busy with the chores of being CO of the Observation Squadron and teaching cavalry officers about airplanes. His only flirtation with a real problem came when he permitted a young boy to ride in his airplane. The boy enjoyed it but the father, a major, threatened to have Arnold court-martialed. Fortunately, calmness interceded and the matter was dropped. There were two distinct plus items: one came via a note of appreciation from President Coolidge's chief of staff for Arnold's handling of the President's mail during summer vacation; the other was a highly complimentary efficiency report from General Booth.

In the military system, some persons follow what they think is the correct format to reach a goal of job or rank. Others follow their preference of taking on a job and doing it well. For the former, two military schools were considered essential on the record: The War College and The Command and General Staff School. Arnold applied for the latter, but had doubts that he would be selected in view of his banishment. At the time, not many aviation officers applied for the school, as they thought in terms of command, not staff, assignments. The fliers wondered if they could still manage to get a plane up and down, because of the very limited number of in-commission airplanes at the school. Arnold was selected to attend.

Unknown to many, even personal friends, Arnold had reached a time in his life to make a ponderous decision. In 1925, while serving as G-2 (intelligence) he had occasion to study a German airline's request to provide service to U.S. cities. Although it was turned down, he found the system interesting and decided to organize a program to provide air service from Florida to the Caribbean and Central America. He selected the name Pan American Airways. One of the participants was a naval pilot who had the necessary connections on Wall Street for financial backing. About the time Arnold was ready to go, the Mitchell activities overwhelmed other considerations.

After the Mitchell affair more or less settled, Arnold learned that Pan American Airways was in operation and the naval officer was in charge of operations. Its problem was the lack of a chief officer. Arnold received an offer to become managing director, then move to President. There were good considerations: a well compensated job with stock and options. It was now 1929, and Arnold felt he was probably looking at the last great civilian opportunity. On the other hand, the 1926 Reorganization Act had established the Air Corps and it was moving, even though at a snails pace. In the end, Arnold's first love won out and he turned down the airline offer.

Arnold had made contact with General Fechet, now Chief of the Air Corps, requesting that he not be returned to duty in Washington. He received his answer that the training command at San Antonio would be his next assignment. Unfortunately, Frank Lahm, who now was a Brigadier General, commanded the Air Training Center and did not approve. Fechet advised Arnold that it would not be wise to serve under Lahm. After considering all the possibilities, it was decided he would take command of the Fairfield Depot at Dayton. The purpose of the depot was to overhaul airframes, engines and instruments. It was not to Arnold's liking. He preferred to make things better as opposed to keep them running.

Conditions were changing in Washington. President Coolidge was gone and MacArthur had been named Chief of Staff. In February 1931, Arnold was promoted to Lieutenant Colonel and assigned to March Field. It had been a primary flight training school, but it was his job to convert it to a base operations with pursuit and bomber groups. Arnold's main purpose was to develop, update and perfect the tactics of pursuit and bombardment. His program called for getting the facts and principles of modern aerial operations regardless of past book rules and regulations. Squadrons were sent to remote fields and placed on their own to create self-sufficiency for several weeks at a time. He stressed night flying and high altitude flights. He soon learned that his combat units could not practice aerial gunnery without an adequate range, and the navy refused use of theirs. He decided to look around the desert and came up with an area adjacent to Muroc. To avoid a California land run, he carefully checked out the land and marked off a piece of the dry lake bed 19 miles long by 9 miles wide. Later, it would become known as the best gunnery and bombing range available.

In his work with the pursuit and bomber aircraft, it soon became apparent that the roles of each in combat had to be examined. That of the bomber seemed relatively easy: give it speed, ability to carry large payloads, endurance, and protective armament. Arnold's idea was to get going fast, carry enough bombs to destroy the target, and get as many home as possible. The program for pursuit was different and needed answers to many questions: Should it be utilized to intercept and attack bombers? Should it provide escort for bombers to and from the target? Could it be a weapon to attack certain types of ground targets after sweeping the skies of enemy pursuit planes? It would take time and technology improvements for many answers to be known, but Arnold wanted the study to start now.

Another matter that concerned Arnold was the method of utilizing boards to provide recommendations for new aircraft. These boards met periodically at Wright Field to consider types and designs for new airplanes. Arnold objected to the system because some members were too young to have acquired sufficient overall knowledge to consider how one airplane would function with another type in actual wartime operations. Arnold wanted to scrap the system and utilize one board with competent personnel to consider the needs for all aircraft. The situation was further complicated by the Air Corps functioning under the nine Area Corps Commands, all commanded by ground force Generals. Although they had little to do with combat air training, they held the authority to direct the use of aircraft and personnel for army missions.

The situation was brought to the surface by an earthquake on March 10, 1933. The quake struck Long Beach, California. Arnold heard about it from a news flash. He immediately contacted Capt. Ira C. Eaker, who was in Los Angeles. He asked Eaker to go there and get a report for him concerning damage and need. Arnold called the commanding officer at Fort MacArthur, but he could not be located. Not willing to wait, Arnold followed up on Eaker's report by sending a detachment of Air Corps men with emergency supplies including medical, bedding, and tents to help the injured people. The press gave praise and credit to Arnold and his men for their fast action and assistance. The next day, however, word came to Arnold from Corps Area headquarters that Fort MacArthur was in charge of the matter. He was also charged with violating regulations. Arnold was dumfounded and immediately flew to the Presidio to see the commanding general. Gen. Malin Craig was an astute officer with many years of war and peacetime service. Nonetheless, he was surprised when an obviously angry Lieutenant Colonel stood before him asking "why am I in the dog house?" After Arnold detailed his story of events, the General accepted it and, following a friendly discussion, agreed to visit March Field. He visited, and after reviewing the troops complimented Arnold saying: "Your men marched as well as any infantry troops I've seen." Arnold had made an important friend.

In May 1933, another problem dropped in Arnold's lap. For sometime at the urging of President Roosevelt, efforts had been underway to create a new Civilian Conservation Corps whose purpose was to send unemployed youth of the country to work doing reforestation, flood control, national park development, and other outdoor projects. The program had been given to the Army Chief of Staff, General MacArthur. His job was to organize camps for 275,000 recruits in 47 states by July 1, 1933. General Craig informed Arnold that he had accepted 1500 recruits to arrive at March Field the following week. In addition, Arnold would be Chief of Staff to General Westover for the spring air maneuvers involving 300 pursuit and bomber aircraft. Arnold received sympathetic comments from all concerned, but still had both assignments to fulfill. The camps were set up in California near Bishop, Monmouth, Silver Lake, across the high Sierras in Nevada, and at Lake Tahoe. Twenty-five camps were organized and Arnold visited them when he could. For him it was a restful time when he could relax and visit with the young men working to survive during difficult economic times in the country.

On February 19, 1934, airmail contracts with the commercial airlines were canceled and the Air Corps was to begin delivery of airmail 10 days later. Arnold received notice he would be in charge of the Western Zone. It comprised the West Coast, interior desert, and the Rocky Mountain region. His headquarters would be at the Salt Lake City airport. Arnold immediately alerted his officers to the plan of operation and assigned them their areas of responsibility. He then established his own headquarters at the Salt Lake City airport. Much of the land mass to be flown over was mountainous. Arnold reported that none of his pilots had acquired sufficient experience with the rapid weather changes in those areas. His report was tragically correct as three pilots were killed during bad weather while attempting familiarization runs on their routes. Newspapers gave the accidents front page coverage. Overlooked, however, was that 23 pilots were killed while undergoing their normal training during the previous six months.

On the day of the inaugural flights only a few runs could be made. The run to Cheyenne from Salt Lake City was canceled as Arnold stressed safety in flight would be adhered to. The flight west to Los Angeles required three en route landings to scrape ice off the wings and windshield, however, it did arrive at Burbank eight hours late with its full cargo of mail intact. The task of flying mail gradually settled down, with sporadic spells of winter weather, but the pilots were getting the system to work and mail was being moved.

Although Arnold suffered with the mail program, worse problems were going on in Washington. The political battle had heated up on all fronts and various committees were attempting to find people to blame. The Air Corps was caught in the middle and politicians were chewing on it like a pack of hungry wolves. The President and Postmaster General wanted the blame for losing so many pilots in bad weather pinned on someone other than themselves. The army and its GHQ felt the Air Corps had not performed as expected and wanted changes made. In an effort to officially place blame, the Secretary of War appointed a civilian board chaired by Newton D. Baker, former Secretary of War. The board of 11 persons met for three months. During that time they questioned 100 witnesses, visited several air bases and aircraft facilities. Arnold appeared as a witness and testified that his airmail commanders and staff recommended that the Air Corps budget be separate from the army; have a separate promotion list; its own provisions for retirement; rank commensurate with duty; regular commissions; extended active duty for reserve officers; and a classified cadet status. Arnold did not ask for complete separation from the army, but recommended a GHQ Air Force to be in charge of all training. It was a change from Arnold's previous thinking, but the airmail experience made him recognize the magnitude of logistic and management problems necessary to going it alone. Many others submitted suggestions with the total separation of Air Corps from army the dominant theme. Unfortunately the recommendations, through a maneuver by the army, were not presented in a manner to affect the board's findings.

Very little of a positive nature came from the proceedings of the board. Jimmy Doolittle, a member of the board, reported to Arnold that he had been naive in thinking the purpose was to take action to establish a strong Air Corps when it was obvious the reverse was true. He advised that the army stressed the need for a strong control over the Air Corps. Five years before the beginning of WWII, the Baker Board supported the army that air power alone could have no decisive effect on the outcome of a war, and those who believed differently were visionary. Some good did come from the findings: the lack of suitable appropriations; need for emphasis on instrument flying; exoneration of Air Corps mail pilots from criticism; and support for negotiated contract purchases of aircraft. At the conclusion of the review one good improvement was in progress. That was the beginning of the GHQ Air Force. Frank Andrews was the active organizer and scheduled to lead the command to an active status. However, as with so many other board and committee programs, nothing of substance came out of the Baker Board hearings toward giving the Air Corps the basics to create the kind of air force needed. As usual, it illustrated the determination of the army to maintain a tight control over the fledgling air service.

Meantime an historic flight was being organized. The task of command was handed to Arnold. Having just been passed over for a brigadier general's star, Arnold felt his selection to lead the formation of B-10s to Alaska was a sop. In his mind it wasn't ego, but the fact that at 48 he had reached his plateau in military life. To rub more salt in the wound, when he inquired of General MacArthur why he hadn't been selected he was told that his name had not been submitted.

As Arnold headed east to Dayton, Ohio, his thoughts turned to the job of preparing and organizing the formation flight of 10 B-10s. He had to select pilots and get the B-10s restored to the original configuration following the changes made to haul mail. He also thought of the historic public relations impression its success could make following the bitter pill the newspapers had created over the airmail debacle. The press started to crowd him for information, but Arnold let it be known he was in no hurry and would be certain that the flight was properly organized for the long trip. He realized such actions would not set well with the press, but he was not about to create another doubt for the American public concerning the Air Corps. By July 4 only two of the B-10s had been made ready for the flight. Calls were coming in daily for the date of departure. Arnold was firm. The answer would come when the pilots and B-10s were ready. On July 17 the 10 planes departed for Washington. They landed at Bolling Field three hours later. The arrival ceremony brought out all the Generals, pilots, and the Secretary of War. The Secretary wanted a ride and Arnold obliged giving him a 10-minute flight over Washington. The festivities lasted two days. When the flight took off, Arnold swung his aircraft around and unintentionally gave the well wishers a strong dusting off from his propellers. At every stop along the 3500-mile flight Canadians met the planes and royally entertained the crews. Five days after departing Washington they arrived in Fairbanks.

During Arnold's stay in Alaska, a German, who claimed to have been a pilot during WWI, visited him. He advised his purpose was to start an airline operation. He told Arnold he had inspected the B-10s and thought them inferior to ones being built in Germany by the Nazi regime at the Dornier, Heinkel, and Junkers plants. The unsolicited intelligence information was unsettling, but correct for the future. After two weeks of poor weather, conditions improved and the mapping work could be started. It was finished in three days and on August 16 the population of Fairbanks turned out to watch the flight depart, its mission completed. They stopped to refuel in Juneau and then made the 1000-mile flight to Seattle nonstop, another first. It was significant that the flight was mostly over water. They landed at Bolling Field three days later on August 20. The most notable comment to Arnold concerning the mission came from the Secretary of War who stated: "I will use every effort to put into effect the recommendations of the Baker Board with the purpose of placing the Air Corps where it belongs in the first rank of world air power." The promise did little to correct the basic differences between the army and Air Corps positions, which Arnold believed were wrong for national defense.

The B-10s had barely returned from the long Alaskan flight when Arnold received secret orders to move them back to the East Coast for army maneuvers. The exercise had been set up by Army HQ with a enemy force attacking the East Coast to find out how efficient the Air Corps GHQ could be in getting aircraft into position to defend and attack. It was difficult to understand why, under the circumstances, the B-10s were used as enemy aircraft. Instead of determining what the bombing force could accomplish, it was an army logistics study of getting the planes into position to support army troops. The method of assigning command air missions by army Generals eliminated any real functioning of the Air Corps GHQ on its own. In fact, the whole exercise had been arranged to support the Baker Board findings in view of the Howell Commission just underway.

Once more the army moved to prevent any information given by witnesses that was not approved by the GHQ. In this instance, however, Arnold had already discussed his views when he stopped in Seattle en route from Alaska. Arnold was ordered to report to Washington in November. When he asked those in charge why, no reason would be given. Actually, the general staff was aware of his discussion with the Commission Chairman in Seattle and intended to have him refute those recommendations not approved by the GHQ. Arnold understood his position. At this time of his professional life he had no desire to strike out at the GHQ, doing harm to both the Air Corps and himself. When he was finally called to the stand he answered carefully for three hours then a loaded question hit home. He was asked point blank if he could straighten the Air Corps out. Arnold considered his answer and its consequences for a moment. Then, as though he had lifted a heavy weight off his chest, stated he could do it if he had the authority.

Arnold was invited to see the President who had intended to commend him for the successful Alaskan flight. Arnold reported later that the 10 minutes had been devoted to a discussion about the landscape of Alaska but nothing about the capabilities of the B-10 bomber. He was also discouraged by the information that the recognition of the flight by the pilots would be no more than a commendation. An army Major turned down the recommendation for the *Distinguished Flying Cross*. In addition, problems in aircraft maintenance were beginning to crop up on the new B-12s and P-26s. Problems beset him almost every way he turned.. Also, a close friend, Lt. Col. Horace Hickam, had been killed during a landing at Fort Crockett, Texas. Arnold had lost many friends since starting his flying career, but none hit quite as hard as this one.

While on his way to Washington in October, Arnold stopped for refueling at Wright Field and visited with Lt. Col. Frank Andrews. The Board had been reconvened to determine a tentative framework for organizing the GHQ Air Force. On October 17, Andrews was officially assigned to the G-3 section of the GHQ to work out the details of the new combat arm. Eventually, a program was developed and approved by General MacArthur only to find certain agreements concerning coastal defense were in error and had to be corrected. When Arnold learned of the situation his comments revealed his consternation over the entire procedure. A large number of air officers were considered for command, which called for a major general. In December, Andrews was selected. Since he was now a lieutenant colonel, regulations provided he could only be jumped two ranks to brigadier general. Later, he would be promoted to full rank. When Arnold learned of the appointment he wrote Andrews: "I know of no one in the Air Corps I would rather serve under."

On April 3, 1935, Arnold received orders to report to the Adjutant General in Washington. The reason was not given. The long awaited promotion to brigadier general had finally come through for the March Field commander. Arnold speculated on his present orders since they mentioned nothing about a hearing and uniform was not specified. Upon his arrival in Washington, however, he was surprised to find many of his close friends present in civvies. He was notified by the Executive Officer that his appearance before the House Military Affairs Committee would be expected the following morning at 10 o'clock. Arnold had not expected to give testimony on the subject of a National Defense Department and had no notes. When he was called he expressed the thought that such an arrangement needed to be supported by army, navy, and air on an equal and self-supporting basis. The Air Corps GHQ was moving along, but needed commanders and staffs that it does not have. Such a situation, he noted, will require time to develop. When it does, then a National Defense system would work. Arnold expected no praise from his colleagues, but believed he had stated the situation fairly. Testimony given by a number of other Air Corps officers represented a consensus of Arnold's position. After the hearings, Arnold departed Washington for Langley Field to visit his friend and boss, Frank Andrews. A squadron of his command was scheduled for a flight to Panama but Andrews informed him the flight had been called off. Andrews did not believe the B-10s were in the tip-top condition he wanted for the difficult flight to Panama. He discussed the type of training he expected prior to making the flight. It was far more difficult than the one Arnold had made a few years earlier. Andrews was also concerned about the rainy season and planned scheduling the flight to arrive after the bad weather. Instrument flying was also of concern and he wanted all pilots to be proficient. Arnold agreed with all the items listed by Andrews and concurred with him on the planning. He had always planned with a safety factor and was pleased.

Soon after Arnold returned to March Field his outfit ran into a series of aircraft accidents. He reported to Andrews that his pilots must be the worst in the world: "As far as I can see the only way to stop the accidents is to ground the planes. Starting with a cadet who had the whole of March Field to land on, he runs into a boundary light. Ken Walker, supposed to be one of our best pilots, overshoots and hits a concrete block, damaging the wing. A B-12 lands at Medford, Oregon, and the landing gear retracts by accident. Captain Malone, on a night flight over the desert has engine trouble, drops a flare and lands at Palm Springs only to hit a clump of weeds and destroys a P-12."

Arnold realized that some of the trouble came from the aging airplanes and some from attitude. In addition, he was losing Ira Eaker, who was ordered to attend the Air Corps Tactical School. Eaker had collaborated with him on a book published by Funk & Wagnells in 1936 entitled *This Flying Game*, aimed at the young man considering a career of military pilot. Arnold respected Eaker's writing ability and considered him a friend. At the beginning of 1935 Arnold had agreed with Andrews to work toward a test of the table of organization and increase combat efficiency. The program had bogged down mainly due to the lack of new and replacement aircraft. Accidents and aircraft out of commission for parts had steadily reduced the ability of units to improve or even maintain their combat training.

Bomber and pursuit held considerable discussions concerning the effectiveness of the two combat branches. A main item was the speed factor concerning the ability of pursuit to intercept bombers and the role of pursuit in escorting bombers to their targets. During the West Coast maneuvers, Arnold reported that B-10s had been able to press the attack without interception by the Pursuit. He sent a copy of the report to the Air Corps Tactical School, which brought an immediate response from Claire Chennault, arguing that the method of using the Pursuit was wrong. Arnold penned across Chennault's letter: "Who is this damned fellow Chennault?" The close of 1935 brought changes. Arnold was assigned as Assistant Chief of Air Corps, a move he felt interrupted his unfinished work with the 1st Wing. He deplored returning to the Washington merry-go-round as the bad experiences from his prior encounter remained in his memory.

One of Arnold's main duties was procurement. During the previous September he had bulled his way through on final approval to go ahead on Project D, the XB-19. A term of *Balanced Budget* had become popular in political circles, and its purpose was to prevent too much planning for heavy bombers. The new B-17 was once more ready for service testing and Arnold proposed an additional 29 be projected for the 1938 budget. The Secretary of War promptly disapproved, saying "it was too costly and not proven capable." The first B-17, flown by Maj. Barney Giles, arrived at Langley Field on March 1, 1937.

As the procurement for next year's aircraft grew near, Arnold received inquiries from Andrews seeking support for the B-17 over purchase of the B-18. The 17 B-17s already approved were being delivered, but Andrews insisted to Arnold that he wanted no more twin-engine bombers. The problem was not with Arnold, but the insistence by the War Department that a greater number of less expensive airplanes was better than a small number of B-17s. Arnold recognized the fallacy of this thinking, since in his opinion the ability of the bomber to attack an enemy's resources represented the true value of air power to national defense. The B-18 did not have that capability, and it made no difference how many were purchased.

The war activity in Spain and China was producing some information relating to the use of air power. Arnold had received reports indicating that Japanese bomber losses without fighter escort were catastrophically high, using the twin-engine types. On the basis of the report, Arnold instructed that data from both wars be compiled into a report. The position of Air Corps senior officers who advocated long-range bombers believed this supported their contention of procuring B-17s over B-18s.

In April 1938, Arnold received a top secret letter from the office of the Secretary of War. Arnold was Acting Chief of the Air Corps during the absence of General Westover. It concerned a request from the British Government for a trade mission to examine combat aircraft available for purchase and dates of delivery. It raised the same questions as those of the recent French request to fly the P-36, which had been approved by President Roosevelt. The main concern of Arnold and others was whether countries acquiring the latest in military aircraft were going to be friendly to the United States later on. The matter was settled in a meeting with the State Department to the effect that sales could be made to all countries for older aircraft and those about to be released in the near future. Sales were to be encouraged from Lockheed and Vultee. As it turned out the British were interested in purchasing 200 Lockheed Hudsons and 200 North American trainers. They had no interest in the B-17. The French also purchased the P-36.

The continued effort by the Secretary of War and the army to prevent further development of four-engine planes was evident anytime the subject came up. There was an almost unanimous effort by Air Corps officers to disparage the B-18 as being of no combat use. Arnold was caught in the middle of the tug-of-war created by the GHQ who wanted the B-18— mostly because of the low cost—and his own service. On the other side was the B-17, which he knew little about. He had not been in on the original planning, and his day-to-day operation brought him in close contact with his boss, General Westover. He was following the army line in the procurement matter. In addition, his good friend Andrews was constantly seeking a larger budget for more B-17s. In the final analysis, he agreed with the numbers supported by the Office of the Chief of Air Corps. They reflected the *Balanced Program* between the Air Corps and the GHQ Air Force. Arnold found himself between friends and policy, not a desirable position.

Arnold was handed a request to procure a twin-engine attack-type plane at the time when he was involved with Assistant Secretary of War Johnson on another matter. Afraid that the program would be rejected if he went through normal channels, Arnold indicated to the Assistant Secretary that it would probably be turned down unless some other way could be found. He said the program was needed and highly desired to update the attack combat section. The Assistant Secretary believed it would be a feather in his cap and agreed to take it directly to the President. He called Arnold back the next day to inform him that the procurement was approved. One way or another, Arnold believed he was building the Air Corps bit by bit.

The complaints about the B-18 continued and Andrews suggested a board be appointed to visit the Douglas plant where the B-18A was being built. Arnold appointed a board of five persons, including three from the Air Corps, to make suggestions for improvements. Arnold believed the criticism voiced over the B-18 was the result of poor procurement, and that very little could be done about it. He was not pleased with the P-26, the Seversky P-35 or the Curtiss P-36 and considered all were products of a poor procurement policy. By this time Arnold had become relatively astute in working out problems that arose in military/congressional politics. He attempted to keep Andrews current as to items that affected his command, but too often decisions were made to which he was not privy. He also faced a situation in which his boss concurred with the army on most matters that affected the Air Corps, matters that he disagreed with if asked. One of these was the substratosphere long-range bomber YB-20. Arnold did all he could to justify funds for its development, but failure of the YB-15 to perform as planned provided the War Department with the reason not to fund it. Later, Arnold received notification that the project would not be funded and funds for Fiscal Years 1939 and 1940 would be limited to those aircraft designed for close support of ground troops. The 67 B-17s contained in the 1940 budget would not be funded.

In September 1938, army and navy aircraft performed for the cheering crowds at the Cleveland Air Races. No one, of course, at those races suspected the internal problems that existed for the air force. Following the air races, the American Legion held its convention Los Angeles. The B-17s from March Field, and the XB-15 were to participate but at the last moment were called off for political bickering about who would be invited. Arnold remained in Washington, but his boss, General Westover, and General Andrews attended the affair. The next day, Westover continued his inspection tour and departed for the Lockheed plant at Burbank. During his final turn the plane stalled and crashed, killing Westover and his crew chief.

For three years, Arnold had been dealing with the War Department, the navy, the Congress, aircraft manufactures, aviation magazines, and individual members of the GHQ. He had learned the hard way to deal with each and had become more amenable in matters where the core interests of the Air Corps could be protected. There were, however, differing opinions about whom should be Chief of the Air Corps. During the period of consideration, a rumor circulated that Arnold was a drunk, allegedly developing during his tour in Hawaii. Since Arnold had never served in Hawaii it was obviously the work of someone peeved over a decision or a slight. Arnold decided to seek advice from two close friends, and the decision was to take his record to Harry Hopkins, a confidante of the President. It was a correct course and Arnold was appointed to be Chief of Air Force. His first caller of congratulations was Andrews who assured him of his support and that of the GHQ Air Force.

In assessing and weighing the many pressing and important tasks ahead, Arnold placed the task of procurement at the top. He had current information on the air strength of the European nations, but very little on the Japanese. There was no line of first resistance for the United States to the west and protection must rely on the long-range bomber. All efforts to change the Secretary of War's thinking relative to the need for big, long-range bombers had failed. Arnold's approach to the problem became one of watch and wait for the right opportunity. A problem closer to home was whether the existing runways would provide the length needed for heavy loads. To this end he had a plan. He arranged a scientific meeting at the National Academy of Sciences in Washington and invited several noted scientists. Among them was Dr. Theodore Von Kamman, noted aerodynamicist, assistant to Robert Millikan at Cal Tech. Also Professor Jerome Hunsaker, director of the MIT Guggenheim School participated. Arnold gave them two problems he faced: windows in bombers that would afford good visibility at high altitudes, and rocket thrust to assist heavy bombers into the air from short runways. Arnold advised that he had $10,000 to help provide research on the rocket assist system. Hunsaker said he would take on the windshield job, and Kamman could handle the rocket assist. Karman returned and enlisted the aid of some graduate students, which became the Jet Propulsion Laboratory. It is to Arnold's credit that the early work started in this field of jet propulsion.

Secretary of War Woodring had been requested to leave Washington to assist in the upcoming presidential race for Roosevelt. For the time being there was the possibility that some help might be forthcoming in the procurement of new planes. Arnold received an interesting letter from Charles Lindbergh. He advised Arnold that he had been able to check on the air capability of France and Germany. The French had no aircraft industry and would have to purchase combat planes where they could find them. The Germans had substantial aircraft manufacturing and were producing fast capable fighters, bombers, and dive bombers. He volunteered to send information to Arnold as it became available which he did.

President Roosevelt was also receiving current information on aircraft and decided to call a press conference. He announced the situation demanded a fresh look be made at the nation's air defenses and capabilities. He also committed 2000 new planes to the French, more than the Air Corps had been authorized in five years. Louie Johnson, acting Secretary of War, was told to make immediate plans to greatly increase aircraft production. Johnson's plan called for 31,000 planes in two years and 20,000 each year thereafter. Arnold was asked to provide his estimates. After calling in his best people they could recommend only 1500 combat planes for the Air Corps. Arnold made them count again and this time they came up with 7500. He wrote the figure down and left the number on the blackboard as a future reference to think big.

Arnold submitted his own figures for the army air force at 7000 and a supporting production of 10,000 per year. He added: "Strength in long range bomber type should be in an amount and performance second to none." He was, of course, thinking of Germany and its bomber program from information provided by Charles Lindbergh. From his early experience with the B-10 flight to Alaska, Arnold honed his skills of computing speed and distance and he was thinking in much longer distances to targets such as the United States. He made a point of Germany operating their Heinkel He-111 from bases in South Africa to West Africa to South America. The Heinkel had a reported range of 3300 miles. This caused a sensation and raised the thinking of national defense to a higher level. Obviously, current military thinking was totally inadequate and made up of assumptions that were out of date and possibly dangerous. Arnold also supplied the latest data on four-engine bombers for German, British, Italian and Russian air forces, comparing them to the U.S.

On Monday November 14, 1938, a secret meeting took place in the White House. Top administration people attended, including General Malin Craig, GHQ Chief, General George Marshall, and General Hap Arnold. The meeting changed the course of the Air Corps and the career of Arnold. The Commander-in-Chief did the talking and it centered basically on the immediate need of combat aircraft. He stated that Congress would be asked to approve a force of 20,000 planes and a production capacity of 24,000. He anticipated the number would be scaled down. He estimated the number could be reached in two years by utilizing private plants and seven new ones provided by the government. He said nothing about the need of the army. He asked General Marshall for his opinion, who answered: "I'm sorry, Mr. President, but I don't agree with it all." Roosevelt gave him a startled look and concluded the conference.

Arnold was to refer to the meeting as the Air Corps Magna Carta. There would be heavy going for the air force, but the new resolve for an air force came from the White House and although the course ahead might be altered, the now determined leader and the coming events orchestrated its future. Arnold's next move was to appoint a three-man secret committee: Tooey Spaatz, Joe McNarney, and Claude Duncan. Their job would be to draw up an expansion plan that would total 10,000 planes in a two-year period and the personnel to operate and maintain them. "You will have a month and there will be no publicity," he said. In addition, they were to provide a breakdown of costs for use with the Congress. A smiling Arnold gave the instructions as he told them: "go to work, this is what we've wanted."

The reason General Marshall did not agree with the President was his belief that a balanced budget was necessary for a national defense consisting of army, navy, and air. The theory of such a program advanced by Marshall, Craig, and the Secretary of War Woodring was that each branch depended on the other during war. The budget worked up by Arnold for the Air Corps was added to that developed for the army and navy and totaled $2 billion. It was a hefty sum but long overdue as the defenses for the nation's security had eroded. In hindsight, it might be speculated as to what would have been the situation after Pearl Harbor if rebuilding had not been started.

Big numbers aside, Arnold realized that the planes required pilots and crews. Randolph Field was sending some 165 pilots for advanced training to Kelly Field annually. The air staff came up empty of ideas for increasing the load needed for the new budget. Arnold who looked beyond the capabilities of the military to the civilian pilot schools for a solution. He would make a deal with those civilian schools to follow military decorum and system, train pilots through primary then send them to Randolph and Kelly for intermediate and advanced work. His advisors were against any such plan of taking training away from the military, but there was no choice. Once established, the system soon functioned well and pilots finished training in the thousands. It had been a gamble, but Arnold had made a gamble of his entire career. He would have to make many more as the war progressed.

At the height of Arnold's exhilaration, he became involved in a political intrigue that almost banished him from Washington for the second time. It was not of his doing. The French government, having been promised 2000 military aircraft by Roosevelt, sent their representatives to conclude a purchase of 1000 bombers, fighters, and attack bombers. They wanted to examine the planes, test them, and fly them. Arnold disagreed as he didn't want to divulge classified items to foreign governments and believed the building of the planes would deprive the Air Corps of planes it desperately needed. His views were known by the War Department and to a lesser extent by the Administration. The White House had arranged through Secretary of the Treasury Morganthau to secretly get the planes to France in defiance of neutrality laws. The French were thus given authority by Morganthau to proceed with their purchasing. Shortly thereafter, a French pilot and a civilian pilot were killed during a test flight in California. The news was headlined and Roosevelt's political enemies were out for blood. Morganthau needed a goat and blamed Arnold for the problem. During a subsequent meeting at the White House, the President looked directly at Arnold and said he was going to get the planes to the French as that represented the first line of defense. He also added that there were places where Generals could be sent who interfered with his plans. Arnold candidly admitted he thought he should pack his bags. Although he was not invited back to the White House for nine months, neither was he dismissed as Chief of the Air Corps. In his absence, General Andrews had carried the ball for the air force in public announcements. In one speech some toes were stepped on when he warned about interference in building the Air Corps. His hopes of being re-appointed for another four year tour as commander of GHQ Air Force were ignored. Understanding the vagaries of Washington politics, Arnold regretted the decision as he knew no one could replace Andrews with his knowledge and competent management. Delos Emmons was appointed to replace Andrews and the command structure was changed placing GHQ Air Force in direct command line under Arnold as Chief of the Air Corps.

In April, 1939, Arnold received word that Charles Lindbergh was returning to the United States and sent a cable to the liner *Aquitania* requesting Lindbergh to contact him on arrival. Arnold was on his way to West Point when he heard from Lindbergh and requested that he meet him at the Thayer Hotel at West Point. There, they could discuss matters in quiet and free from the constant press following Lindbergh. The luncheon lasted for hours as the historic airman briefed the head of military air power with information letters could not provide. The two men appreciated each other and the solid air capabilities they represented. Later, Arnold asked Lindbergh to come on active duty in grade of Colonel and take some of his "savvy" and combat know-how on a tour of bases[1].

Arnold later assigned Lindbergh to the Kilner Board to assist in getting a well-funded research and development program underway. Lindbergh would work with Arnold for six months in various assignments, some secret, and then be posted to combat duty in the South Pacific after declaration of war had been declared.

In late April 1939, the term of General Malin Craig ended, and General George Marshall was appointed as Chief of the GHQ. This would bode

---

[1] Author's note: As a Second Lieutenant in the 20th Fighter Group, I served as Officer of the Day when Lindbergh landed at Moffett Field in 1939 flying a P-36. He was gracious and pleasant as he inquired about duty and flying the P-36.

well for Arnold as the Air Corps could look forward to a much better treatment in its expansion efforts. With the appointment of Marshall possibly his first act was to notify Andrews that he would serve on the prestigious General Staff as its Assistant Chief of Staff for Operations and Training G-3. The assignment and promotion to permanent Brigadier General of the line was a tribute and honor for a fine officer who served his country well and with devotion. Arnold was pleased, and as he flew to the West Coast on September 1, 1939, he sent a message of congratulations via the plane's radio to General George Marshall, flying in the same air space. Much lay ahead for both men.

Gen. Henry "Hap" Arnold, United States Air Force
who served beyond duty and honor is recognized as a
Legend of Air Power

Frank M. Andrews

There were two squadrons in formation high above, sitting, waiting in the sun. They waited, holding for his signal. Then it came and they peeled off, plummeting down guns ready!

These guns were not to shoot. Leading was Lt. Col. Frank M. Andrews with two squadrons of Boeing P-12s signaling a welcome to General Italo Balbo, flying a S-55 Savoia Marchetti Flying Boat just arrived on a 6100-mile venture from Orbitello, Italy. The date was July 15, 1933. The army GHQ staff officer said the momentous flight had no bearing on the future! Such would be the denigration of the Air Corps until a short year before the Japanese attack on Pearl Harbor.

Among those who struggled to keep the effort alive to provide the protection of air power to his country, none did more than Frank Maxwell Andrews. His name is enshrined on the number one base, Andrews Air Force Base, Washington, DC[2]. Andrews' death occurred while flying a mission for his country during wartime, and he joined the legion of other pilots who died in their nation's service, during those combative years of WWII.

Frank Andrews, born in Nashville, Tennessee, was probably the youngest would-be pilot to be grounded. It occurred when he attempted a jump from the roof of his home holding tightly to the family umbrella. The flight resulted in damage to his mother's flowerbed and young Frank was grounded by his father. Later, he attended West Point, graduating in 1906.

---

[2] The author served as Deputy Base Commander when the enthronement took place in 1944, and later as its second Commander.

Gen. Frank Andrews

Subsequently, he attempted to be transferred to the air branch, but was thwarted by a Major whose daughter he wished to marry. He commented he didn't want his daughter to become an early widow. Such was the view of army officers in those very early days of military flying. That concluded the matter as under existing law married officers could not enter flight training. The law was changed later with the advent of WWI and he was assigned to the Aviation Section. He graduated from flight training school at Rockwell Field in April 1918, and received the rating of Junior Military Aviator.

Andrews was not sent to France during World War One, but remained assigned to headquarters with temporary rank of Lieutenant Colonel. When Billy Mitchell returned from France in 1919, Andrews was Chief of the Inspection Division and member of the Air Advisory Board. Andrews, whose approach was low-key and steady, offset Mitchell who was dynamic and boisterous. Mitchell was to learn that Andrews was a basically sound and thorough officer with a good understanding of the potential of air power. They complimented each other in their efforts to pursue the role of the Air Corps in national defense. A year later, Andrews was promoted to permanent rank of Major and transferred to Germany as Chief of the American Air Service in Cobbles. His flying was done at Weissenthurm air station with an assortment of 13 planes. He and the pilots assigned kept busy flying trips to visit the various air facilities in the countries around them. In 1922 Mitchell stopped by to visit while conducting a tour of Europe's developing air facilities and forces and the two men had much to discuss. Between them they determined that although Germany was racked by inner turmoil and economic collapse, it was not a defeated nation. Andrews returned from Europe in 1923 and was assigned as Commanding Officer of the Advanced Flying School at Kelly Field. Mitchell was exiled to San Antonio in 1925.

The two men spent much time together discussing various problems and the best ways to address them. Andrews tried but was unable to keep the determined Mitchell from continuing his crusade.

Although Andrews was a quiet person and wanted firm ground in making decisions, he was not robotic or stolid, but willing to take chances with a well designed and thought-out plan. The following episode occurred while Andrews was attending West Point illustrates this. Andrews' platoon was bivouacked not far from a community dance hall, which was off limits to cadets. By design he pitched his tent at the end of the platoon line. After waiting until everyone was settled, he got up and stowed his tent and pack in the nearby woods, then beat it to the party. Since bed-check would be made by tent occupancy, he figured he would be in the clear. After a fun-filled evening he returned, re-pitched his tent and slept until reveille. It was a little dangerous, but well outweighed by clever planning of a strategic mission. In future years, his planning and strategies were marked by well-thought out approaches designed to bring successful conclusions to his efforts.

Andrews was an excellent pilot and strove to improve his abilities. He believed all pilots should be qualified to fly on instruments, and to improve as new technology provided greater capability to deal with weather. He did not buy the doctrine that since pursuit and attack pilots do not fly in cloud conditions or when visibility is poor to zero on a mission, they don't need to be instrument qualified. Neither did he agree with the premise that bomber pilots did not need to fly by instruments because they could not bomb if they were in the soup and couldn't see the target, nor that there was no need for all Air Corps aircraft to have the proper navigational aids and instrumentation. Andrews would not accept these excuses for pilots not to be qualified enough for flying on instruments. He reasoned that if the real potential of air power was to be achieved, then all pilots must be able to fly on instruments when encountering weather conditions. Not one to criticize but not perform, Andrews ferried an aged Keystone bomber from Langley Field to March Field during poor weather. Then, in 1932, he led a flight of five ragtag planes from Kelly Field to France Field in the Canal Zone. They were antiquated Keystone bombers and a pair of Douglas amphibians.

Andrews planned to fly ahead and make necessary protocol, arrangements at stopovers for refueling, maintenance work, and quarters. The flight covered 2200 miles without problems or mishaps due to planning and good maintenance. It required 25 hours of flight time and 2 weeks en route. Andrews believed it would be safer to fly in the morning hours when the weather was good and avoid the afternoon thunderstorms. But, he believed the military airplane must be capable of operating anytime as most certainly enemy aircraft would be. When Andrews returned, he immediately applied to take the course for instrument flying at Kelly Field. Afterwards, he kept in practice by flying in actual weather conditions. Graduating air cadets were required to learn the rudiments of instrument flying and be able to perform the tried and true *needle, ball, and air speed* system. That and the 180-degree turn saved many pilots caught in unexpected bad weather.

In 1931 Andrews became unexpectedly involved in a bad-weather fiasco. After protracted negotiations, the navy agreed to permit the use of a old ship hulk named the *Mount Shasta* as a bombing target. Andrews got caught up in the idea and helped promote it to the press. It was billed as the second Mitchell battleship bombing of the century. The 2nd Bomb Group at Langley Field, commanded by Bert Dargue, led the group out to sea in bad weather on the first day. They couldn't locate the old tub and got royally fouled up milling around the Atlantic. The second day, flying in rain squalls, they spotted the target and dropped 42 bombs, making only one minor hit. The navy sank her with its own guns and the Air Corps had egg yoke smeared all over while the navy rubbed salt in the wound. Andrews let his displeasure be known and believed the lack of instrument flying ability was largely to blame.

In 1933, Andrews was ordered to Selfridge Field to command the 1st Pursuit Group. He had completed a three-year stint of duty serving as the Executive to General Foulois, Chief of the Air Corps, and also completed the Army War College. Earlier he had completed the Command and General Staff School. Andrews was highly regarded in the upper levels of the army for his capabilities, and in 1929 had been one of three pilots in the Air Corps placed on the eligibility list to the General Staff. Andrews had enjoyed a close relationship with Arnold who referred to him as "Andy" starting with their days at West Point. He was one year senior to Arnold in rank.

Following the *Mount Shasta* affair, Andrews returned to his post at Selfridge Field determined that the pilots in his group would become proficient instrument pilots. However, he had no sooner returned than he was assigned the flying mission to welcome the Italian flying group. As it turned out the incident provided an example of what instrument flying was all about. It was exactly the thinking behind Andrews' push for instrument proficiency. Balbo's crews had spent months in training for the long flight. Their planes were equipped with the best instrument and navigational equipment available. On the long and weather-dangerous leg from Reykjavik, Iceland, to Cartwright, Labrador, the efforts had paid off. The crews had fought heavy turbulence, headwinds, fog, and severe icing, but came through safely and without delay. The aeronautical axiom was made clear in Balbo's report: *The air forces can, like the navies, confront the problem of moving squadrons. With the Atlantic flight, Italy has furnished proof of these possibilities . . . aviation can make gigantic strides with improvement of machines, crew training, and organization of meteorological, logistic and technical services which are still too insufficient.*

Andrews had published virtually the same message in his paper written at the War College titled: "The Airplane in National Defense." He had also complained that peacetime limitations imposed a lack of funds and that there was a tendency to judge by past performances *during wartime without regard to changing improvements.* Here, he was making reference to the reports sent from Italy during the preparation of the flight, but never forwarded to the Air Corps from Army GHQ as they weren't considered pertinent. With the festivities at a close, Andrews was eager to return to his command. In order to start instrument flying in his 1st Pursuit group, he decided to take inventory of the needed equipment. To his dismay, he found that not one airplane was equipped with a gyrocompass or gyro horizon, both essential to instrument flying. In addition he knew the aircraft compasses on the P-12s were not reliable and gave incorrect readings. The radios produced by the Signal Corps were not reliable and many provided only one-way communication. In addition to these problems, the BT-2 he had hoped to use as a trainer had been wrecked in a taxi accident.

During the summer and fall, Andrews sent letters through channels to Washington and Wright Field. He found there was ready agreement to the problem, but no money to solve it. Maj. Hugh Knerr, Chief of Field Services, wanted to hold his limited resources for new equipment coming on line, rather than spend it on the existing items that would soon be obsolete. Andrews didn't agree, commenting that it was better to have the best available now than to have nothing at all. Andrews knew also that the Air Corps people in Washington agreed with him. He decided to keep up the effort hoping that by starting a campaign early, there might be a better chance of getting the necessary funds.

An important reason for improving instrument flying and navigation was the Coastal Defense mission assigned to the Air Corps. It was the driving force behind all Air Corps programs. Andrews understood the difficulty in making the Army GHQ knowledgeable concerning the need for instruments and navigation aids. Consequently, if they could not sell the army on essential funds, they must find some other way to obtain those funds.

Air Corps strength was declining, not growing. Only 33 cadets graduated from Kelly Field in the fall. Many of those were seeking jobs with the airlines, due to the restriction of funds for 2nd lieutenant pay for active duty. A few cadets volunteered to stay on for a year. Those going with the airlines would probably be lost for good, and those returning home would probably forget most of their training. It was a bleak picture. There was a recommendation to cut 15 percent of all pay, and the President had been given authority to cut flight pay altogether. In addition, Roosevelt had made an arbitrary reduction of Air Corps funds from $40 million to $7.5 million for new aircraft.

Andrews was leading the 24th Squadron to Miami for a public relations appearance at the All-American Air Races. It was an annual affair that gave the Air Corps a chance to perform for the public. It was a must to prevent the navy from getting all the press and newsreel coverage. After the hoopla was over and during a quiet moment in time, Andrews realized he would reach the age of 50 within the month. His days in the air would be over as more important tasks would be assigned. One, most important to the Air Corps, would require all his skill and patience. That was the efforts of those who opposed control over the nation's air arm by army officers, and their removal from office and otherwise denigrated. Not just the army but politicians as well meted out the punishment. Assignment to high office in the Air Corps could be a sacrifice for those die-hard stalwarts who supported a separate air arm.

During the proceeding October, the Drum Board had recommended that the Air Corps set up its authorized Air Force GHQ. Nothing had been done by the army to follow through, and there was concern that the navy might move into the breach with its own plan of Coastal Defense. On October 17 Andrews was officially notified that his new assignment would be with the G-3 Section of the General Staff. His work would be sorting out the details of organizing the new GHQ Air Force. Problems started immediately. Waiting for him on his desk was a plan already worked out by the G-3 section that had the approval of the Chief of Staff. The tables of organization provided for a number of promotions for those in the command section. The G-3 resisted that section of the tables, objecting to the rank increases. It wasn't the resistance that bothered Andrews, but that he didn't know whether General MacArthur would be re-appointed as Chief of Staff. Andrews considered him the driving force behind the GHQ Air Force. MacArthur was known to want a combat air arm, but was concerned about the joint Army-Navy Board's acceptance of conditions of a GHQ Air Force. The provisions could create ambiguous and contradictory command authority between the two services pertaining to coastal defense in time of war. It had to be corrected before the final date of organization.

Regardless of the delays placed in his way by the G-3, Andrews submitted the tables of organization on December 11 to General Drum. By that time it was known that the GHQ Air Force was soon to be activated. Many Air Corps officers were being considered, but on the day Andrews delivered the tables to General Drum he was notified of his selection to be the Commanding General of the GHQ Air Force. Official notice was made on December 26. Congratulations and good wishes poured in from many persons in the military and civilian communities, including the navy and government. The appointment brought general good feelings but Brigadier General Frank Andrews had no office to hang his hat and no desk or chair to sit on. His staff consisted of 1st Lt. Pete Quesada who had been assigned as operations officer to the GHQ Air Force along with his boss. Quesada was a savvy energetic officer and a good pilot. He had served as Executive to retiring Secretary Trubee Davison. His office was located in the State War and Navy Building on the second floor and was still vacant. He made the necessary arrangements for the space and escorted his boss to the new office of the new GHQ Air Force headquarters. It was on Pennsylvania Avenue, just a stone's throw from the White

House. Quesada soon realized that under the apparent smooth feelings between Andrews and the GHQ there was an ugly undercurrent being generated from the G-3 Section of the War Department where Andrews had been working on the tables of organization. He satisfied himself that it did not come from the top echelon but from the next layer of Colonels who were either jealous or disgruntled over the ascendancy of Andrews. He ascertained they had placed roadblocks to thwart Andrews in his work on the tables of organization and were still at it. Andrews, aware of the situation, said nothing and continued to work around their stunts.

On January 10 Andrews received a directive from Secretary of War Dern to have the GHQ Air Force organized by March 1. He would start with a staff of four officers, a chief of staff, and three assistants. He was free to make his own selections. His choices were based on experience, age, qualities of energy, dedication, and determination. He selected three Majors and one Captain, all with approximately 20 years of service. Three had prior combat service and all were considered to be pros in the business of flying. Andrews received a constant stream of letters from pilots in many places offering their services and loyalty. He explained the smallness of his organization, which would be only 23 officers and 85 enlisted personnel. He answered them all, and kept track of them. He was wise in the ways the military functions and knew changes would be necessary for schools and growth that would eventually take away good men.

Andrews found himself being criticized for his manner of selecting personnel. Some said his loyalty to close friends made him blind to their shortcomings. He disagreed. If he could see strength he could overlook weakness, and that was how he sized up his choices. Those he appointed worked hard to give their best for his fairness in return. He was fully aware that within the exclusive structure of military life, prejudice, jealousy and personality often played a part in who gets what or went where. Although he was helpful and protective of his friends, his actions were always within the proper framework of the structure.

One example of the Andrews approach was his friend, Walter Weaver. He had transferred from the Infantry to the Air Section of the Signal Corps in 1917. He was a West Pointer and his father had been Chief of the Coast Artillery, retiring as a Major General. Weaver was able to quickly establish the Air Corps' first aviation mechanics school, in face of a negative bureaucracy. Starting in 1919, and for the next two years, he served with Andrews in different capacities. Andrews then attended War College and Weaver went to the Army Industrial College. Weaver earned his wings in 1921 and classified as bomber pilot. He was considered an average pilot, specializing in training and logistics. He and Andrews were friends and golfing pals. In 1922, as CO of Mitchel Field, he converted it from a run-down and deteriorating installation into one of the best bases in the army. He was considered a fierce competitor with strong opinions, especially on the use of air power. He was serious and conscientious, a strong believer in strategic air power and a firm friend of Billy Mitchell. He had written a strong attack on an Army Board report for publication, however, the editor thought it might get him in trouble and it was published under Billy Mitchell's name. He was a believer in publicity and had written Andrews, Arnold, and two others to join him in a publicity effort to tell the story of the Air Corps. Andrews was able to work out a position for Weaver as the Air Inspector. His rank would be Lt. Colonel. Andrews advised him that would be the top rank for the job in accordance with the Tables, but he would try to get him put back on flying status. Weaver's reply of appreciation also contained a proviso that he would never place Andrews in the position of having a problem over his appointment.

Information provided by the press indicated that the organization of this new GHQ Air Force was a huge air component capable of protecting the nation from attack, and with the ability to destroy the enemy. In fact, the outfit was in reality a paper tiger. Andrews described the fundamental mission of his command this way: "To organize and train so as to operate efficiently in any weather and against any proper objective within range of the equipment available . . . If we can deny a potential enemy air base, fixed or floating, from which he can operate by air against the Continental United States, then, and only then, are we in a position to accomplish our mission."

The army, with General MacArthur's approval, had recommended a complement of 1245 pilots and 980 planes of which Andrews had 555 pilots and 446 aircraft on hand. Only 176 planes were considered modern and suitable. Command headquarters was located at Langley Field. On paper, the three Wings of bombers and pursuit squadrons looked formidable, but lacked the teeth to really bite. Unfortunately, overly-ambitious writers led the public into believing the force was in being. Much of this was the fault of the army in its publicity releases. In Europe, attention was quickly given the story. In Germany, Hitler let it be known openly what had been going on in secret for a year. The German Air Force, or Luftwaffe, was now an independent arm of the Reichswehr. Air Minister Hermann Goering would be in command. Goering immediately informed the world that Germany demanded "equality" in the air, while his subordinates in the huge, newly built Air Ministry were engaged in a crash program to attain air superiority. The French lodged a protest with the League of Nations as a violation the Versailles Treaty. At the same time, a British delegation meeting with Hitler in Berlin assured the German leader they wanted peace.

The Air Corps Act of 1926 included a provision pertaining to temporary promotion for duty commensurate with the rank required. If the temporary rank did not become permanent while the officer held it, he could be rotated to another duty and revert back to the lower grade. This meant loss of pay and the sudden change from Brigadier General to Lt. Colonel overnight. There was much complaint and in a short time the army issued its Circular 7 recommending expanding the opportunity for temporary rank. As a result, 616 out of 1333 regular officers in the Air Corps received promotions. This was in line with Andrews' wishes, and regular officers and reserves received equal treatment. The real goal was a separate promotion list of the Air Corps, which Andrews now believed attainable. The agreement by the army to bring the GHQ Air Force into being, its help on the promotions matter, plus the desire of the army to keep Coastal Defense, convinced Andrews that a better understanding now existed between the two. However, the command structure of the GHQ Air Force soon proved it was a convoluted situation that could not work. This was pointed out to Andrews by Lt. Colonel Ralph Royce, commanding Selfridge Field. He was accountable to four commanders. These included: The Chief of the Air Corps for personnel and technical inspection; the Chief of Material Division on matters of maintenance; the Commanding General of the GHQ Air Force for tactical training; and the Commanding General VI Corps Area for matters relating to courts-martial and administration of non-Air Corps troops assigned. Andrews considered it a system that demanded too much time of his commanders, and he was determined to bring changes. He had two main problems within his command: personnel and divided authority. One would require appropriations to increase strength, and the other would need reason and persuasion.

Andrews held hope that the Howell Commission would provide recommendations helpful toward the separation of the Air Corps from army control. On January 22, 1935, the report was given to the President. Unfortunately, it made no recommendation concerning a separate air force, but supported the GHQ Air Force concept. Andrews expressed his disappointment. However, he concluded there would be little reason to aggravate the situation, at least not for the present. He called a meeting of the senior officers in his GHQ Air force and recommended they follow his thinking in the matter.

Andrews believed he should let the public know about the GHQ Air Force, what it could do and could not do. He appeared before the Rotary

Club of Newport News and discussed the protection of having bombers to attack the enemy at its air bases, and its factories making the arms of war. It was strictly a defense-monitored theme, but cleverly included the potentials of strategic warfare for those so interested. He also contacted a well-known radio personality who had given good reports on the GHQ Air Force, inviting him for a visit. An ex-RAF pilot, he was appreciative of Andrews efforts and became a reliable source for release of information to the public.

A problem faced Andrews in the matter of the announced flight to the Panama Canal Zone. It was his feeling, which had been expressed to Arnold who had a squadron involved, that after inspection of the aircraft, crew training, and general ability to make the flight under safe conditions, it wasn't ready. Also, the planning called for a 900-mile stretch almost entirely over water. Andrews believed the decision-making belonged to him as Commander of the air force. The Assistant Chief of the Air Corps disagreed and it was taken to General MacArthur for a decision. He sided with Andrews. The decision was not permanent, but temporary, and when the deficiencies were corrected it could be rescheduled. He then listed several items of concern: The aircraft weren't equipped with segregators necessary to remove water from fuel. The squadron engineers had done nothing about installing them and indicated there was no planned need. Andrews remarked that was a sloppy attitude, indeed the aircraft would be operating in an area of heavy rain and high humidity. In the matter of instrument flying, not all pilots were as proficient as needed and should be assigned to the instrument course planned to start at Wright Field. He also wanted the type aircraft selected, B-10 or B-12, to be thoroughly inspected and that a 1500-mile flight be made to include flying through fog without loss of contact or control. He had requested Arnold to have the pilots making the flight visit Langley where he could talk with them. He explained that the political effects of having anything unfavorable happen could affect the future of the GHQ Air Force in its role of national defense. There must be no chances taken with this mission. Arnold agreed with him. Andrews had no sooner taken care of the matter, and soothed some hurt feelings of pilots who wanted to make the inspiring flight, than a political matter of great concern arose.

Through a clerical error in the office of the Chairman of the House Military Affairs Committee, secret testimony given by Andrews had been released for public consumption. The testimony related to a scenario "what if" a foreign government made an attack on the United States. Andrews had discussed the theory of defense and the probable response. In the abstract, Canada had been named in the discussion as a possible target for bombing and the press blew it sky-high. Roosevelt, the State Department, and all of Congress were indignant and demanded an investigation for those responsible. The press had named Andrews and, of course, there was a clamor to fire him. Older and calmer voices were heard and the whole thing died down. General MacArthur wrote a severe admonishment, castigating Andrews for his testimony. This caused a confrontation with MacArthur without satisfaction. It violated Andrews' code that senior officers protect those below. Andrews saw MacArthur's action as an injustice done to cover himself and the war department. He would not again hold MacArthur in the same light of respect as before.

After the press had run out of print space on the story, Andrews got down to a matter that was of extreme importance. It was the badly needed appropriations bill for additional funds to the Air Corps that MacArthur had requested in February. The Secretary had approached Congress and requested an immediate appropriation of that amount in addition to the regular budget. He received information the next day that the request was being made to the full military affairs committee. Woodring advised he would go with the chairman, if it were approved, to see the President for his approval. It appeared to Andrews that, at last, something was going right. Wrong! The visit to Roosevelt was not made. The request was made again but the source of funds had been used up, and when it was taken up with Roosevelt, he refused to do anything about it. The funding would have to be requested through regular procedures.

After the discouraging news, Andrews returned to face other stacks of problems. Of constant concern was the increasing load of training requirements throughout his command without the addition of qualified officers. The number of regular officers on whom he could rely was backed up with reserves whose tenure was uncertain. He commented: "Because in our units today we have three or four regular officers, and the rest untrained youngsters, our units are far from measuring up to that standard of efficiency to be rated an M-Day force. I am also afraid this shortage of experienced officers is affecting our accident rate, particularly with the pressure of additional training which we are facing in all our wings." Andrews believed that to command meant to lead. Consequently, he passed on his ideas that might be helpful to those struggling with problems. One idea to eliminate the source of accidents was to establish a system whereby his inspectors would classify aircraft defects under two classifications: those that might cause a forced landing or crash and those that would not. Each month he would post a chart showing the class of defects in each squadron and the results. When a large disparity developed between squadrons, he moved to find out the reason and reacted accordingly.

In August, Andrews commented to Arnold that he believed the GHQ Air Force was catching on in Washington. He said the outfit is definitely on the map as an important part in our defense forces, adding that training regulations coming out soon would give a definite status and that the Wilcox bill recognized the GHQ Air Force in legislation.

In December, the first real service test would be made. The first six months of organizing the GHQ Air Force had passed with many gains posted. Andrews' staff in its meeting worked toward the purpose of the test, which was designed to test the mobility of moving the air units. Toward that goal and also to take the sting out of canceling the Panama Canal flight, Andrews called on Pete Quesada to give him a check out in the B-12 on pontoons. It was the only one of a kind. Andrews was an active pilot, having accrued more then 3000 hours of flying time. The B-12 had only one cockpit, so it was a talk-through check out. Andrews found his hands full. It was a trick to break water at the right time and took a little doing to get the hang of it. The landing was even more tricky and took fast talking from Quesada to get the bird down. After the lesson, Andrews remarked to his instructor, "Gee, Pete, it isn't as easy as I had thought." But, he stayed at it and in time became proficient.

The staff took note and came up with an idea that would demonstrate the ability of the GHQ Air Force to operate over water while setting a speed record. And more, it would demonstrate the ability of its premier pilot to fly as well as command. On August 24, Andrews lifted the B-12 off from Willoughby Spit at Hampton Rhodes and set course for Floyd Bennett Field, Long Island. The plane carried two 1100-pound bombs. By the time Andrews completed the 2000-kilometer course (1200 miles) he had broken three seaplane records set by Charles Lindbergh and Ed Musick in a Sikorsky Pan American Clipper. The record was for the 1000-kilometer course only as he experienced spark plug trouble toward the end of the flight, reducing his speed. Head winds were given as the reason but the real trouble was reconditioned spark plugs. In addition to the shortage of funds for essentials, the shortage of officer personnel was retarding the efforts of Andrews and his staff to develop the GHQ Air Force. Congress continued to play its games. In August it authorized an additional 1650 officers, and 50 regular commissions for flying cadets. However, it failed to provide the funds that were needed. If the authorized strength were to become reality, then it would have to be provided in the 1937 budget. When General Malin Craig was appointed to replace General MacArthur, Andrews made a status report to him concerning GHQ Air Force. The shortages of officer personnel continued, aircraft shortages increased and the shortage of parts hindered combat efficiency.

Also, the continuation of corps area control interfered with good command structure. He was pleased to report that 75 percent of the pilots were now instrument qualified. In 1938, it was the goal to see that all pilots were qualified. A final item to discuss was the future of the B-299 to be known as the B-17.

Shortly after delivery of the first B-17 model to Wright Field, it had crashed on take off. It was a devastating blow to Andrews. He was relying on the four-engine plane to move into an updated theory of strategic tactics with a long-range bomber that had speed and could carry a heavy load of bombs to the target. He wanted to know precisely what had happened. It was not complicated: the lever locking the elevator in the tail section had not been released, thus preventing the pilot from having the necessary control on take off. Now, funds would have to be procured for a second plane. Meanwhile, Andrews had received some good news concerning bombing accuracy from Hap Arnold. He decided to fly west to March Field. He personally observed the bombing accuracy and related his pleasure to Arnold. But another problem had come up, a lack of oxygen for use at 18,000 feet. Arnold advised he couldn't get it and when they used it the liquid oxygen leaked making it necessary to abort the flight. It was suggested that gas oxygen would be a better method, but as yet, bombers flying at 18,000 feet were rare.

It became obvious that it would take considerable help to get the B-17s. The B-18 had been approved for purchase and while it was unable to perform the mission, it was cheap. Andrews was prevailed upon to take the matter to the army staff and convince them to recommend the purchase of 13 four-engine bombers. He suggested they be purchased under experimental funds and the army staff accepted his suggestion. The conformity within the Air Corps for the B-17 did not extend itself to the Pursuit plane. Two were in contention: the P-35 and the P-36. Andrews disagreed with the method used in selecting the plane by the board. He contacted Robbie Robins at the Material Division to determine how it was done. He learned that in the process a number of board members were selected from the field and one from GHQ Air Force who had not discussed his position when appointed and consequently had little input. This Evaluation Board determines what is available and selects the desired. Little testing was done in flying, shooting, or communications. The decision was made on the basis that the plane might make 300 miles per hour against the Curtiss plane that was set at 280 MPH. Robins said his people had nothing to do with the decision and suggested that next time the GHQ Air Force board member should be better instructed. Andrews indicated his displeasure with the method, and so advised the

Chief of Air Force. He wrote: "This is your pigeon and I'm staying out of it, but it was a sloppy job by your Evaluation Board." He received no reply. Robins, who had been catching heat on procurement, suggested that maybe it would be better to purchase planes based on quantity rather than quality. Andrews came down hard on that idea. "I can't imagine the navy buying wooden battleships because they cost less. It's our job to get the plane that will do the job. It will cost more, but we must educate the congress why a certain airplane is important."

The continuing effort by the navy to assume the coastal defense assignment continued to bother Andrews. The navy intended to go ahead with a striking force of at least 1000 shore-based airplanes for that purpose. Andrews had cause for concern about an upcoming service test, which was to prove the capability of the air force for the coastal defense mission. The exercise would be a mock attack against the United States and the Panama Canal through the Caribbean area. Because his staff was considerably below strength, Andrews decided to accept the Tactical School's offer to help. He suggested that the school develop and test communications methods. Air Force Headquarters would control the exercise during the December 2 to 10 period. Combat units moved out on December 1 and all were in position within 23 hours at seven selected bases. Arnold's 7th Bombardment Group made it in 21 hours. This led Andrews to report to Craig that, given the proper advance notice and barring unusually bad weather, he could place a force anywhere in the United States within 24 hours. During surveillance, contacts of ships at sea were reported as enemy and pursuit aircraft took off to intercept, some as far as 100 miles at sea. In spite of navy claims that army planes couldn't navigate that far over water, they found the targets and returned to base. For pursuit interceptors, the targets gave their locations as if a radar net covered the area, and were intercepted without difficulty. Andrews could scramble 36 pursuit planes airborne and on their way to intercept in six minutes from the time of alarm. Pilots were in the ready room and, on signal, grabbed a 'chute and made a run to their planes. While they hooked up in the cockpit, a truck drove along the flight line with a big sign giving magnetic course, altitude and estimated distance from point of attack. It was considered quite an ingenious and effective plan. News media covered the event and there were no slip-ups or accidents to mar the exercise. The basis of Andrews' plan was later used in the Battle of Britain to defeat Hitler's raids.

Florida residents were impressed with the number of aircraft engaged each day. What they saw was the total force. Although it was successful and looked impressive, the reality was that the Air Corps was seriously under manned and not capable of a sustained effort against any aggressor.

Not long after the exercise, Andrews received notice of his promotion to Major General as authorized for the commander of GHQ Air Force. Other changes took place and a new Chief of the Air Corps was appointed. Andrews' held a philosophical reaction to his promotion. "It's only temporary and can change with the April showers, and at any time I have a different point of view with the powers that be and I'll be out." His promotion brought a huge number of congratulatory letters and calls from all sorts of people, in and out of the service. Claire Egtvedt, president of Boeing, summed it up: "It is very gratifying to know that you and GHQ Air Force, which you command, are being recognized not only by this significant promotion but by leaders of importance throughout the country who feel that your command represents something real in national defense."

Lowell Thomas, a popular news commentator of the time, invited Andrews to share the microphone with him during the evening of January 13. Andrews accepted. At the interview, in answer to questions, Andrews stated: "Uncle Sam is woefully unprepared for defense. Of 980 planes authorized for the air force, probably only one-third would be available at year's end. Landing fields are badly needed and without them a big concentration of planes is useless. Certainly the public should know, as should the Congress, to provide for an adequate defense."

Command exercised by the Army Corps Area commanders over the air bases had been irksome since its inception. The only purpose for it to exist was that it represented a method to control Air Corps activities. Andrews had worked continuously to get it changed. Finally, he was able to convince the Army GHQ that it worked to the disadvantage of Air Corps commanders and the system was discontinued. No sooner had that command problem been settled than Andrews faced another. The Chief of Air Corps had been lobbying to get the GHQ Air Force under his command. He spoke to Andrews about it, but he disagreed as to how it would be arranged. Both men were Major Generals and vital to the entire air program. One reason given to promote the idea was to reduce bickering between the two staffs. Andrews, however, was unconvinced, and didn't like the idea of losing his entree to the Army GHQ. "It would work fine in peacetime but not in war," he commented. Andrews went on to explain that a basic War Department Training Regulation stated that in time of war the GHQ Air Force would be under the command of the Chief of Staff and not the Air Corps. Andrews made his point but the Chief of Air Corps was upset over the lack of support as he saw it, and strong words were uttered.

In May, the Chief of Air Corps ordered George Kenney, the G-3 of GHQ Air Force, to duty as an instructor to the Infantry School. Andrews wrote Army GHQ that to lose Kenney would be a set back for the entire air force as he represented the heart of training and operations, and he pointed out, that three of the last G-3 assignments had been lost for one reason or another. The response was sympathetic, but the request for Kenney had come from the Chief of Infantry and there was no replacement available. This was another serious point of contention for Andrews. He felt the interests of air force were ignored in the reassignment of its personnel and indicated he thought such changes should be channeled through air force for comment before they were announced.

George Kenney's G-3 section gave considerable attention to the impact of public demonstrations of Air Corps aircraft and personnel involved in tests and record-setting events. It was a method of getting the Air Corps picture before the congress and public. The section put forth the idea that a long-distance flight by one of its planes flown by the commander would be impressive. The plan called for a twin-engine Douglas amphibian plane *The Big Duck* to double the distance flown by Andrews on his previous record-setting flight. Andrews agreed to the proposal. He would make a non-stop flight from San Juan, Puerto Rico, to Newark, New Jersey. This would double the distance of his previous record-setting flight from San Juan to Miami. The official purpose was to test long-range navigation equipment and to inspect landing and servicing facilities in Puerto Rico. He selected his crew and also invited Maj. Gen. Frank McCoy, 11 Corps Area Commander, to go along and inspect an infantry unit he commanded there. Also, Andrews wanted to illustrate the feasibility of air force flight over water. The flight from Langley Field to Florida was made in heavy rain, and the men remained overnight in Miami. The next day they continued on to San Juan. Andrews spent a few days looking at potential field sites. The wind blew strong the morning for departure and the water was choppy, requiring an extra-long run for takeoff. About 400 miles out they encountered a line squall and Andrews bored into and through it for 10 minutes. The turbulence battered the plane with heavy rain that restricted forward vision to zero. Once through it, they traveled the next 1200 miles in brilliant sunshine. Andrews commented in his log: "We did not see a sail or a bird, nothing but ocean." Stronger than expected headwinds forced the flight to land at Langley Field, but a distance record had been set.

Andrews had indicated his dissatisfaction with the command structure as it existed between GHQ Air Force and the Air Corps, and once again aired his feelings to the Army Chief of Staff over personnel changes. He made this suggestion: "The creation of an Air Division of the War Department's General Staff would do much to allay the clamor for a separate Air Corps. It would weld the Army Air Corps firmly together as an integral part of the army and would prevent the recurrence that had made it necessary to separate the tactical units from the Chief of the Air Corps." Andrews received no reaction to his suggestion and once more experienced the intense frustration that seemed to dog him in almost every aspect for improving his GHQ Air Force. It seemed that every small gain to advance helpful ideas succeeded only in falling by the wayside of time. One day he had them, the next day they disappeared.

Andrews tried to resolve some of the difficulties between the Air Corps staff and his own by assigning one of his officers to work in Washington in the Air Corps office. It didn't work. The officer found himself virtually ignored. He couldn't find a place for his desk and no help was forthcoming for a secretary. It seemed that every effort made to eliminate the eternal bickering between his staff and that of the Air Corps Chief was doomed to wither away. He received no respite from the personnel problem and his top people were being sent to schools or rotated.

War had come to Spain and the German Government was deeply involved in getting its Luftwaffe combat trained and its aircraft battle tested. Intelligence information gathered by American officers was sent to G-2 of the GHQ, but it never found its way to the Air Corps or the GHQ Air Force. Andrews looked forward to the new Congress in 1936 with a feeling of intensity and hopefulness. New people were coming in and the situations abroad served to bring those in office a concern for the future. Out of it all Andrews hoped to have two Groups of B-17s: one on the West Coast and one on the East Coast by 1938. On January 18, 1937, a new bill, known as the Wilcox bill H.R.3151, was introduced in Congress. Its purpose was to create an Air Corps under the Secretary of War, to be known as the United States Air Corps to consist of the regular Air Corps, the National Guard air units and personnel while in the service of the United States and the Air Corps Reserve. Andrews explained that the purpose was to recognize air power equal to the army and navy in the scheme of national defense. Secretary of War Woodring told Congressman Lister Hill that he and the GHQ were unalterably opposed to the Bill. He concluded his remarks by adding: "During the past 11 years, four previous attempts to offer similar proposals have been received. None has added to the national defense."

During the phase of discussion about the Wilcox Bill, Andrews had been quietly checking into a old theory being advanced by the Army GHQ to harness the build-up of heavy bombers in favor of the balanced Air Corps. This new plan would be the political and military determination by the Secretary of War, together with the Army GHQ, to prevent the Air Corps from creating a strategic bombing force. Working against Andrews to increase the purchase of B-17s was the lack of experience with the plane and its damaging crash on the first test flight. Whenever Andrews made a pitch for funds to buy more B-17s he was rebuffed by cost and a lack of substantial support from operations. As a result, when the 2nd Bomb Group, under command of Bob Olds, was equipped with the first B-17s, Andrews made it a point to explain why nothing must go wrong—even down to a broken tail wheel. Andrews met with the Olds and Hal George, his executive officer, to brief them on his thoughts: "This is one airplane that can't be cracked up, not even in a minor way. One accident could be used as an excuse to stop additional procurement funds. The army would use any excuse to stop buying them, even accusing the Air Corps of not having pilots competent to fly them. Your pilots must be the best qualified to fly instruments and go anyplace in the world, over land or sea." The first B-17 arrived at Langley Field on March 1, 1937, a day the Air Corps took a giant step to achieve air power.

In May the entire bombing strength of the air force was assembled in California for maneuvers. An area in the desert was designated as Los Angeles. One part of the bombing force would act as a decoy to draw off the Pursuit, while the second would attack and bomb the target. At the conclusion of the exercise, Andrews spoke to the news media and was interviewed coast-to-coast. Andrews said defenses were weak. If the United States were attacked on two fronts, he said, there would be only enough forces to defend one. Not one injury occurred in the three weeks of mock exercises involving 300 planes and 3000 men. His salient point was that three years after the approval to build a force of 1000 combat planes he could still muster only a third of that number.

On June 1, 1937 Andrews presented a detailed analysis to the War Department on why all heavy bombardment purchases should be in the four-engine class. The B-17 can be utilized for long-range reconnaissance or heavy bombardment. He pointed out that the twin-engine bomber now on contract would equip two Groups and three reconnaissance squadrons by 1939. Unless four-engine development is encouraged now, he warned, the United States would be hopelessly behind the state of aeronautical art and be equipped with outmoded, outclassed, and obsolete bombers. Only a four-engine bomber could reinforce the Hawaiian Islands. In spite of the plea, the Secretary of War and the GHQ were dead set against the B-17 bomber increased authorizations. The proposals were not supported as Andrews had hoped. He was requested to provide B-17 supporting data, which of course, was not yet available. By year's end, Andrews had made at least six major attempts to change the War Department's attitude on the matter. In August, the Secretary of War rejected the Air Corps recommendation to purchase 13 more B-17s.

By the end of August, 1937, dramatic data concerning the operations and capabilities of the B-17 became available. Andrews passed it to the General Staff. However, in the fall of 1936, the President changed all arguments by requesting information on what the army bombers could do against a fleet. To gather this information, on July 10, 1937, it was announced that the exercise would be held in August on the West Coast. That would be the worst time for the air force, as much of the area would be fogged in. Thirty B-10s, four B-18s and seven B-17s would be used as the attacking force against the Battleship *Utah* using 50-pound water bombs, new to the air force. The navy was to use reconnaissance planes to locate the ship and report its position to the air force, which would then fly out and attack. Lt. Curtis LeMay was selected as lead navigator for the air force. Although a pilot, he was considered much too young and inexperienced to pilot the B-17. As a navigator, however, he was considered the best. Three days before the exercise was to start, the navy finally located the water bombs and turned them over. On August 12, the entire West Coast was socked in solid from heavy fog that extended seaward 200 miles. At 3:37 P.M. the navy signaled it had located the *Utah*, but the message was not forwarded to the air force until after four o'clock. The B-17s and B-18s scrambled and after taking course direction on the first report, received another navy report that the ship was 40 miles east of the first sighting. LeMay computed a new course and time of interception. When they arrived over the location, they were over a cloud bank. The lead B-17 descended to 700 feet and broke out, but the *Utah* was not in sight. They did a square search pattern, but found nothing and returned home. LeMay was asked if he was sure about his navigational plot. He nodded his head, and made another celestial sighting that indicated his first plot could not have been off more than one mile. He said: "to prove it here is the heading for San Francisco and this is the time of arrival." At 10 minutes from time of arrival over San Francisco, LeMay took a position between the pilot and co-pilot and watched. The fog covered San Francisco, but at the exact time he had computed, the glow of lights could be seen through the fog. His boss and pilot, Col. Robert Olds, turned and asked: "How could we have missed the *Utah*? Andrews had the answer. "All the navy scout planes' reports were incorrect and not corrected until nine-thirty that night." Just a small error of one degree, reported the navy. That meant an error of 60 miles at sea in the fog. Had it been intentional? The answer would be "Yes" if asked of any Air Corps man from Andrews on down.

The fog forced the ships to land farther inland at Sacramento Municipal Airport for the night. With coffee and hot dogs for dinner, the crews slept on the cockpit floor overnight. Olds awakened LeMay in the morning. "Come on, have some coffee," he said. He advised him that the navy had admitted its mistake, and his attitude indicated to LeMay there would be no further question about his accuracy in navigation.

The following morning the fog still limited all flights. The navy scouts, which were supposed to keep contact on the *Utah* had lost her during the night. Colonel Olds made the decision to get his planes airborne and Andrews joined him. The navy reported a sighting of the battleship. Olds took the flight of B-17s down through the fog, breaking out and deploying his planes line abreast to make one last effort. Instead, there, in what LeMay called "the greatest happenstance in the world," lay the *Utah*. She was 285 miles off shore, her crew spread out on the deck taking their ease. Excited conversation broke out from the other B-17s as they prepared to attack. The crew on the *Utah* was in wild disorder, a wild scattering of seamen making for the hatches. LeMay, who had made his way to the nose section saw the first water bomb hit the battleship's deck, then in the wild excitement three more made direct hits. There were a number of near misses that would have gutted her had they been real bombs. Everyone aboard the B-17 cheered as Olds put the airplane in a climb up through the fog bank. LeMay, on checking the bearing provided by the navy was again one degree off according to the *Utah's* real position. The navy attempted to claim the attack meant nothing since the ship was unable to maneuver away from the sneak attack. As a result, Andrews demanded another test, this time from altitude. The navy agreed, anxious to redeem its position that a battleship couldn't be damaged to any extent by bombs. This time the weather was clear and the *Utah* took evasive action. The B-10s, B-18s and the B-17s bombed from altitudes of 8000 feet to 18,000 feet. They scored 37 direct hits. This time the navy was unable to duck the damage done to the battleship's reputation. Possibly, this one action more than any other, established the four-engine bomber as the real air defense for the United States.

The navy brass desperately tried to hush up the entire affair, but they were thwarted by a newscaster who not only described the whole test but had pictures to prove what he said. The navy was furious and the GHQ Air Force was questioned in no uncertain terms about the leak to the newscaster. Pilots at Langley Field knew nothing and said so, even with smirks on their faces. From that moment forward, Andrews boasted the accomplishments of the B-17 every chance he had. In an account he gave at the Army War College that October, he drew attention to the superiority of the

B-17 over all other GHQ Air Force bombers. He closed on a somber note saying: "The air power of a nation is essentially what it has today. That which is on the drafting board are the statistical tables of resources and manpower and can only become its air power five years from now, too late for tomorrow's employment." It could have been considered an arrow from his quiver directed straight at those who seemed determined to downplay the need for B-17s as an urgent tool for National Defense. In any event, he received a letter of commendation from Chief of Staff Malin Craig, praising the efficiency and dependability of the GHQ Air Force.

With all of Andrews' attempts to change the thinking about air power at high levels, nothing seemed to dent the hard rock encasing the negative ideas that prevailed. The XB-15 was completed in the fall of 1937. A number of items, including gross weight being too high for the engine power and the top speed too slow, prevented it from acceptable consideration. Andrews believed it should be continued with an improved and modified version constructed, but this suggestion was rejected at GHQ level. His objections were voiced at the highest levels, but to no avail. Later, however, when he expressed the same concerns in an article written for the Army Ordnance, an in-house organ, exception was taken by some in the GHQ general staff. They objected not for Andrews' opinions about air power or the B-17, but over his statement that because of personnel shortages it had been necessary to make use of reserve Lieutenants and Cadets as "airplane commanders with far less flying experience than required for copilots flying commercial transports." Those responsible for shortages that Andrews wrote about were quick to comprehend its implications, straight up to the Secretary of War. The Adjutant General's office declared it to be in violation of specified requirements. Andrews was aware that the demand for an explanation could be a form of warning. Andrews also knew his efforts to build air power over the objections of the entire military establishment treaded close to the edge at times. He had made his decision. Nothing was acceptable but the immediate growth in personnel and aircraft essential to air power.

Andrews felt the pressure of events that drew war closer to the world. There was his realization that Germany was rebuilding its Luftwaffie, the civil war in Spain that permitted Germany to test its aircraft and pilots under combat conditions, the threat of Japan's militaristic government throughout Asia, and the United States' weakened financial condition from the long Depression. Drums of war sounded ominous to those in tune with realistic developments. Japan had provoked open warfare with China. On December 12, 1937, the U.S. gunboat *Panay,* moving on the

Yangtze river, was struck in broad daylight. Her decks were clearly marked and identified with the American flag painted on its deck. Twelve Japanese bombers flew over and deliberately dropped their bombs from low altitude in clear weather. The American government quickly hushed up the incident. It could not, however, overlook the insolence and arrogant disregard of international laws concerning a nation's freedom to move safely in neutral waters. Another discordant problem facing Andrews was the method of dealing with the 2320 military aircraft approved as a goal for the Air Corps. The army insisted on its *balanced program* for buying aircraft, which was a dodge to buy poor quality planes in numbers to meet the requirement. Andrews was dead set against the method and wanted a substantial number of B-17s and other four-engine types. He was not alone in this thinking, as Arnold, Emmons and Knerr agreed. It would be to no avail to try and build the GHQ Air force with antiquated aircraft or other types not designed to do the job. To these men that meant the ability to carry large bomb loads over thousands of miles and armed for its own protection against enemy fighter aircraft.

Secretary of War Woodring had been a thorn in Andrews' side refusing to provide the financial assistance essential to a buildup of the four-engine bomber airplane. Woodring refused to even consider the needs expressed by Andrews. The President had recently appointed Louis Johnson to be the Assistant Secretary of War and indicated he would eventually become the Secretary. Eager to get the President's ear on anything, Johnson kept moving in on Woodring's decision-making.

Woodring, Johnson, Andrews, and most of the Army GHQ attended a meeting in the late-fall of 1937. Andrews bought up the matter of long-range four-engine bombers, saying he believed there should be only two types of bombers: the heavy and attack. Johnson asked Andrews to provide a program along those lines and Andrews promised to do it forthwith. Not long afterward, Delos Emmons, commander at March Field, advised Andrews that he had asked Johnson about the program and Johnson had indicated positive interest but said it couldn't be accomplished so long as Woodring was secretary. On January 25, 1938, Andrews met with Johnson at his office and went over the presentation planned for a procurement program for 1940 to 1945. Johnson was willing to back it on all points. At that meeting, made up of the same personnel as in the earlier meeting in November, Andrews stressed his point about restricting the bomber development to two types. He then stated that the 31st Bomb Squadron, ordered to Hawaii, would be moving by boat because the B-18s couldn't safely fly that far. With the B-17, the move could have been made by air and avoided the costly permanent change of station. He stressed his point by stating: "Airplanes that can be flown to theaters of operation, continental, insular possessions, or foreign, in which this country might become engaged, and which can be transferred by air from one theater to another, have an obvious national-defense advantage with our limited shipping and in our particular geographical situation." Andrews' presentation changed no army minds. However, an event was about to take place that bore real significance for the GHQ Air Force.

The State Department requested a mission of six B-17s be sent to Buenos Aires. Woodring turned down the request, saying it would cost too much. Johnson heard about this, made an appointment with the President, and sold him on the idea. The President, intrigued with the idea of bombers flying almost 6000 miles, called Woodring and ordered him to support the flight. Andrews selected Bob Olds to command the goodwill flight. Lieutenant LeMay was selected as the lead navigator. The White House indicated it would like for the flight to arrive in Buenos Aires the day after it left the U.S. To comply, Olds timed his takeoff from Miami at one minute after midnight, giving the flight 68 hours to arrive in Buenos Aires. They made the first stop at Lima, Peru, for refueling. Weather had dropped to zero-zero at departure time, and the takeoff was made under instrument rules. The flight arrived in Buenos Aires the next day on time. The entire visit was carried out without incident. The President praised the good will created by the flight and personally honored Olds and his men for a job well done. After the hoopla had died down, it was back to the books for Andrews and his staff. Andrews was brought back to reality by the loss of top personnel to rotation and schools. He had hoped to keep Hugh Knerr assigned to his staff, but the outspoken Knerr was assigned to Fort Sam Houston to the same job in which Billy Mitchell ended his career, and the same office.

As the signs of war in Europe drew closer, the French and English governments desperately tried to find bomber and fighter aircraft. They sent buying commissions to the United States to examine and determine what could be used and the availability. Two pursuit planes, the P-35 and the P-36, and one bomber, the B-17, were at a stage of development for consideration. These were the mainstays for Andrews and his GHQ Air Force. This was dictated by the shortage of funds he experienced since organizing the air force. When asked for recommendations for 1938 funds, Andrews and his commanders agreed that the best course would be to solve the problems involved building a military pressurized cabin to be adapted later to a production bombardment airplane; and to start the procurement of design data for a 250,000-pound bomber. That proposal, Andrews later noted, was met with the comment that there was no need to consider anything larger than the B-17.

Andrews directed his total attention toward the 1938 maneuvers of his air force, slated to be the largest ever held with more than 300 aircraft stationed on 19 airports, of which only 4 would be air bases. A total of 3000 officers and men would participate. The exercise plan would have the aggressor attack with planes, ships and troops, aiming to capture the industrial territory in the Northeast. The fleet was busy in the Pacific, so it was up to the air force to prevent a landing along the eastern seaboard.

Andrews explained to a local politician: "The exercise is primarily for the training of commanders and their staffs, but there would also be a spectacular problem, the blackout of Farmingdale, Long Island. At a fixed time all lights in the area would be turned off while searchlights probe the sky for bombers." These "aggressors" would be seeking to bomb the Republic Aviation Factory, dropping bombs from 15,000 feet. Interceptors took off to meet the attackers, and the Coast Artillery Regiment blasted away with anti-aircraft guns.

During the exercise a significant plan came to light that would not only bring reality to the exercise but also front page news concerning national defense and the GHQ Air Force. The idea was to intercept an incoming ocean liner, which would represent an attacking enemy force. As luck would have it, the Italian liner *Rex* was making its crossing, bound for New York. The press was invited in on the plan. The top air force photographer, Maj. George W. Goddard, would shoot the capture of the *Rex* far at sea. Approval had to be obtained from the War Department and the Steamship company. Both approved. Three B-17s would be the attack force and Andrews designated Group Commander Olds to select the pilots. A three-man crew from NBC would ride in one ship, and C. B. Allen of the New York *Herald Tribune* in another. The New York *Times* correspondent, Hanson W. Baldwin, would ride with A.Y. Smith in the third plane. Lieutenant LeMay was named to be the lead navigator. News coverage was complete, but weather was foul with rain, high winds, and poor visibility forecast to remain. It would be much worse at sea. The three B-17s landed at Mitchel Field to await takeoff time. LeMay was given the first report from the *Rex* and he and the other two navigators calculated the ship should be about 600 miles off Sandy Hook at noon the next day, approximate time of intercept. Given the weather forecast, the time element and the fuel supply, finding the Italian ship would take a combination of expert navigation, flying skill, and a smile from some heavenly saint. That was the consensus of the three navigators.

When the sodden dawn arrived, LeMay was already up and checking weather. No improvement occurred, and the *Rex* had sent no additional reports on its location. As the big planes taxied out, there was a sudden pounding on the hatch and LeMay was handed a soggy paper with a new *Rex* position report. After he had re-figured his calculations, it appeared the ship was farther out at sea than the first report indicated. The revised ETA would be later than his first estimate. Unknown to LeMay, the NBC announcer was broadcasting on a coast-to-coast hookup to millions of Americans. Low ceilings and rain forced the three planes to fly at almost sea level. LeMay continued his calculations. When the plane suddenly broke out of the rain into clear weather, he found that airspeed was slower than he had figured, which meant more fuel used. At about the same time, one of the pilots came back to check the course. In the discussion, LeMay learned for the first time that the flight was being broadcast all over America. He was thunderstruck! Everything had been based on his original calculations. LeMay realized fuel could not be used to increase speed as they would be on the edge at ETA. He went forward to advise the pilot of the change in his calculations, but the only response was: "You're the navigator, Curt!" He made his way back to the navigator's table just as the plane entered towering clouds of another cold front system. The wing planes were instructed to move out as they slammed into the wall of the front. For 10 minutes they were battered back and forth, up and down, with hail stones beating on the windshield. Suddenly they broke through and were again in smooth air with blue skies. At higher altitude, they set a search line 30 miles apart. Everyone knew the enormity of their effort to locate a 900-foot ship in the Atlantic. At 12:21 P.M. LeMay noted the sun had been blotted out by a squall. Two minutes later they had cleared the squall. Then a few minutes more and Connie Cousland boomed out: "There she is, dead ahead!" LeMay was to report later that it was like a movie or a dream, happening to someone else.

The three ships formed up and headed down to circle the *Rex* with her red-white-and-green-striped funnels. Goddard got his camera ready. He took shots of the passengers streaming out on deck to wave and cheer. News of the interception was flashed back to Mitchel Field, and communications were established with Captain Cavalini the ship's master. With excellent courtesy, he invited all the crews to drop in and have some delicious fine Italian food. The invitation was regretfully declined. On the stern, a group of passengers jumped up and down and waved. Later, it was learned they were Americans singing *The Star Spangled Banner*.

The celebration soon evaporated aboard the three B-17s as they headed for home. Weather they encountered returning home proved to be much worse than that on the way out. Once the planes entered a front, violent winds raged in an unbelievable fury, one moment the plane was suspended, the next it was slammed 1000 feet downward as the propellers clawed the air to hang on. At the bottom of the fall it stopped suddenly, then shuddered and emitted sounds of groaning and sighing as if its innards were being ripped out. Anything loose was flung around the cabin, sometimes suspended when negative forces created weightlessness, then suddenly smashed against the fuselage as crewmen ducked. The pilot tried to hold the yoke, pulling and pushing to oppose the forces and keep the plane upright. Turbulence became so violent that the B-17 would drop several hundred feet, hit bottom like a rock in a dry well, and then shudder from nose to tail. No new altitude provided any relief to the pounding. Golf-ball size hail stones battered the fuselage and threatened to smash the Plexiglas windshield, and lightning crackled and ran along the wings as if in some weird game of chance. Finally, like a spent tornado, the plane tore itself loose and flew into benign and calm air as the exhausted crew collected themselves. One thing was firmly and forever established in the mind of each, no question could ever be raised about the ability of the B-17 to withstand any test nature could provide.

The mission took almost eight hours and covered more than 1500 miles, mostly over water. It located a ship in the Atlantic Ocean, a target smaller than the proverbial needle in a haystack. What the B-17 had accomplished was totally unrecognized in the War Department. Only those in the Air Corps knew its full meaning. The success of the mission was reported from coast to coast in every form of news agency release, as well as around the world. The *New York Times* reported the lesson to be learned was valuable to the aerial defense of the United States. Wherever Andrews spoke about the flight, he was quick to remind those listening that the mission was a routine operational performance.

While the air force basked in the glow of the doting press, it was soon to dim. At a staff meeting with Air Corps officers, Andrews was interrupted by a call from the Chief of GHQ. It was short and sweet: "Henceforth, all over-water flights by the air force are to be restricted to a distance of 100 miles off the shore." There was a stunned silence after the call. Whatever the reason had been, whether the navy had complained, or someone's ego in a uniform or a politician's suit got tweaked, the order had been given with little concern for the national defense of the United States. The order was never put into writing.

During the summer of 1938, Andrews found himself with a constant problem of trying to find out what decisions were being made in Washington that concerned him and the GHQ Air Force. His principal worry was procurement of the B-17. Seemingly nothing had changed in the Army GHQ or Secretary of War's thinking about the B-17 bomber. Andrews had faint hopes of getting procurement in 1940 for 67 since the procurement for 1939 had been dropped. In accordance with a decision from Woodring, those were dropped in favor of two-engine light bombers to provide ground support. The one bright spot for the summer was the appointment of George Marshall to the new War Plans Division of the Army GHQ. Andrews had not met Marshall but knew he was held in high regard. Later, Andrews invited Marshall to accompany him on a tour, which Marshall accepted. The trip gave the two men an opportunity to visit and discuss problems Andrews faced. Afterward Marshall wrote a note to General Pershing outlining the trip: "I flew from Washington with General Andrews of the GHQ Air Force to Selfridge Field, Chanute Field, Minneapolis, then on to Billings, Montana, and across Yellowstone Park to Spokane where the air force had concentrated. From there I flew over to Fort Lewis where another element of the First Wing had concentrated, did the Boeing plant at Seattle—where B-17s were being made—and stopped at Vancouver Barracks for the night where another Group of the 1st Wing was concentrated. From the Northwest I flew to San Francisco, Sacramento, Los Angeles—the air plants there—Denver, San Antonio, Barksdale Field, Shreveport, and home. Altogether, I had a very interesting trip professionally and a most magnificent one personally."

The two men enjoyed each other and formed a bond of friendship. Marshall was open and voluble with Andrews, later referring to their journey as the point where his education on air power began. As the summer passed into fall and in Europe moved swiftly toward the brink of war, Andrews learned of the decision to drop the B-17 procurement for 1941. His own tour as commander of the GHQ Air Force would end March 1, 1939. The decision to scrap the plan to buy more B-17s was just half the problem. Planes were beginning to come off the production line, but a lack of funds prevented having pilots and mechanics to use them. By July 1, 1939, the Air Corps would be short 900 officers and more than 2000 enlisted personnel.

The public was totally unaware of the deficiencies. The September Air Races at Cleveland excited the crowds with the proficiency of the Air Corps pilots, and later the American Legion convention would be held in Los Angeles where the show would be on again. By this time, however, the question on most minds was a single one: Was there to be a war in Europe? Prime Minister Chamberlain had met with the French Prime Minister to discuss Hitler's demands over the Sudetenland. Even at that moment, the abandonment of Czechoslovakia was under way. Andrews and the Chief of Air Corps had attended the American Legion event together and discussed many of the problems they faced as heads of the two largest air power elements of free America. What they said was never known, but it's safe to say it dealt with their concern over the coming war. It would be their last visit. The next day, while landing, General Westover crashed and died. He had stalled the A-17 while turning on final in rough and tricky winds. After the shock was over, the task of determining a new Chief was paramount. Andrews stood at the top of the list, both in seniority and grade. After much discussion from all concerned, President Roosevelt announced Arnold would be the new Chief. Andrews immediately sent his congratulations. In mid-October, George C. Marshall was named Army Deputy Chief of Staff. Andrews sent a long letter of congratulations with a rundown of items essential to the air force. Considering Andrews' worries and anxieties during the four years of his efforts to build the GHQ Air Force into a believable and combat ready organization, and to the consistent and continuing fight for the B-17 build-up, his joy on hearing of the new program of procurement could be understood.

On Monday, November 16, 1938, a secret meeting took place at the White House. The purpose of that meeting with President Roosevelt was to discuss the immediate buildup of combat and allied aircraft for the Air Corps. In the process, aircraft would also be included for sale to friendly nations. Funds would be requested to provide the pilots and enlisted ranks necessary to fly them. It would bring to the Air Corps all the upheaval and explosiveness of a revolution. For Andrews it was, indeed, a revolution. The mission of the Air Corps was of great importance to Andrews. It no longer consisted of just the muddy waters of coastal defense, but now encompassed the broad parameters of hemispheric defense. At last, the true mission and purpose of four-engine bombers would be recognized for its proper inclusion in the scheme of air defense and strategic warfare. In the months that followed much infighting developed between the Administration and the Congress. Roosevelt was the catalyst in the expansion of military aircraft, so much of the blame for the nation's position in the military arena found its way to the White House. Those who looked with great concern on the possibility of American involvement argued for isolationism; those for adequate protection wanted military strength, especially air power. Roosevelt was sorely pressed to improve the country's military posture. However, suddenly calling for spending a huge amount of money raised the question: "Why are we in this mess?" That is a question no sitting president cares to answer. It was also a question that the War Department, with its *balanced air corps* program idea, hoped would not come up. But, it did. At year's end, Secretary of War Woodring had made the following report to the President:

"There has been provided a powerful defensive in the form of the General Headquarters Air Force. In creating this extremely important arm, it was necessary to do more than merely procure increased numbers of airplanes. A balanced air force had to be established in personnel, ground installations, training and supplies. In the gradual development of this air force, we constantly strove to keep abreast of rapid development of aviation equipment and technique, and simultaneously provide military aircraft of unexcelled quality. Considering our initial deficiencies, it is my opinion that we have built wisely and well in developing our General Headquarters Air Force. The efficiency attained by that force in a few short years of its history is a most noteworthy achievement. We have a substantial framework for the extension, which now appears essential."

On Monday, January 16, 1939, Andrews was the featured speaker at the National Aeronautic Association Convention dinner in St. Louis. He supported the items the President had outlined in his speech to the Congress. In addition, he stated the United States was a fifth- or sixth-rate air power. Once more, he pointed out the need for building around the long-range bomber, things he had repeated many times before. This time, however, he was saying it to a very select air-wise audience and a press that was eager to report his comments. "Our air forces are inadequate . . . the entire army combat force in continental United States . . . numbers only slightly over 400 fighting planes." The press reported his statement on air strategy, as meaning a good offense is the best defense, a totally opposite picture than the War Department's axiom of defense. "There are only two ways to stop an air attack" he said. "One is to prevent the hostile air force from getting close enough to launch an attack, the other is through fear of retaliation to stop the aggressor from even planning an attack." He spoke about the vulnerability of U.S. targets; the Panama Canal, the northeastern Atlantic seaboard. "Eighteen power plants," he pointed out, "supply 75 percent of all electric power for the New York metropolitan area. It would not take a large force of bombardment planes to accomplish the destruction of those plants." Later, he answered a question about an effective air force saying, "This means equipping our air force with enough planes of sufficient range and bomb-carrying ability to enable them, from available bases, to reach any locality where an enemy might attempt to establish air bases, either land or water." He agreed that geography played a part in determining the makeup of an air force, but the side that had the longer-range weapons was the side that had a distinct advantage. A year before, Andrews had said the same thing, but now with Austria annexed, the Munich Pact seen as surrender, and Roosevelt's call to build air power, Andrews words were in line with a developing administration policy. It was likely that the White House was in full agreement, but ears in the War Department burned. Andrews' speech flew squarely in the face of Woodring's statement to the President as well as the claims by the War Department. Woodring, with General Staff agreement, had put a halt to procurement of long-range bomber production. The comments were Andrews' way of sticking the *balanced air corps* theory under their noses. Also, this was the first time the bomber theory had been stated for public consumption. It was in direct contradiction to the position outlined by the Secretary of War. Probably, it was never known what effect the Andrews declaration had on the President or the Secretary of War. However, it had to be a direct attack on the credibility of the Secretary of War. As to the effect on Andrews' position in the War Department, he fully realized his vulnerability, but was not about to leave his position on March 1 without a clear understanding of why the GHQ Air Force was unprepared for its mission. Of course, the glowing terms expressed by the Secretary of War over the excellent growth of the GHQ Air Force under Major General Andrews' tutelage left little room for a poor efficiency report.

Nevertheless, Andrews was concerned. He was at the apogee of his career and wanted a challenge in his next assignment that could benefit from the experiences he would take with him. Two potential assignments interested him: command of Maxwell Field and the Air Corps Tactical School, or the Air Corps Training Center at Randolph Field. The latter would be his preference because of the pilot training work with the GHQ Air Force. The true position of Andrews in relation to the War Department was unknown. He knew he had enemies. Command placed one in the limelight, created many friends, but also faceless enemies. The G-3 section of general headquarters could fit that bill.

A few days before his official transfer he had business to discuss with Air Corps. When he arrived at the War Department office he was handed his orders. His new assignment was as Air Officer to the VIII Corps Area, the same job given to Billy Mitchell following his court martial, and just a year earlier to Hugh Knerr. It called for a reduction in rank to Colonel. Secretary of War Henry Woodring had signed it, very likely suggested it. Andrews accepted the assignment philosophically. He understood the vagaries of military life. His many friends in and out of the military wrote him letters of support. None said it better than Devon Francis of the Associated Press: "I want you to know with what regret I learned about the finish of your tour as the head of the GHQ Air Force. I need not tell you that the newspapermen who have had the opportunity of 'covering' you bear you an affection seldom bestowed on a news source. But that is understandable. Few men have the patience, kindliness and confidence that you have shown us. For myself as an individual and as Aviation

Writer for the Associated Press, and as President of the Aviation Writers Association, I wish you Godspeed and success in any new undertaking."

That assignment defined as nothing else could the degree of animosity and contempt with which the senior air force commander was held by the army brass. The description of stogy, stiff-necked and spiteful old men taking their vengeance out on an airman who had succeeded in creating a specialized command from nothing, fitted them perfectly. Obviously, little or no attention was given to the desperate position that existed within the nation's air arm. Granted, it would be difficult to see into the future and know that Hawaii would be bombed, but the situation in Europe was worsening and there was little not to understand about militaristic Japan. Aside from that, however, a cursory examination of the War Department decisions, deliberately designed to deter the orderly and essential buildup of the GHQ Air Force, should have been sufficient reason to ask why. The struggle by Andrews to do the job was well known inside and outside Washington. A farewell celebration was held in honor of General Andrews, marked by sadness and disbelief. The majestic attitude of Andrews, however, kept it on even keel. He criticized no one, offering no bitterness or remorse. He has seen such action taken before but took no part in such activity. Treating loyal officers in that manner smacked of petty jealousy and vindictiveness. If Andrews had any complaint, it was the genuine sorrow he felt in not being permitted to continue with his work.

On April 8, 1939, he received a note from George C. Marshall. It was addressed to Maj. Gen. Frank M. Andrews. "I did not find the opportunity to have a talk with you at the time of your final relinquishment of command of the GHQ Air Force, and since then things have been happening so rapidly that I must admit I lost track of the matter. You know full well that you created, more or less out of whole cloth, a splendid tactical command, but I should like to add my appreciation of this fact, along with the statement that I think you gave a remarkably fine exhibition of leadership in the development of discipline, tactics, and general progress, in organizing and rounding into practical shape the GHQ Air Force. I should like to have been able to look forward to some more agreeable and highly instructive trips with you like that of last summer, which, incidentally, was of tremendous assistance to me this winter. Not that one can acquire an intimate knowledge of the Air Corps in nine days, but it gave me a perspective, as it were, against which I could sort the facts which I collected during the following months. It was probably as well that I knew so little at the time, rather than having started out with too many preconceived notions. However that may be, it was a thoroughly delightful and highly informative experience. With warm regards, Faithfully yours, (Signed) George C. Marshall.

At the end of April, the President announced that George C. Marshall would replace Malin Craig as Chief of Staff. Andrews sent a letter of congratulations. Marshall was on a trip west with Hap Arnold at the time and hoped that he could see Andrews. However, on his return, he was slated for a trip to Brazil and missed connections. He advised Andrews he would return in July. In the meantime, Andrews was taking care of his duties, enjoying the scenery and his many friends. It was a relaxing but unnecessary interlude, payment for his refusal to knuckle under. Marshall returned in June and took over his new job near the end of the month. On June 30, Andrews received a wire from the War Department: *The President has submitted to the Senate your nomination for appointment as Brigadier General. Wire acceptance.* In a few words it had happened. Frank Andrews was back doing his job. Never mind all the petty, two-faced stabs in the back, all the efforts to prevent his air force from growing to become an essential part of the nation's defense. Andrews had won. Arnold had called him first to advise he was a general officer of the line, no temporary stuff. In the middle of July he received his assignment orders. He would be G-3, Assistant Chief of Staff for Operations and Training for the entire United States Army. He would be the first air officer to have attained such heights in the War Department structure. Marshall had fought hard to get the acceptance for Andrews in the Secretary of War's office. However, after the announcement and briefing on the accomplishments of Andrews not one word of discontent was heard. Had there been, it would have been drowned out by the cheers. During the last weeks of his official rest, Andrews settled into his new office. It would take a little time to get settled, organized, and tuned in with his new boss, but with his knowledge, training, and sense of organization no time would be lost. He faced a gargantuan task to build a modern army, but there would be no bets against its taming by the new Assistant Chief of Staff for Operations and Training.

Lt. Gen. Frank Maxwell Andrews, GHQ Air Force
who served beyond duty and honor is recognized as a
Legend of Air Power

Carl A Spaatz

Cadet Carl A. Spaatz was graduated from West Point in 1914. Two things happened to him while at the Academy that would stay with him the rest of his life. The first was the endowment, by an upper classman, with the nick name of *Tooey*. The name had no particular significance other than it had been the nickname of an upper classman who also had red hair. It stuck

Gen. Carl A. "Tooey" Spaatz

and he would answer for the rest of his life to the call of *Tooey*. He had no problem with that, so he and the name became one. The other item was connected to the Hudson River that flowed by the Academy. Glenn Curtiss used it as a course to fly his Pusher plane. Tooey liked the idea of flying like a bird and it snared him forever. At that time the army did not permit its new officers to join the Aviation Section until after they had served in another branch, so Tooey joined forces with the Infantry for awhile.

In November 1915, he started flight training at Rockwell Field near San Diego. He made his solo flight in a Martin tractor-type airplane after only 50 minutes of instruction. Most of the instruction period on the airplane was spent overhauling the engine. After the solo, Spaatz (pronounced like spots, not spats) was able to get about 20 minutes of flying a day, if the plane was flyable and the pilot was healthy. Other than learning to take the engine apart and balance the propeller, the sky was wide open for exploration. The theory of flight had not yet been explained and few had any idea why an airplane flew. Tooey graduated in the spring of 1916 and was designated as a Junior Military Aviator (JMA). After graduation he was assigned a JN-2, affectionately known as the Jenny. Tooey was to fly it to join Capt. Benny Foulois, who was to take the squadron into Mexico to support General Pershing's punitive expedition again Pancho Villa's marauding guerrillas. The squadron was the first U.S. aerial combat force and equipped with eight Jennies. The squadron saw no combat. However, the myriad of problems trying to fly and maintain the planes made veterans out of its men before the action ended.

Once the squadron reached Mexico, the problems of orientation began. With no maps of the area, it was pure guesswork to find where Villa was rumored to be operating. It was easy to get lost during bad weather and hard to find where the refueling was set up. Rugged terrain made it difficult to keep the landing gear from collapsing. As a result, planes were scattered all over the area and it was impossible to know whether they were flyable from one day to the next.

Spaatz was ordered to France in late 1917. In October, he was flying bombing missions with the French and solo observation and reconnaissance patrols. After a month in action, he was assigned as Officer in Charge of the 3rd Instructional Center, training pilots at Issoudun, well back of the front lines. He was there for several months and had his fill of training. Billy Mitchell was dissatisfied with the pilots and wanted to send Spaatz back to America to improve training methods. Normally a quiet, taciturn type, Tooey suddenly became very vocal when he heard of Mitchell's idea, and succeeded in getting assigned to the front for two weeks. By this time Spaatz had been promoted to Major and knew the Lieutenants flying in the 2nd Pursuit Group and Charlie Biddle's 13th Squadron would not take kindly to having an inexperienced brass hat to mother around. Consequently, when Tooey walked in, he left the oak leaves insignia in his kit bag. After a few flights, his skill was quickly recognized, and Biddle made him a flight commander. In combat on September 20, 1918, he shot down an enemy fighter. Reluctant to leave, he remained on duty another week. The St. Mihiel-Verdun Offensive was then under way. Spaatz stretched his stay for another week, and on September 26 he and his patrol engaged a German unit of unknown strength. At one time, six German Fokkers were on his tail, and Charlie Biddle came to his rescue. Spaatz shot down two Germans and chased a third deep into enemy territory. He ran out of fuel and crash-landed his plane near a shelled out hill. He found he was unhurt and immediately took evasive action. He soon heard voices speaking French and knew he was in friendly territory.

The Frenchmen arranged a party for their comrade-in-arms and celebrated the brave American pilot with a few bottles of choice French wine. When Tooey returned to his base, another celebration took place. As they were making one more toast, Billy Mitchell and General Mason Patrick walked in. Tooey was congratulated, then reprimanded for disobeying orders and not returning after the two weeks were up. Major Spaatz was cited for bravery under fire, and received the *Distinguished Flying Cross*, plus the irreversible designation of Military Aviator. Mitchell sent him back, but promised when he returned he would have his own Pursuit Group. However, the end of the war stopped that possibility. After his return, Spaatz organized and commanded the Far West Flying Circus. He organized it for support of a Victory Loan drive, but in putting on stunting and dog-fighting exhibitions over a large part of the nation he was also generating interest in the Army Air Service. The job was mostly hard work and little glory, as keeping the pilots and mechanics organized was a massive operation. They flew wherever a show was scheduled and the people were thrilled to see a wartime hero. In their helmets, goggles, boots, and flying jackets, they were a romantic bunch and the girls loved them. Tooey was not the partying type, although he could enjoy a get-together with other pilots and hangar talk all night. His love was flying and he was one of the best at it.

After the exhibitions, Spaatz joined forces with Billy Mitchell to organize the Transcontinental Reliability Test. It immediately attracted the attention of Congress and the public. It took place in 1919 and was the first air race, but more like a trading maneuver. Thirty planes would take off from each coast and fly round trip between New York and San Francisco. At that time there were no air routes and no airports along the course. Since the range of the planes did not exceed 300 miles, it was a rugged challenge for Tooey and the other participants. An average of 40 refueling stops was required to make the continental circuit in an average elapsed time of about 39 hours, provided each applicant was able to complete the course. Each pilot had the problem of maintenance, refueling, food, and weather conditions to cope with. Flying a course during daylight hours was one thing, but flying at night was another. There were no highways with automobile lights to navigate by, no beacons flashing their signals, and no radios to furnish pertinent information. Also, there were no route maps and not many highway maps available for navigation. Even the telephone service was in its infancy. If a pilot went down with engine trouble he had bailing wire and pliers available in his kit. The route would run through the rough mountains and desert areas from San Francisco to Salt Lake and through the Wasatch Mountain Range, with its peaks to 12,000 feet, and on to Cheyenne. From there the route went across the plains, with its high winds and sudden thunderstorms, and finally into New York City. The route would be reversed into San Francisco. Many did not make it. Nine were killed in crashes due in part to the terrain and unpredictable weather. Tooey made it flying his favorite SE-5. Most entries flew the DH-4. Spaatz completed the trip, winning the event. He received a commendation from the War Department for his excellent planning and airmanship.

The event was run for two purposes; to demonstrate the need for airways, and as an example that isolationism would not survive in a world with the airplane. In 1927, another Army Air Corps pilot, Charles Lindbergh, would demonstrate the point much better, flying solo nonstop New York to Paris in The Spirit of St. Louis. During the next two years, Spaatz was assigned a number of duties. He was stationed at Rockwell Field with Hap Arnold for a short tour, then moved with him to Crissy Field, at the Presidio of San Francisco. The commanding general of the Presidio was Hunter Liggett, who had commanded the First Army in France. Liggett was highly thought of and had the opportunity in France to see military aviation and its uses. He encouraged Arnold and Tooey's aeronautical ventures and they were many. Mainly, both men hoped to keep the Air Corps in the limelight without bringing any undesirable reports to the public. When Arnold was assigned to Rockwell Field, Tooey went back to school. He attended the Air Service Tactical School at Langley Field, and was then assigned as Assistant G-3 for Training and Operations in the office of the Chief of Air Service, next door to his friend Hap Arnold. While at the Tactical School, Spaatz was ordered to Washington to give testimony before the House Military Affairs Committee on the Curry Bill providing for a separate Air Service. While en route on the train, he scribbled his thoughts for reference:

1. National policy as to army based on assumption that navy in being will keep out enemy until army is mobilized and trained. Navy cannot. Air force can.

2. Army will not seek increase of air force at expense of men or independently of army. Would rather have a capable mechanic with a peg leg take care of my airplane than best disciplined soldier in army who had no mechanic's duty.
3. Army is different from navy. Could not operate as part of army.
4. Air Service is just as different from army and navy, as army is from navy.
5. Air Service cannot operate under army or navy any more than navy could operate under army. Air force must be available at outbreak to defend coasts. If separate, can be centralized to be flown to either coast—if under navy would be close to shore and split up. If given to navy—stations built up along the coast no line of retreat except to flanks. Therefore, cannot defend in depth.
6. Army still has coast defense.
7. At outbreak of major emergency air force operates independently.
8. As soon as armies are raised the air force would be needed by army.
9. If under navy as soon as navy fight is finished has no further need of air force.
10. Large strength will be idle. Under army will operate under conditions unfamiliar.

Spaatz testified accordingly in favor of the bill and then sent a quick letter to William Stout, who was to become one of the principal developers of the Ford Trimotor passenger airplane. He wanted his support and also that of more prominent citizens, like Henry Ford, to espouse the idea of a Department of Aeronautics similar to the Curry bill. Spaatz received a reply from Stout indicating that Henry Ford believed he should take part only when a national emergency was involved. However, he went on to say there was still a chance of getting Ford to change his mind. As had been the result of other bills when the administration and congressional support was sought, the Curry bill also fell prey to the traditional army-navy position against the fledgling Air Service.

Spaatz was ordered the next month to once more testify before the Lampert Committee, which was conducting an investigation into U.S. aviation. Regardless of the hearings, it was impossible to understand the conditions that surrounded the reality of a career in the Army Air Service. At Langley Field, Tooey was concerned almost daily with the tactics of flight and some of its harsh effects. On Sunday, May 10, 1925, he wrote an entry in his diary: "Benedict was killed last Friday by colliding with a balloon he was attacking. At our age, muscle reactions lag behind mental impulses. Aviators over 30 years must allow a large majority of safety in their flying." The next day he wrote: "Class met for first time since Benedict's accident. Mental effect on men like Jake Fickel and Walter Frank who have had little direct contact with crashes, is terrific. My mind must be case hardened since my reactions in these cases are not severe." Later on, he added: "Led a Martin bomber formation, which never did get together. Some said I climbed too fast, others said I flew too slow and the remainder said I flew too fast. Judging from the flying today the effects of Benedict's crash are still lingering in a few brains. A crash always does make one slightly apprehensive and a little more cautious for a more or less extended period." The next day he made another entry: "But to pass an interval between two eternities raking in gold is simply absurd to me. My creed up until now, but henceforth I am to acquire sufficient gold to cease any worry about my old age. It may be ridiculous for an aviator to worry about old age, but I do coupled with apprehension that someday I may quit my army career either through my own volition or otherwise." Tooey was thinking about an experience with Davey Davison. Davey wanted to be a rancher, and had convinced Tooey that he, too, should consider being one. There was certainly no future in the Army Air Service the way things were going. They took a trip into Imperial Valley in southern California and came back to their wives with glowing stories of the spread they had found. All it would take was $50,000 apiece. Tooey flew east to Boyertown, Pennsylvania, where he had been born and raised and where his father had owned the local newspaper. He went to see Dan Boyer the banker, who said the bank would make the loan. He flew back with the good news only to learn that Davey had been seriously injured in a crash. Davey would never be a rancher or a pilot again either.

While thinking about that incident, Spaatz also thought of the "otherwise" condition of leaving the army. He was thinking of testifying at the court-martial of Billy Mitchell. He knew such testimony could be costly for young flying Majors. Arnold, Dargue, Eaker and Olds would also be there. Tooey would be one of the first witnesses. He had been warned to be careful in what he said. In answer to the air strength, he said the number of planes in the United States, modern and available, was 51. He pointed out that there were no properly equipped pursuit planes, and to put 15 of them in the air would require taking all the administrative officers from their desks in his office. When the defense counsel asked Tooey if he thought aviation was being retarded by the War Department, the prosecutor vigorously objected but not loudly enough to drown out Tooey's "I do!" A General on the jury questioned Tooey: "Major, you are an officer in the United States Army?" Spaatz replied he was. "Well, what do you mean by criticizing the War Department and the General Staff?"

Spaatz was silent for a moment and then said: "Well, I'd like the recorder to read back over my testimony and read exactly where I criticized the General Staff." It was near the noon hour and after the recorder had spent some 30 minutes trying to find something that would satisfy the General's implication, the question was withdrawn.

After lunch, the court heard Captain Olds testify concerning superior orders that lacked judgment or knowledge. Olds recounted the incident in Hawaii when Major Wheeler crashed trying to return to the field for a forced landing because Major General Summerall ordered forced landings to cease and issued orders requiring pilots involved to pay damages if they landed off-airport. Olds said Major Wheeler and his mechanic were victims of "run-down equipment and bone-headed orders." Tooey and Wheeler had been close friends since their days at West Point. In his estimation, it was a perfect example of why the authority and control of military flying belonged in the hands of those who understood flying and its problems. Spaatz hoped publicity would give the public an awareness of how the General Staff viewed the Air Service and would insist that it be corrected. However, like other efforts to promote and build the Air Service, Billy Mitchell's trial and conviction were soon forgotten.

In the fall of 1928, an incident in which Spaatz wasn't involved resulted in his being chosen to lead a project. The Junkers Company provided one of its planes to attempt an east-west flight across the Atlantic in reverse of Charles Lindbergh's 1927 epic flight. The plane, named the Bremen, was attempting to fly from Baldonnel, Ireland, to Mitchel Field, New York. It carried a crew of three. The overloaded low-winged Junkers just barely made it into the air on Friday the 13th. As time passed with no word, fear arose that the plane was lost. Later it was spotted near the coast of Labrador on tiny Greenly Island. The crew was safe. Although the plane was 1000 miles off course, it had spanned the ocean east to west. The Junkers Company wanted the plane back and sent their chief pilot to fly it out. In Washington, Assistant Secretary for Air Trubee Davison asked Ira Eaker to assist the company pilot. Eaker pointed out that the area would be ice covered and he couldn't land, but he would fly over for the company pilot to parachute drop into the area. The company pilot agreed to the idea. The rescue flight ran into difficult weather conditions but finally got to a position so the pilot could make his jump. He was successful, landing near the plane. Eaker dipped his plane's wings and set a course for Portland, Maine. During the return flight, low fuel was becoming a problem as they were flying above an undercast into Portland. With only a small amount of fuel left in the tank, Elwood

Quesada, one of the crew for the flight, made a let down, sweating out the ceiling height under the clouds. He broke out of the cloud cover just in time to land. That night, as they talked over the flight, Quesada observed that it would have helped to have a gas station up there. The chance remark led to the *Question Mark* endurance flight. Tooey Spaatz was selected to lead the venture.

The idea was to stay in the air as long as possible. Since no one knew how long that would be, they dubbed the plane the *Question Mark*. Funding was not available from the government for their meals during the flight, which the crewman later figured was par for the course. Spaatz chose the Fokker Trimotor for the flight. Refueling planes were Douglas C-1s. Pilots assigned were Ross G. Hoyt, Irwin Woodring, Auby Strickland, Ira Eaker, Quesada, Tooey, Harry Halverson, and Sergeant Roy Hooe, mechanic. The *Question Mark* flew more than 11,000 miles taking on more than 5000 gallons of hand-pumped fuel, also oil, food and water. The flight remained airborne for almost one week with the crew living in cramped quarters and deprived of the normal every day comforts, including a bed and toilet. The teams accomplished refueling by using a borrowed fire-department hose. The line was extended from the refueling plane, about 20 feet above to the *Question Mark*, and inserted into the fuel tank of the Fokker. The system worked fine until one refueling effort when Tooey took the line and inserted the nozzle into the fuel tank. Both planes jolted in rough air and the nozzle yanked free. Raw fuel spewed over Tooey as he struggled to get the nozzle back into the tank. He was drenched with high-octane fuel that could burn skin. Eaker turned the controls over to Quesada and went to assist Tooey. Sergeant Hooe stripped Tooeys flying suit off and rubbed him down with rags and oil. Tooey yelled: "If I'm burned, I'll bail out," he said. "Keep this plane in the air and that's an order!" He wasn't burned, but was quite a sight, half-naked and covered with oil. Following the flight, Tooey and the rest of the crewmembers received the *Distinguished Flying Cross*. President Coolidge authorized the citation:

> For extraordinary achievement while participating in an aerial flight on Jan 1-7, 1929, He commanded the airplane Question Mark in a refueling flight, at or near Los Angeles, California, which remained in the air a total of 150 hours, 40 minutes and 15 seconds, a period of continuous flight longer than any previous flight ever accomplished. By his endurance, resourcefulness and leadership he demonstrated future possibilities in aviation, which were heretofore not apparent and thus reflected great credit upon himself and the Army of the United States.

The real accomplishments showed that flight was limited only by the amount of fuel, and that aviation had advanced far enough to provide engines and other mechanical parts that would run much longer than thought. It also struck at the heart of isolationism, which was sweeping the country. It demonstrated the vulnerability of targets that could be attacked by air from any far-off base, and it showed that if army airplanes could stay aloft, so could commercial aircraft. It also demonstrated man's ability to overcome obstacles and expand his presence into this new medium—airspace. In the not too far distant future, what the *Question Mark* had accomplished would lead to in-flight refueling that would extend the range of modern fighters and bombers thousands of miles as they flew regularly across oceans to bases in foreign lands.

Tooey's tour at Rockwell Field ended with his transfer to March Field. He was there at Thanksgiving in 1931 when Hap Arnold and his family arrived from Washington. Tooey was assigned as Executive and Wing Commander under Arnold. The job was to convert March Field from a primary flight training school to a major tactical operation. Tooey would have the benefit of another World War One pilot, Capt. Frank O'D. "Monk" Hunter, who commanded the 17th Pursuit Group. Hunter had been an active pursuit pilot during the war, shooting down eight German planes, received the *Distinguished Flying Cross* five times and the French *Croix de Guerre*. He was an expert in his field, and intended to stay that way. He had served for three years in the office of the Chief of Air Corps, and described his service as sitting on every important pursuit board that provided entree to all the testing and the recommendations of what fighter aircraft should be procured.

Many discussions centered on fighters and their role. Tooey maintained that fighters assigned to escort bombers would probably be slower because of the increased fuel loads. He put his finger directly on the crux by raising the question: should a distinct type of airplane be developed for escort, or can the bombers be armed to protect themselves?

The summer of 1933 was the time March Field became the camp-organizing base for the Civilian Conservation Corps (CCC). With Arnold in charge of the program, Tooey would have to represent him during the spring maneuvers that would involve some 300 combat airplanes from different parts of the country. Tooey scheduled the use of the new bombing range at Muroc and directed the combined fighter, bomber, and attack techniques in combat. Arnold had expressed interest in that phase of the maneuvers. At the conclusion, and after the CCC program was concluded, Tooey received orders to report for duty in Washington. He would head up the G-3, Operations and Training Section in the office of the Chief of Air

Corps. For staff assignments this was the highest possible in the Air Corps and an honor to even be considered. Tooey had demonstrated his ability in command positions and was considered a competent leader.

Tooey's experiences epitomized the bad promotion system under which the Air Corps was forced to operate. He had been a major for 17 years, a pilot for 19, and an officer for 20. He was 43 years of age but he held jobs that called for at least two grades higher. It was a system devised by the army to disinterest the young officers graduating from West Point who might consider a flying career. After World War One, and the Air Corps became more certain of its existence, air officers were added to the one promotion list controlled by the army. Pilots were placed at the lowest number possible. It was wrong and contemptuous of the army, causing extreme hard feelings between ground and air officers.

Many air officers comparable to Spaatz in service and rank found little interest in attending military schools. These assignments, of course, were considered a must for army officers who noted from the promotion list their chance for rank and higher position. Tooey expressed himself on the subject in a note to a friend: "I cannot see myself taking the course at Leavenworth. I fully expect to put in for retirement March 1, 1940, and I see no reason to spend two of the next six years at that place." He saw these schools being of no benefit to those in aviation. Learning where a Lieutenant should place his machine-gun squad is no help while I'm cruising at 30 thousand feet looking for a strategic target to bust up.

At times, Tooey scribbled down his thoughts concerning those things he considered important to the Air Corps:

- "Morale—built up belief you are doing something important or useful in the scheme of things, plus confidence in the controlling agency.
- Knowledge that you are being treated fairly. Lack of effective doctrine—policy and plans.
- If we are a first line of defense, why do we permit units to become ineffective from lack of equipment and personnel?
- Why do we send our most needed personnel to schools, or put them in command of CCC units?
- The growing need of air power development is coming but vigorous leadership not available under present system of diversified control.
- Where is growing strength? Navy completes a five-year plan with growth; we finish ours with fewer airplanes than we started with.
- Lack of sufficient personnel in Chief's office resulting in overwork and hasty decisions of important papers. The seeming fight for air power with army rather than to face the enemy."

Tooey's position on air power and its future was, of course, in keeping with most of those associated with him. None were aware of the challenges that lay ahead to test them in the coming tides of political war.

On February 19, 1934, when the President gave the job of delivering airmail to the Air Corps, its Chief immediately instructed Spaatz and the rest of the staff to obtain the data pertaining to mail delivery. In the G-3 position for plans and operations, Tooey had to assemble the nationwide status on aircraft available for use in transporting the mail. He knew the enormity of the mission and responsibility attached to such a prodigious task. Airplanes would be away from their base of maintenance and would probably operating beyond normal inspection dates. Delivering parts and mechanics to distant points and away from places of military control would be very difficult. That meant pilots would be flying night and day moving mail, and also must find time and a way to get maintenance just to keep airplanes flyable. Into that picture, Tooey computed the problems of instrument flying, night flying, and the effects of winter weather. That meant ice on airplanes that had no de-icing equipment, and cold starts on engines where no heating equipment was available. Worse, the airplanes available had no baggage space in which to store mail. Sacks of mail must be thrown into empty cockpits, meaning there would be no security for mail in the event of crash or forced landings. Tooey knew there was nothing but pride that could see the mission survive. The belief in the ability of the Air Corps to do the job would determine its outcome. Tooey had expected some help from the airlines—it wasn't the fault of the Air Corps that a political decision had been made. Most critical of all needs was the radio system utilized by the airlines. The loan of that alone from the commercial carriers would be of immeasurable help. Not only was help not forthcoming but the airline bigwigs cast dispersions on those in the Air Corps attempting to deliver the mail. Nor was there any assistance from the army. In fact, certain high-ranking officers on army staff indicated a mocking delight over the trouble the fly-boys were in. The heaviest blow came from the need for funds. Apparently the administration thought the money would be spent anyway, so what's the difference if it's spent flying the mail? Of course, that wasn't the situation at all. Most activity was away from base and that meant incurring expenses at airports for space, food, and quarters. Officer-pilots would be away from home and need per diem. None of this was provided. Officers and enlisted men were existing on their own meager funds, or signing chits.

Spaatz had other problems. He found that of the 281 pilots selected to fly the mail, only 31 had more than 50 hours of night flying, and the rest had less than less 25 hours of instrument training. Funds for flight hours had grown smaller and smaller as the years went by. It meant that pilots could become proficient up to a point and stop. This, he believed, would show up under sustained flight operations, specifically in night and instrument flying. Tooey remembered a communication from Arnold pertaining to flight hours: "Unfortunately, instructions were received which cut down flying time of our Air Corps pilots to such an extent that it is impossible for us to carry out any mission away from our home station during the rest of the fiscal year. This cut in flying time was made due to the shortage of gasoline and oil." Squadron and group commanders could fly a total of 16 hours, other tactical pilots only 10 hours. This was pitifully small when compared to the average of 100 hours a month for airline pilots. Much of that included a great deal of night and instrument flying. One area of help came from the Commerce Department, which agreed to place its weather stations under the Air Corps for weather information to pilots flying the mail routes. Tooey greeted with great relish the fact that the Air Corps would be on its own. The army would have nothing to say about it, a sort of air autonomy at least. This alone, he believed, would move mountains if necessary to get the mail delivered. Tooey realized that regardless of planning he might do, the ultimate job would be in the hands of the pilots who were assigned a route. They would make the decisions and fly the mail.

Tragically, some of those decisions were deadly. While flying practice runs the day before starting regular mail flights, three pilots met with disaster from weather. The headlines of most papers carried the tragic news in bold type the following morning. It would serve as a presage of things to come. It was stunning news, but nothing out of the ordinary for Air Corps pilots. In the previous six months, 23 Air Corps pilots had lost their lives in flying accidents. Spaatz knew from his own well kept statistics that the loss rate of pilots was defeating its effort to grow. He approached the problem from the method used by insurance companies in the issuance of life policies. The difference was that he wanted to determine the cause of death to prevent it; the insurance company's purpose was to make money.

Spaatz noted the mail was moved during the harsh winter months, in spite of all the accusations hurled at the Air Corps by the Congress, the press, and from individuals throughout America. During the 78 days of activity, Air Corps pilots flew more than 1.5 million miles, carried more than 388 tons of mail, and completed close to 75 percent of their flights. He agreed with the comments by Horace Hickam: "It is believed that no report on the Air Mail operations can be complete without commenting on the special efficiency, resourcefulness, fortitude and initiative of Air Corps personnel in all ranks and grades. Adverse weather conditions and inadequate facilities seemed only to spur evidence that the Air Corps can successfully meet any emergency, provided the necessary facilities and equipment are available." As Tooey had predicted, it would be pride and belief in the Air Corps that sustained the effort. There could be no question about the loyalty and the willingness to die in their determination.

As in all government programs started for political purposes, when they prove to be unpopular or just plain stupid a culprit must be found to take the heat off the higher-ups. Roosevelt started the idea of firing the airlines by charging them with illegally getting mail contracts. He knew nothing about airmail contracting but believed the Republicans had rigged it. Someone had to take the blame. The innocent reply by Foulois earmarked him to be the goat—an example of the narrow line that military personnel walk when involved in political matters of government.

On May 28, Tooey was assigned to assist Andrews in preparing the outline for a new combat unit with great mobility, the GHQ Air Force. He joined Andrews, Horace Hickam, Hugh Knerr, B.Q Jones, and Edwin House. The officers worked almost without a break and completed the task June 16. Aware that arrangements were under way for a flying venture to Alaska, Tooey and Andrews hoped to be involved. In the initial arrangement, Tooey was to be one of the pilots. However, when Arnold was named to command the flight he reduced the number of pilots and Tooey lost his spot. It's likely that Arnold wanted some of the younger pilots to gain experience. After the flight returned, the participants gathered in Tooey's office to go over the details, an exercise in debriefing. They were excited and effusive as they described the events and sometimes all were talking at once. Tooey sat back, lit up, and let them talk as he made notes. They were all invited to the Carlton Hotel that night as guests of the Air Corps personnel stationed in Washington.

Spaatz described the climax of the affair in a letter to Walter Weaver, vacationing in New York: "I don't know whether any one has written you about the dinner which was given for the Alaskan flyers at which were present the Secretary of War, General Drum, and of course all the Air Corps personnel in and about Washington plus the Alaskan flyers. The Secretary of War made quite a lengthy talk stressing particularly his keen satisfaction with the finding of the Baker Board as being a means of developing the Air Corps. At the conclusion of his speech our Chief gave a talk which ended by saying he hoped he was addressing officers of the army. He then called for three rousing cheers for the Secretary of War. Whether the call was rather unexpected or for other reasons, there was a long and awkward pause followed by a rather feeble attempt at cheering. Perhaps the gesture represented the opinion of the Air Corps concerning the Baker Board."

Tooey's report included the following: Its salient point was the need to establish an Air Corps base in the Territory, primarily as an advance supply depot where tactical units essential to the air defense of Alaska, may be based on a temporary basis and that special projects such as this flight be given to a tactical unit to execute[3].

In 1936, Tooey was approached about attending the Command and General Staff School. Even though still holding the view that military schools at that time offered very little to the air officer, he considered this offer. An old friend—Strat Stratemeyer—an instructor at Leavenworth, promised to stay for the extra year if Tooey would attend. This, combined with a weary feeling of the Washington circus, and getting his family away from the summer's heat, made up his mind to go. Also, he had been promoted to temporary rank of lieutenant colonel, the first promotion in 17 years. He wrote a note to his friend George Brett inquiring about squash courts, and noted that he was looking forward to the change. "It will be a relief to get out of this melee here."

Tooey completed his tour of the Command and General Staff School after one year. He left the school feeling the same as when he entered. His new assignment took him to the 2nd Wing as the executive officer, which pleased him thoroughly. Shortly after taking that assignment Hap Arnold named him to head up an Evaluation Board on Flying in Washington. Soon after his arrival, Arnold called on him and Ira Eaker for advice about handling the false rumor that Arnold was a drunk. Tooey and Ira came up with the same tactic: Contact the President's trusted advisor, Harry Hopkins. Arnold did and Hopkins quickly squashed the dangerous rumor and gave his support to the appointment, which was announced on September 28, 1938. Following the appointment, Tooey returned to his work with the GHQ Air Force.

Arnold faced a huge responsibility after Roosevelt determined that air power was necessary. Now, Arnold and his small group of air power enthusiasts could acquire the people, the airplanes, and the industry to make them, and build what they had struggled for so long and so hard. It would be too late for some firebrands who had etched their name in history such as Billy Mitchell and Foulois, but the war would historically

---

[3] Author's note: As operations officer with the 18th Pursuit Squadron we arrived in Alaska in February 1941 with P-36s. Only the very bare necessities greeted us at Elmendorf Field—short runway, no hangar, no way to remove the two inches of Cosmoline that covered each square inch of the P-36 fuselage and separated wings. The temperature hovered near 10 degrees and there was no heater. The building to be a hangar was a shell without glass in the doors over a dirt floor. Obviously, no one paid any attention to Tooey's report.

prove the positions of these men were correct and the country was better off for their sacrifices.

Arnold appointed Tooey Spaatz to head a three-person board that would include Joe McNarney and Claude Duncan. This would be the second time he had borrowed Tooey, but this time it was final. Tooey would shortly become Arnold's Chief of Plans, his number one man. None of the three had any idea of what lay ahead. Arnold told them what had occurred and outlined what he wanted done. It was tantamount to revamping the entire Air Corps. Having a free hand appealed to Tooey. For once a program could be designed without worry of having it all chopped up by people who knew nothing of combat military planes or their functions within the roles of bombardment, pursuit, or attack. Tooey had devoted his military years to learning how to plan and program. He was no arm-chair type, however, and enjoyed command in the air. The early years of the coming war would prove difficult because so much time had been lost in creating the force with airplanes, pilots, and mechanics trained and ready for combat. It all had to be done in a hurry and men like Tooey Spaatz took on the challenge of responsibility and command.

General Carl A. (Tooey) Spaatz, United States Air Force
who served beyond duty and honor is recognized as a
Legend of Air Power

Ira Eaker

Ira Eaker was close to almost all the good and bad things that befell the Army Air Corps from its early days before World War I through to the beginning of World War II. The latter conflict proved his and his compatriot's theories about air power and its vital need to the national defense. During the court-martial trial of Billy Mitchell Eaker was detailed to provide any documentation concerning the charges against him that Mitchell wanted for his defense. As the trial progressed he carefully studied the General Officers making up the Court. There was one characterization that fit each one: they were authoritarians, virtually free of all thought except that emanating from unquestioned obedience to authority. They were the antithesis of the military pilot. In the air, dealing with the vagaries of the weather and his engine, the pilot's mind must be free to think and cope with each new demand. Add to that the dimension of enemy combat and the mind could not survive and function with a rigid thought process.

Gen. Ira C. Eaker

Ira Eaker entered the military air service during WWI. Although he had not served in France, he remained in the army and completed a tour in the Philippines. He returned in 1922 to Mitchel Field, was promoted to Captain and assigned a post Adjutant. He was from Texas, lean and tall in stature, and intense. He moved with grace and ease, dominating the athletic games in football, baseball, and basketball. Congress passed a law in 1923 permitting Captains to resign and receive one-year's severance pay. The purpose was to reduce the "hump" created by the war's end. This fit Eaker's plan. He was eager to obtain a law degree and had decided to leave the service to attend Columbia Law school. He obtained the approval of his commander who understood his purpose but could offer him nothing better.

One evening he was working late at the office when a DH-4 landed and parked on the ramp. The passenger was Air Service Chief General Patrick. His pilot, Billy Streett, was ill. The General asked if a pilot could replace him and Captain Eaker filled the job. The General learned of Eaker's decision and suggested that he consider attending a one-year college course under a plan available to young officers and still keep his regular commission. Eaker made that choice and obtained his degree using the three years earned at the University of Manila to finish the requirements for a degree in law.

Returning to active duty Eaker was assigned to General Patrick's office in June 1924 as assistant to Maj. Moe Kilner, executive officer to the general. This position placed him where he could observe air history in the making. He concluded the only difference between the General's view of air power and that of Billy Mitchell's was in their approach to matters. Central to the feeling of air officers was the opinion that air power could never survive control under the army or navy. After a time of being privy to the discussions from all sides, Eaker became addicted to the theory and support of air power. He saw improvement and advancement in the Air Service in Patrick's dealings with the top brass of the army and the Secretary of War, purely due to their acceptance of him. They trusted him. Conversely, their attitude toward Mitchell was hostile. Prior to Mitchell's exile to Fort Sam Houston in 1925, Eaker had opportunity to know him. He admired his ability to express himself and his ability to get his point across to the press, thus exerting influence on the public. He found his personality to be inspiring.

The winter of 1926 in Washington found Billy Mitchell and Hap Arnold gone and much of the excitement went out of the War Department life. Even though the Air Corps Act of 1926 gave only a small portion of what the struggle had been all about, it was better than nothing. It strongly affected Ira Eaker by bringing him in touch with the top players. A main feature of the Act provided for Assistant Secretaries of Air for the War, Navy and Commerce Departments. F. Trubee Davison was recommended to be the Assistant Secretary for Air due to his family's political connections and his interest in aviation. He had been involved in an airplane crash that severely injured his legs but he had a keen mind and was a top supporter of the Air Corps. Eaker attended Davison's swearing in ceremonies. Afterward, the first request from the new Secretary was a plane ride over Washington. General Patrick told Ira to escort the Secretary to Bolling Field and give him a ride in his Blue Bird DH. After the ride, the Secretary, pleased and exhilarated, asked to be flown to his home near Mitchel Field, Long Island. Eaker obtained the clearance and flew to the base. Davison invited him to his home where Ira met his family. They returned the next day, but Ira now had the assignment as personal pilot to the Secretary. That placed Eaker in the center of the three most important Air Corps seats of power: General Patrick, Assistant Chief Brig. Gen. Fechet, and Trubee Davison.

These were obviously exciting days for Eaker, but he was about to participate in a great aerial adventure that would illustrate what air power was all about. The purpose was to demonstrate American interest in South American countries. It would also illustrate the primitive technology available in the building of an airplane. The venture was the Pan American Good Will Flight of 1926. One can only marvel at the determination of the pilots who strove to be included in the selection process to undertake such a journey. The plane selected was the Loening COA-1. The fuselage was mounted on a wood and duralumin hull. The engine was the war-time 400-hp Liberty, mounted inverted so the propeller would clear the hull. It was an open-cockpit amphibian that cruised about 85 mph. The planned flight would cover some 23,000 miles, not including the extra miles for flying around unknown and unplanned weather fronts with their fog, winds, icing, and heavy rain. The recommendations for pilots were made by Assistant Chief Fechet and given to his boss, General Patrick. Eaker was among those chosen.

The flight would include five planes with two pilots assigned to each. The final list contained the names of 26 pilots. One pilot was required to have an engineering background. Eaker immediately chose Lt. Muir "Shanty" Fairchild. Following the war, Fairchild had become a test pilot, joining a handful of daredevils that included Jimmy Doolittle. Eaker had known Fairchild at Wright Field and Langley. He believed that no one knew the Liberty engine better than Fairchild. The planning called for 56 days for flying and 70 delay days for diplomatic functions and aircraft maintenance. Although no maintenance plane would go ahead or accompany the flight, a number of parts and tools for maintenance went along. No maintenance would be available at any of the stops listed. Following a gala send-off, the five amphibians departed Kelly Field, Texas, on December 21, 1926.The planes were named after principal cities: *New York, San Antonio, Detroit, St. Louis,* and *San Francisco.* Eaker and Fairchild flew the *San Francisco.*

The course selected was that which ultimately would serve Pan American Airways. The daily schedule called for a 4:00 A.M. rising and a 6:00 o'clock takeoff. This early rising was made even more arduous by the nightly diplomatic banquets and dancing. Fortunately, they were all young and rugged men in good health.

Fueling the aircraft in primitive landing areas where few had ever seen an airplane required long hours. The inverted engine mountings caused oil to leak through the rings, requiring frequent cleaning and changing of spark plugs. There were other problems. In Guatemala, Bert Dargue was taking off on a small field surrounded by trees. Just beyond the trees he encountered a 50-foot stone aqueduct that he couldn't clear. He chopped the throttle and landed in a small cornfield, damaging the landing gear and hull. There were no injuries, and necessary repairs were made to the aircraft. The amphibian was taken to a nearby small lake and then flown to France Field in Panama for a complete overhaul. On another occasion, the *St. Louis* developed engine trouble over rough seas off the Colombian coast. The others watched helplessly as two Lieutenants, Bernard Thompson and Leonard Weddington, went down into the high waves. Hours later they were able to get airborne and landed at the mouth of the Magdalena River. They explained it this way: "We could see the waves would break us up and no ships were in sight, so we decided we might as well try to fly and break up in the effort. We gave her the gun and just bounced from wave to wave until we got here." They repaired the leaky radiator, worked the three propeller blades back into shape and were ready to go.

Following three days of banquets and hard work on their planes at Chile's inland capital of Santiago, they flew down the coast from a tropical zone into a temperate one and heavy rain. They flew in close formation just to keep in sight of each other until reaching Valdiva, where they landed. It was a pioneer town populated by Germans who were busy clearing forests to build their homes. The settlers were grouchy and said they hadn't seen a decent day in nine years. The real work for the fliers, however, was to prepare for the 650-mile flight across the Andes to reach the east-coast port of Bahia Blanca, Argentina. They took off the next morning and flew in rain for 50 miles over the forests, then broke out of the rain and into clear weather. In front of them lay a shroud of clouds higher and thicker than any they had seen. It hid the high Andes Mountains from view. Dargue gave the signal to climb while circling, with each plane on its own for the crossing. Eaker was flying and he climbed to 12,000 feet, the maximum altitude for the aircraft, considering the three tons of fuel and equipment aboard. He leveled off, just on top of the cloud layer and could see sharp peaks jutting up from the clouds. After about one hour of flight, the Liberty engine started coughing and threatening to quit. Ice had formed in the carburetor and there was no way to clear it without going to a lower altitude and warmer air. Ira knew he would have to descend into the clouds as the engine was losing power. The only alternative was the parachute. He yelled to Fairchild, asking if he wanted to jump. Fairchild said "No!" with emphasis. At that point, Ira decided it was a toss-up, stay with the plane and chance a blind collision with a mountain peak, or jump and end up on a peak holding the chute in his lap. At that point, Eaker's plane was just above stall speed and flying down into the gray cloud that surrounded them. He could see nothing beyond wing-tips. Ira was flying blind and on the only instruments he had. He could see the altimeter steadily winding down and kept close attention to the needle, ball, and airspeed. As they waited, their eyes darted from side to side, hoping for a break in the cloud. That day the air gods were kind. Like a glimpse of paradise, a lake appeared below through a cloud gap.

At that point, Fairchild became excited and stood up in the rear cockpit holding a piece of paper with a crudely drawn terrain sketch. A British engineer he once knew had surveyed a route across the Andes and marked the pass with the lake below. Through incredible luck, they had managed to bring their plane down over the valley thus avoiding the surrounding mountains and peaks. Eaker circled the lake for a possible landing, but the air had warmed and the Liberty coughed up the melting carburetor ice. Ira put the *San Francisco* back on its course over the Patagonian plains.

At Polmar Field, Buenos Aires, luck that had sustained the pilots of the Pan American Goodwill Flight thus far was about to run out. As they passed over Buenos Aires, the four planes were in a diamond formation escorted by three Argentine Army planes flying alongside. Over the city, Dargue in the lead plane, signaled to break formation. The two wing planes were to pull up and turn left away from the planes underneath. However, distracted by a landing gear problem, the pilot of the left wing plane failed to pull up and remained at the same altitude as the lead plane. They collided. The two pilots remained in the wreckage and perished. The pilots in the lead plane jumped and survived. Eaker, flying in the diamond spot at the rear, had been able to observe the entire tragic affair. The accident happened over the city and the two planes and debris fell on the streets. At the funeral the President of Argentina and his cabinet marched in the procession, honoring the pilots.

As Eaker flew up the long coast of South America on their return fight, another problem developed with the Liberty engine. While over rough seas near Montevideo, Uruguay, a blockage developed in the carburetor. It had the potential of catching fire. Looking at the rough waves, Eaker decided he would as soon go up in flames as drown, and headed for shore. Reaching the shoreline they landed, but faced additional trouble when the tie-rope broke from the anchor in high waves. A huge wave hit the plane and drenched the engine as Eaker was trying to get it started. He worked frantically until it fired and they were able to move away from the rocks. The waves literally tossed the plane onto the beach and natives rushed out with a rope and helped pull it to safety. After repairs the next day, they took off safely and rejoined the others at Santos.

On May 2, 1927, the adventure concluded at Bolling Field in Washington, having taken 175 days of travel and grief. Before a large crowd of friends and military brass, President Coolidge greeted the eight pilots. Major Dargue presented messages of good will sent the President by 23 Latin-American countries. Coolidge, in return, presented a newly created medal, the *Distinguished Flying Cross*, to each person for outstanding performance in an aerial mission of great importance. They were the first to receive the award

Over the next few years, Ira Eaker would be in a position to watch and observe the development of the Air Corps from very high places. His demeanor, willingness to work, and his timing concerning important issues assured him of the implicit trust from those whose work was so important to the early development of the Air Corps, and, indeed, of air power. His participation, first hand, in when and how important decisions were to be made and their results gave him insight that few military airmen enjoyed.

Most supporters of developing air power selected public relations to advance their cause. This was one area where hidebound military authoritarians had no ability to function and could be exploited without fear of reprisal, provided it didn't go too far. Of course, a certain amount of credit would fall on the War Department when aviation programs such as the Pan American Goodwill Flight, the intercept at sea of the Italian Liner *Rex*; and the flight to Alaska received favorable nationwide publicity. Such planning, however, was in a way subversive to the army idea that the only function of the Air Corps was to serve the battlefield needs of the army.

Ira Eaker understood such a course and had the skill to add to it. A competent writer, he was aware of what was newsworthy for public interest. The Air Corps supporters and defenders believed that advancement in technology served an interest of the public and therefore made an effort to publicize new developments as they occurred. Eaker quickly saw in Trubee Davison, the ability to soothe over and heal the caustic demands for air independence that had taken Billy Mitchell out of action, leaving his supporters lost for a leader. Davison was aware of the navy's desire to take over the Air Corps' position in national defense and believed that publicity would help defeat the effort. He confided in Eaker that a public image of the Air Corps should be more refined, especially with Congress. He believed the War Department restricted it either from a lack of understanding or its own desire to prevent the Air Corps' point of view from being publicized. To help get the Air Corps point of view better understood, Davison employed a newspaper writer and friend to work as his legislative aide. He assigned Eaker to assist him by supplying the military background or data for whatever the writing—a speech, a hearing concerning the Air Corps, a flying training mission of unusual dimensions concerning a long distance bombing, or new equipment received. Davison saw to it that a close informative relationship was maintained with the House committees on military and appropriations. As a result, Eaker often flew members of Congress to bases and installations to educate them on where money was needed and how it was spent. Eaker noted that Davison pursued matters he felt were important and essential to Air Corps needs and growth with the General Staff. Many times the Staff complained about his persistence, but never his attitude or methods. Ira saw to it that his boss was always current in aviation matters and spoke on solid ground when making a point of contention. Captain Eaker represented his boss at some hearings and was aware of the consequences if his facts weren't exactly on the mark. Crusty old Generals would have eaten the Captain alive.

Davison wasn't Eaker's only boss. Gen. Jim Fechet was the other, a convert to air after 20 years in the saddle as a cavalryman. He had ridden the Mexican deserts chasing Pancho Villa and his horsemanship placed him on the Cavalry Team of 1909. He was commissioned from the ranks during the uprising in the Philippines and was wounded at San Juan Hill in Cuba. He was a rough, tough man and admitted that logistics bored him. His comment about the subject was succinct: "I've got a staff for that sort of thing." He referred to Ira as "I-ree", and treated him like a son. The two made a pleasure trip out of an order to pick up two Douglas O-28 planes from Rockwell Field, near San Diego. Fechet had learned to fly after his cavalry days and recognized his age and his lack of the finer points of piloting. He suggested "I-ree" lead them back home. They departed the West Coast on a fine, clear day. Ira looked back a couple of times and saw Fechet was doing fine. When Ira landed at Winslow, Arizona, the General didn't follow. Ira checked to see if anyone had seen him fly over. They had not. Ira was preparing to retrace his flight path when someone yelled, "There he is!" Fechet landed, looking a little sheepish. He confided to

Eaker that he had dozed off in the warm sun and suddenly awakened to find himself off course and close to the ground. He and Ira decided to get some sleep.

Ira had his share of good and bad flights. When the P-12 came off the line, he arranged for a publicity stunt to show it off. He would make a dawn to dusk flight from Brownsville, Texas, to France Field in Panama. In addition, a new air route was being opened from Brownsville to San Antonio. The Brownsville airport was new, the inaugural transportation flight was new, and the P-12 was new and about to set a new record. The combination events attracted a large crowd and the news services. At the correct time the P-12 appeared overhead, landed and Ira taxied up to the speakers' platform. General Fechet's wife was there to christen the plane as the *Pan American*. Ira took off the next morning at dawn and headed for Panama. A short distance outbound he ran into foul weather, strong head winds, and poor visibility. By the time he made Nicaragua, he knew he could not reach Panama before dusk. He landed at Managua and continued on to France Field the following day. He prepared for a return flight the following day, hoping to set the record in reverse. After checking the plane over, he retired for the 4:00 A.M. takeoff. Once more, he ran into bad luck. The weather was worse than the day before. He missed his refueling stop and was forced to plan a landing at Tampico, but ran short of fuel before getting there. He landed in a mud hole during a downpour. When he finally returned to Kelly Field, he stated without rancor that the culprit was weather. And, it was true. Ira would see the day, however, when weather was no longer the cause of missed flight records or canceled flights, only the most severe of conditions would prohibit flight.

About a month after his attempted record flight to Panama Ira made the flight to drop the company pilot near the aircraft on Greenly Island that resulted in the idea to try aerial refueling.

As the Air Corps matured and better equipment came along, questions arose about the radio equipment provided by the Signal Corps. Compared with the airlines, military equipment was second-rate and unreliable. Reception was poor and the two-way feature was defective. Several sources were attempting to improve it. For one thing, the weight of the radio in pursuit planes was too heavy. Eaker became involved by testing a P-12 with the radio unit's battery stowed directly behind the cockpit. It weighed 54 pounds and he wanted to test the plane's stability. At 5000 feet, he put the plane into a spin to the left. Recovery was sluggish. He climbed to 7000 feet and put it into a spin to the right. While in the spin, the nose came up and the plane continued to rotate in a flat spin. Ira could move the control stick around without response, even though the control surfaces were also moving. Nothing he did changed the rotation of the plane as it lost altitude. The weight of the battery had caused uncontrollable instability. At 500 feet he bailed out, banging his nose and leg on the stabilizer. He had waited too long to give the 'chute time to fully open. He went down on one side of a house and the canopy was on the other. He slammed onto a cement stoop, buckling his right leg under him. It was extremely painful as he rolled around on the ground trying to unhitch from the harness.

As he lay there, the back door opened and a lady stepped out and looked at him. She immediately stepped back into the house, leaving him to agonize and hold his leg. He was now aware that his plane had torn down a hen house and was on fire in the adjacent orchard. As he was wondering how to get out of the predicament, the door again opened and the same lady came out to help, and full of remorse. "Let me help you!" she cried, and kept urging him to let her help. Together they got the harness unbuckled and she assisted him into the house to a couch. Ira still felt miserable but her kindness soothed him. He asked if she would call Bolling Field and she agreed. "First, let me tell you why I didn't help you right away. I had to call the newspaper first. They give five dollars to the first person who calls in an ambulance case." Sometime later, Ira learned from reporter and columnist Ernie Pyle that was the deal.

Eakers had a bum foot as a result of hitting the concrete and the doctor had him in bed for rest. Tooey Spaatz came to see him. Spaatz told friends that the net effect of it all was that the General and I-ree play cooncan (a form of rummy) all the time instead of occasionally." Ira was lucky. He didn't solve the weight problem the way he wished but one thing was certain: no army pilot would be taking off with 54 pound radios stowed behind the cockpit on pursuit type planes.

In 1930, Ira was invited to attend a Thanksgiving party given by his friend, Lt. Newton Longfellow. Ira was introduced to Ruth Apperson, a graduate of George Washington University, whose home was in North Carolina. One year later they were married.

The military social situation in Washington for wives of high-ranking husbands in the army was determined by the "pecking" order. The invitation list established the status according to the rank of the husband. It was a closed affair and closely monitored. The right people had to be invited to an event, which was social and military in nature. Size of the event would determine who in the pecking order would be invited. It was almost like royalty, but instead of Kings, Dukes, Earls, and Princes, it had Generals from one star to four, Colonels, Majors, and a few in the lower ranks, usually aides. The social order was tightly controlled and the position on the list changed only with transfer, death, promotion, or new arrival. It was a snobbish arrangement to keep people in their official social place. Sometimes, of course, if the matter were serious enough, a de-listing would occur for some poor soul who dropped from acceptable social graces.

The Air Corps, on the other hand, was totally different. The promotion list that was zealously guarded by the army meant very little to Air Corps wives. They knew about it but their husbands had difficulty explaining it and seldom tried. Air Corps wives knew the basic concepts that drove their husbands—flying! They lived it during the day, talked about it in the evening, and dreamed about it during their sleep. Of course, the dreams were far ahead of the actual product. Wives, generally, didn't like the airplanes they saw, and they didn't like their husbands flying them. But, like women folk who accompanied their husbands across the frontiers for their dreams of the future, so did Air Corps wives understand what drove their husbands to fly and seek how to fly better. There was much more camaraderie between the few Generals in the Air Corps to the Lieutenants because they all shared in the same dreams and hopes of building the Air Corps. There was also the intimate bond of flying among pilots and regardless of rank, pilots in a flying suit all spoke the same language. That's not to say there wasn't respect and discipline for higher ranked pilots—they had earned it. However, when on a flight together and stuck in a small town because of weather, regardless of rank they stayed close to one another.

In 1932, Captain Eaker was placed on detached service to study for a journalism degree at the University of Southern California. He and his wife were out driving late one afternoon, she taking a driving lesson. Suddenly, the entire road began to tremble and shake with an ominous rumbling sound. Ira thought the car had a flat or something was wrong with the steering. As it got worse and they saw people running from their homes he knew it was an earthquake. It had just struck in Long Beach. Ira took the wheel and drove quickly to their home. It was a mess with dishes all over the floor and the piano moved across the room. As they were deciding what to do, Hap Arnold called and asked Ira to drive to the Long Beach police headquarters and get an estimate on what was needed. He did, with parts of buildings and rubble falling all around as he drove carefully through the streets. Ira talked with the police chief, the Mayor, and the relief people and called Arnold with the report. Arnold went to work and sped relief assistance to the area. When Ira completed his school assignment in journalism he was assigned to March Field. He got there just in time to take part in flying the airmail.

The "bashing" given the Air Corps concerning the weather problems its pilots were facing day and night irritated Eaker. News reports ignored the real difficulties confronting the pilots and zeroed in on the sensational crashes, which in most cases were caused either by weather or a lack of proper instruments for navigation. News media reported them as "untrained pilots" or "poorly maintained " planes. Nothing was mentioned about the tonnage of mail being moved in spite of great problems. Ira used his writing skills to defend the pilots. He wrote one article that was published in a New York magazine. He wrote another concerning the critics who were more interested in selling newspapers than reporting facts about flying the mail.

Eaker believed that adding copilots would provide an excellent method for checking out new pilots on the airplane, giving familiarization runs on airmail routes, and relieving pilots for rest periods. He prepared the idea as a presentation and sent it to Arnold who approved and forwarded the recommendation for inclusion in the training program.

Shortly after the conclusion of the airmail operation, Ira received his promotion to Major. He was eligible for the Air Corps Tactical School and assigned to the next class. Hap Arnold had recommended him for the course and had ideas of a future assignment for the brilliant officer. Ira had two great assets for handling school courses: his legal and journalism training. The legal training provided an ability to organize and formulate his ideas; the journalism gave him training in written presentation. Ira took a break from school in June. He had been given permission from the school heads, Bert Dargue and John Curry, to present an idea to Arnold for approval to fly a P-12 on instruments over an extended route of navigation. The idea was to demonstrate flight accomplishment in extended navigation using radio and instrument aids. Ira planned to fly in the P-12 himself, and be accompanied by Maj. Bill Kepner in a chase plane. The program was approved by Arnold and blessed by Washington, and on June 3 the two P-12s took off from Mitchel Field.

The course was from Mitchel to March Field, and just a touch of the Pacific Coast. Nine landings would be required, the first at Bolling Field, Washington, DC. Eaker would be under the hood on each leg, going on instruments directly after takeoff until reaching the landing stop. Considering the refueling and rest stops, the flight required four days. Over Texas, the flight encountered bad weather conditions and Ira instructed Kepner to fly close formation and he would lead on instruments. Ira had practiced the routine while flying at March Field with his squadron, regularly taking his formation up through cloud formations. It was a new record for Ira, and in the doing had demonstrated how far the

Air Corps had advanced in its ability to fly weather. One thing was certain: any place the P-12 could go certainly the bombers could do likewise. It led to the record flight by General Andrews flying a twin-engine Douglas amphibian *The Big Duck* on instruments.

After completing the Tactical School, Ira decided to complete his school requirements by attending the Command and General Staff School. It was during this period that Pursuit moved forward to the P-26, the Seversky P-35, and the Curtiss model P-36, considerably advanced over the P-12. Unfortunately, the P-26 did little to improve the pursuit combat capability and the others were well below the German and English models. Ira was promoted to Lt. Colonel and assigned as Assistant Chief of Air Corps under command of Arnold. For Ira it was a move up in rank and assignment. He had been diligent in his preparation for a military career, having completed his formal education with two pertinent university degrees, and the essential military schools for his rank level. He had managed to keep up his flying and greatly improve his instrument flying. Few other officers could match his all-around flying expertise, and he had managed to survive some near fatal accidents. In the coming years when military air would finally reach the independence sought by Billy Mitchell, Ira Eaker would be there to serve his country and its people.

Assistant Secretary of War Louis Johnson made a speech to the American Legion comparing the relative strengths of major nations. He had been criticized for using incorrect figures and assigned Lt. Colonel Eaker to supply correct information. It was Ira's first assignment in his new job. He quickly learned that current figures from the Army Intelligence were more than a year old. The numbers of planes represented all types, civilian and military. The British headed the list with 5600. Italy and Russia were next with each having about 4100. The United States was about equal to Germany with 3200 followed by Japan and France at approximately 2300 each. Ira put an asterisk by each number indicating it represented anything that had wings and an engine mounted on a fuselage. To conclude his report, Ira drew attention to quantity and quality of the planes involved.

Officially, Ira Eaker, as Chief of Air Corps Information, did a voluminous amount of public relations work writing articles, speeches, news releases, as well as background information for other officers. He let nothing slip by that was creditable for the Air Corps. His contacts with the press were wide and varied. Ira Eaker could not know that in a short span of time he would be called upon to provide leadership in high command. There, he would be able to prove that the theories he had fought so hard to develop were correct when applied to the ordeal that faced air power in the tumultuous times of a world at war.

General Ira C. Eaker, Army Air Corps
who served beyond duty and honor is recognized as a *Legend of Air Power*

Legendary Comrades

Behind the *Legends* during the early formation of what would become air power as the world would know it stood great airmen in their own right. They took the plans and commands and turned them into missions accomplished. In the coming maelstrom of madness concocted by Hitler and his madmen, each and every one of these men would serve his country with bravery and astuteness, rising to the heights of military air supremacy that dominated all other countries, indeed the world. They are not listed in any order, just by name: Follett Bradley, Laurence Kuter, Lewis Brereton, George Brett, Herbert Dargue, Curtis LeMay, Ross Hoyt, James Chaney, George Dern, Muir Fairchild, Jimmy Doolittle, James Fechet, Joseph McNarney, Earle Patridge, Robert Olds, Horace Hickam, Millard Harmon, Elwood Quesada, Delos Emmons, Walter Kilner, Charles Lindbergh, Arnold Krogstad, Conger Pratt, Ralph Royce, Frank Lahm, St. Clair Streett, Nathan Twining, Clarence Tinker, Ennis Whitehead, Caleb Haynes, Byron Jones, Leonard Harmon, Harold George, Kenneth Walker, Barton Yount, Walter Weaver, Hugh Knerr, Jan Howard, Hoyt Vandenberg. Others? Of course.

No aviation program could be planned or developed without enlisted personnel. In the schemes of the bests planners, it has always been the enlisted personnel who start each day whether the mess hall, rolling out the planes, pulling the props through, opening the offices, arranging the "in" basket material to start where it left off from the day before, starting the vehicles and trucks on their scheduled runs, picking up the generals to start their activities with a pleasant "Good morning, Sir." On, and on, and on, until the day is spent. Then, they busy themselves putting all in order for the coming tomorrow.

Not all can rest. Problems written up after the missions are flown must be corrected before the next scheduled flight. It might be into the early hours of morning before the cowling goes back into place and just a few hours before reveille. Even so, you won't catch that crew chief yawning or making excuses. The enlisted personnel perform their duties in a bond of honor with the pilot scheduled to fly the next mission. Enlisted personnel are trusted and revered in their performance of duty. They are a different breed of person—the very backbone of the United States Air Force.

Book Two

Allman T. "Cubby" Culbertson volunteered for army air corps flight training in 1936. A typical Flying Cadet of the time, he completed Randolph Field and Kelly Field training with the class of 1937B. He flew B-17 missions on the first daylight raids over Germany in WWII. He served as Deputy Commander of the 95th Bomb Group. His decorations include Legion of Merit, Distinguished Flying Cross, and Air Medal with oak leaf cluster. After 32 years of service he retired as a Brigadier General.

2

First Stage to Combat

The LEGENDS struggled to overcome many obstacles in their determination to achieve air power to protect the United States. So, too, did the individuals in the 23 classes of Flying Cadets who were to take up the banner and help to put into action the air power that these legends strove so hard to produce. I was fortunate to be one of those individuals.

I remember the day. Hot, muggy, humid air followed a wild thunderstorm that had soaked the red dirt plains of Fort Sill Oklahoma. I was a private in the National Guard field artillery. My duty was to operate the French Aiming Circle in the battery commander's detail when we were firing the Howitzer cannon. My Lieutenant depended on my accuracy in computing the trajectory of shells. Sometimes, I was good—or lucky—when he fired for "effect" and blasted the target. It was 1932 and I was 17. The Great Depression was underway and the Ford Motor Company was closing its assembly plants in Oklahoma City and elsewhere. The oil companies were pumping oil, although a moratorium reduced their production. It didn't seem to matter to the oil people; they kept building new homes.

Some might wonder why I would spend two weeks of my summer vacation on the boiling red clay at Fort Sill. For one thing I liked shooting the big guns, and another was economics. I received $1 per day and food for my work. I had not learned about loyalty but I knew about the Depression. It changed life for most of us and created a day-to-day existence. Dollars were precious and scarce.

Our Field Artillery battery was horse drawn. Six men made up our crew and when we moved the cannon our position was sitting atop the caisson. It's a four-sided metal box attached to the axle housing with wheels on both sides. There are no appurtenances to hold onto; three ride facing the rear and three face the front. We locked arms and pressed our backs against the caisson front and back. The caisson transports the ammunition and its top, where we sat, is very, very slick.

I didn't mind the horses but they disliked thunder and would panic when lightning struck. On one occasion, horses, cannon, and gun crew raced—out of control—across the gunnery range, frightened by a thunderbolt that split the skies. We are all holding on tight with our free hands grasping the caisson's slick sides when the horses suddenly make a right turn. For a moment we are free falling, then we hit the red mud and went sprawling in the goo. I assured myself, while checking my legs and arms for damage, I would never fight a war on the ground. As though emphasizing my decision, three army planes flew over in formation very low. The roar of the engines was deafening, and as I watched, the sunshine peeps from behind the storm clouds, as though spotlighting their majestic departure. I vowed that on my return home from summer training my flying career would start. It did. A small airport operated on the northwest edge of Oklahoma City. It was named after the veteran pilot Wiley Post. A small trainer biplane had been designed for primary instruction and bore Post's name. It was powered by the small engine used in the Ford model "A" automobile, a four-cylinder, water-cooled engine that could literally be repaired with pliers and bailing wire. Post inverted the engine so a propeller could be attached to the crankshaft, and installed a small oil pump for internal lubrication. It was a dandy training plane with two cockpits in tandem. The instruction charge was $5 per hour for dual time, that is, with an instructor.

Money was scarce in 1932. I lived with my widowed aunt who took in boarders to make ends meet. I decided to try finding some cleaning and polishing jobs on airplanes at the airport. I found a few regulars but not many. One Saturday afternoon a bevy of small planes came in for fuel. Help was short and I pitched in helping park and fuel them. Afterwards the airport manager asked if I would be interested in working part time. I still had a month left of summer vacation and could work during weekends and after school. He hired me to clean the hangar and help refueling. I asked if he would credit my work toward flying lessons. He agreed and said the first hour of dual would be free. He was the first of many who offered to help me in my flying effort. My instructor, Dutch Kinder, was licensed by the CAA (FAA later) and had a no nonsense attitude when it came to flying.

At the end of the month I had earned two hours, giving me a total of three. Dutch gave me an orientation flight explaining controls and gadgets and why it flew. He also said he had a girl he wished to marry and had promised her I would be a good pilot. I got the drift and told him I would be his best student. I was just 17 and doing something I had not thought possible. Dutch briefed me during the first hour of dual. Among other things, he flew me around the airport so I could see the approach from different directions. "I don't want you getting lost the first time you fly alone," he said. During the second hour we did some stalls. Dutch took the stick and motioned for me to follow through a few turns. After he led me through several I was able to sloppily perform them on my own. I knew they weren't well coordinated, but I was flying! After landing, Dutch gave me some advice I never forgot: "Never lose flying speed! Some things you will forget, but your life will depend on keeping the airplane in the air. The most common fault by beginners is to insist on pulling back the stick when faced with engine failure at low altitude. Push it forward to glide and keep control."

One beautiful fall day, Dutch had me taxi out for takeoff on the east runway. I was completing my sixth hour of dual. After taxiing into position I did the pre-takeoff checklist of controls and instruments, swiveled my head to check traffic, and eased the throttle forward. The engine surged into high RPM and in seconds I broke free of the ground, entering the beautiful environment of bird life. It's no wonder birds love to sing. There is nothing that compares with the inspiring views, the tugging of the wind against the goggles and the freedom from earthly clutter. Even through the bitter days of the Depression, birds still flew freely and sang their songs of encouragement for all to hear.

Dutch put me through the paces. If I didn't please him the maneuver had to be repeated until acceptable. Finally he motioned me to land. The way he did it scared me. We had been up only 30 minutes, so I guessed I'd screwed up on something that really displeased him. I landed and after rolling to a stop waited for the chewing out. Instead, he crawled out and yelled over the engine noise: "She's all yours!" I did a double take for assurance and he nodded to me. I tried to remember everything Dutch had told me: checklist, look around, smooth power and airspeed. I taxied out, completed the preflight, swiveled my head, and pushed the throttle forward. I broke ground and flew about halfway down the runway gaining about 200 feet altitude when the engine quit cold. Suddenly I'm looking at the prop standing straight up and down. I immediately eased the stick forward to keep flying speed and started to sweat.

At the end of the runway, a highway ran north and south. I could see cars moving on it. Beyond the road was a field in fallow and I disregarded the moving cars. My attention was on reaching that field. I could understand the reluctance to push the stick forward, it seemed more normal to get the nose up to hold altitude, but I knew better. I had done stalls and knew the feeling of flying speed with power off. I relaxed my hand on the stick, reached up to wipe the sweat off my brow, then we were crossing the highway and a fence was coming up. It slid under the wing and I pulled the stick back just as the tires hit dirt. Dutch ran over to see if I was all right and I could see him breathe a sigh of relief. "Damn good job!" he said.

I flew the Wiley Post trainer for another five hours. Three friends, all pilots, checked me out in their Waco, Kinner Sportster, and Fairchild Cabin. They were older men with whom I came in contact through a mutual love of aviation. I think they respected me for attempting the almost impossible task of becoming a pilot without financial assistance during the Depression. On the other hand, I worked hard to keep their planes clean and free of dirt and grease. Regardless, it was their kindness and trust that flowed and helped me when I was a teenager with an improbable dream.

I continued to fly when I could scrape up the cash. During the summers, I flew as part of a crew barnstorming through the farming communities in western Texas and Oklahoma after harvest. Usually three or four planes made the flight. My job was servicing the planes and selling ads to local businessmen. Singer Sewing Machines and Sears Roebuck could be relied upon to take $5 ads. For this they received their names written on the plane's fuselage plus a few free tickets to the show. We also sold rides for $5 for flights around town. Since there wasn't any football, baseball, or television, and very little radio or movies, our shows were well attended. Some figured a crash might occur, but we flew accident free. After the show was over, I usually got to fly one of the planes to the next stop and get the hoopla started. By the end of 1936, I had passed all my requirements for private pilot and three year's of college credits. Also, I was broke.

During college I enrolled in the ROTC for credits toward a reserve commission. We received a bulletin from the army pertaining to flight training at Randolph Field. I read over the requirements and knew I was qualified except for the required physical exam. The army instructor said the physical was tough. Nothing could have stopped me from trying for the flight training; it was the best in the world. Also, I could come out commissioned a second lieutenant. I sent in my application and was ordered to Fort Sill for a physical exam. Unfortunately, the medical people there knew very little about the requirements, but they checked my heart, pulse, weight, and height. I got so excited when they checked my pulse I flunked out. I asked my doctor to check the reason and he thought it was wrong so I sent in another request. This time I was sent to the medical center at Randolph Field for testing. I passed and orders were issued for my assignment to the class starting March 1, 1937. For me, I had just been given the opportunity to join the elite military pilot organization of the world. Climbing out of the dark hole of the Depression into the sunshine of a young boy's dream was like a miracle. The big question was whether I could cut the mustard.

I also had an additional reason for wanting the flight training. When I was 12 years old I heard that Charles Lindbergh was making a flight from New York to Paris. Newspaper accounts increased the excitement and the announcement came over the radio that he had taken off in terrible weather. Nothing was heard until the following morning. Then came the news that he had been sighted and was on his way to Paris. It was one of those great things in memory that stays clear as day, almost as if it happened yesterday. Years later, in 1939, I was officer-of-the day at Moffett Field when Colonel Lindbergh stopped for a refueling in a P-36 on his way to Hamilton Field. General Arnold had requested him to inspect the units flying that type plane. Weather made it a poor weather day for flying and we discussed the conditions going into Hamilton Field. I tried to provide information, but no advice.

Becoming a Flying Cadet

My enlistment instructions required me to take a physical examination at March Field on March 1. Unfortunately, fate, whose presence always comes as a total surprise, sent me to a hospital-operating table with a hot appendix. A competent surgeon excised it and said I should be able to make my enlistment signing on time but the incision would require a few days to heal. I was strap-taped, and made it to March Field. My concern was whether I would be accepted for the March class. Fortunately for me it was a busy day at the hospital. The medical orderly told me to take off my shirt and did the usual weight, height, ear, and eye exams. He sent me to the flight surgeon, who checked the report, asked me how I felt. "Fine," I said, and signed my enlistment papers. I departed by train for Randolph Field the following morning.

The train arrived outside Randolph Field as scheduled. I heard all kinds of shouting and yelling outside my window. "Put your bag down! Pick it up! What's the matter with you? Can't you understand English? Oh, I see, you're waiting for the next train. Stand up straight when you speak to me! Pick up that bag! Get those shoulders back. Suck up that gut! Pick up that bag".

I stepped off the train and immediately received the attention of those whose voices I had heard. This was called hazing, a method of initiating new members into an organization to reduce their ability to think independently, and lower their esteem to eliminate cockiness and superior thought. It's supposed to start the individual on the lowest step of the ladder, then with training, to gradually make him a part of the team. Does it work? There are many opinions on this. Some cases went too far to achieve the intended purpose.

As new recruits, we were required to report to the hospital for our entrance physical. When I undressed, the flight surgeon asked, "What's that?" looking at my stomach. "You're supposed to be in top condition for this training." I explained how it had happened. He said he could hold me over for the next class, or give me light duty for two days. "Can you commence full training then?" he asked. I said the light duty would be fine. On my return to the barracks, I took the slip to the Commandant's office. He wanted an explanation, and I repeated my story. He was irritated by the failure to hold me at March Field, and asked me if I could march. I assured him I could. After the two days I received my full treatment as a dodo. Much of the hazing was reduced after a month when we reported to the flight line to meet our instructors.

Randolph Field and Kelly Field were different in many ways. Randolph was a show house, the Shangri-la of the Air Corps. Many who visit there often refer to the entrance building as the Taj Mahal. Its design is similar to the mausoleum at Agra, India. Randolph Field was to become the school for training pilots and officers who would one day serve in the separate United States Air Force. Although West Point graduates successfully qualified as pilots, their basic training had been army. Their allegiance and loyalties remained, for the most part, to their school and brother officers. Randolph Field, dubbed West Point of the Air by media people, was not intended as a replacement for West Point. Just as the founders of West Point wanted that school's graduates loyal to the army, air power crusaders wanted their officers geared entirely to air power philosophy. It should not be construed that West Point pilots were not welcomed into the Air Corps ranks. Their interest in development of the United States Air Force could be an asset. Some of West Point cadet life was borrowed for Randolph Field cadets. Proficiency in marching, manual of arms, and care of the rifle became a part of Flying Cadet training. On Saturdays, regular inspections and review of troops were conducted. Mistakes resulted in demerits to be walked on the ramp.

When funds were approved to develop the Training Center composed of Randolph Field and Kelly Field, it was necessary that the land for Randolph Field be donated. When the 2300 acres were finally approved, arrangements were made through the City of San Antonio and the owners to acquire the land. Supporters of the project to bring land acquisition to a successful conclusion did much local work. San Antonio not only helped provide facilities for the Air Force, but has always welcomed its personnel, in particular the Flying Cadets.

Randolph Field Air Force Training Base where 1700 Flying Cadets became military pilots between 1931 and 1939. They provided the corps of officers and pilots on which the air power of WWII was built.

As Flying Cadets, we were given $1 a day for subsistence, and the food was excellent. We also received $75 per month, a lot of money during the Depression. For the first time in my life I was dressed in a spiffy uniform, receiving pay, had two-to-a-room quarters, medical care, and learning to join the elite military pilots' club. In a few months I paid off my debt to the doctor and the hospital in Santa Barbara. Then, I started a savings account. Suddenly, my Depression days were disappearing. I had thought the Depression was the worst thing in a man's life. Little did I know what fate had in store for us on December 7, 1941.

The Commander of Cadets inspected cadets each Saturday morning.

The Cadet program required considerable marching and handling of the rifle. Although doubtful we would use the rifle, we were functioning under army procedures. They dictated that persons coming into service know how to march and handle the rifle. A tactical officer was assigned to insure drilling, marching, and manual of arms were done properly. It was his duty to supervise the Cadet program for Saturday inspections and march us in review. I remember him well because I received so many demerits for not having my hair cut. I explained the problem of cutting curly hair too short, but never convinced him. Consequently, I expected the usual number of demerits each Saturday, and got them.

My previous flying would be helpful in understanding terminology and learning to follow pre-flight and in-flight instructions. Knowing that made it possible for me to spend additional time on ground-school subjects. I quickly learned there would be no excuses accepted for dumb mistakes essential to safety. Five of us were assigned to our instructor, Lieutenant Gurr. He introduced himself and called off each cadet's name. "I assume you are here to learn how to fly. I will teach you my method, and whether you are just learning or have flown before, we'll do it my way. He stopped talking, and pointing at me said, "I'll take you first." I felt my heart go into overdrive. I slipped into my 'chute and buckled up the straps. The instructor stepped onto the wing and climbed into the forward cockpit as I settled into the back and secured my seatbelt. He yelled "clear" and the propeller rotated as the radial engine fired and then settled into a steady beat. We taxied out along the ramp onto the sod field for takeoff. He checked engine instruments and magnetos, looked behind, and moved the throttle forward. In seconds the tail came up and we were airborne.

Lieutenant Gurr climbed and leveled at 2000 feet. I kept track of our position with a good idea of the course home. The instructor did a few turns in both directions, then signaled to me. I made the turns with a little pressure on the rudder pedal and stick, surprised at the ease of the PT-3's response.

The indomitable PT-3 primary trainer looking deceiving frail and easily distractible had the backbone of an elephant and the guile of a tiger cat. It could be rammed into the ground, whack a tree limb, and bounced high as a hangar roof. With some glue, fabric, and artificial resin applied to its wounds it would be ready to roll and fly again in the morning sun. The PT-3 was the number-one trainer during the early 1930s, losing out to more sophisticated PT-11s and PT-13s.

I felt very comfortable with it. It brought back memories of the little Wiley Post biplane in which I soloed when I was 17. At one point, Gurr turned to me, swung his head around, and pointed at me. That meant he wanted me to swivel my head more, looking for other aircraft. Many PT-3s and PT-13s were in the area. Possible nearness of other aircraft was a constant concern, although areas were divided into sections for air work. He did a few stalls, then gave it to me to practice a few. He put his hand over his eyes and pointed at me. It was time to go home and I'd better know how to get there. I knew Randolph was east of us, and I had the railroad tracks in view. As I flew toward them, I could see Randolph Field to the south. Gurr shook the stick and took over. At 500 feet he set up his glide and came in fairly flat for a wheel landing. The landing was made on the wheels, with a couple of light bounces and the tail settled onto the ground. I thought that's the way to land this little bird. As he walked away, he stopped suddenly and said, "it's a good idea to always know your way home." I filled out the form and noted one hour of flying time, my first as a Flying Cadet.

The little PT-3 had been in use as a primary trainer since 1930. It could be repaired about as easily as the Model-T Ford. It was a biplane with tandem cockpits. Fixed gear with little give made for a stiff landing. Still, Cadets had to do it the instructor way. As one instructor said: "If I catch any of you trying to make a three-point landing, you'll get a downer." (In a three-point landing, both main wheels and the tailskid—attached at the end of the fuselage—touch the ground at the same time.) I didn't try it. Instruments included a tachometer, oil temperature gauge, on/off switch, starter and a primer. There was also a clock to remind us when time was up and to go home. There might have been others, but the instrument panel was sparse. The PT-3 was made for one thing only—teach the rough fundamentals of how to operate an airplane. They were rugged and tough and could take a beating. Many Flying Cadets held that opinion[1].

The first two weeks went slowly as our instructor worked with each of us. During my next hour, the instructor had me do the walk around—examine the aircraft before takeoff to be certain it is airworthy—and start the engine. We climbed to 2000 feet and did 360-degree turns in both directions. I tried to keep the nose on the horizon and stop on the same spot. Torque, a force acting on the airplane from the rotation of the propeller, attempts to nose the airplane down in a right turn and up in a left turn. This requires control compensation in both directions to keep the

---

[1] See the Flying Cadet IV *Reflections* section for comments by Brig. Gen. Paul Tibbets.

nose level. The problem was eliminated with jet engines. Some cadets were sent up with instructors for a check flight when they couldn't seem to get the hang of it. We finished my second hour with stalls and glides. I flew the plane back and entered the traffic pattern. The instructor took over and landed it. On the ground, he said the flight was OK, but I didn't look around enough. He wasn't pleased.

Flying Cadets learned many things about the military. Ralph Pusey and Ken Martin demonstrate the absolute correct position. Cadet Pusey had one flaw, the head cover tipped slightly to his right side. Martin is a perfect model from top to bottom: arms straight, thumbs touching the pant seams, stomach tucked in, and straight creases in the pant to the top of the shoes.

Our class also attended ground school, studying engines and theory of flight. For many, the subjects were difficult and complicated. Some of us had trouble getting through the exams. We were on a strict honor code system and anyone cheating or seeing someone cheating could be eliminated from training. It happened once in our class when a cadet reported seeing another one copying from his neighbor. The reporting cadet was washed out. The reaction was that he was a "ratter" for having squealed. I thought the cadet who broke the honor code should have turned himself in.

Upper classmen reminded us we were also still dodo birds. Three bells signaled lower classmen to turn out in formation at attention. I thought some of the actions were silly and dangerous, especially leapfrogging over another Cadet while going upstairs and downstairs in the barracks. In my opinion a few upperclassmen carried on with the dodo days too long. The purpose of humility and self-importance had been served, but there seemed more to it with some. They seemed to be taking a shot be-

Three Flying Cadets—(l to r) James F. Starkey, Warren Wheeler, and Ray Toliver— made it. They are smiling because they just moved over to basic training from primary stage. The rate of washout on primary was high: about 50 percent. In basic this failure rate dropped to 10 percent or lower. Toliver commanded the 20th Fighter Wing in England after WWII. He is a world military air historian and writer of several books on fighter aces of the world.

cause of a hangover from their own treatment. However, only a limited number were involved.

One event of the dodo days amused us. At one three-bell, the hazing got louder and louder, with much shouting. Our commandant lived across the street from our barracks. His wife was pregnant and approaching the delivery date. Not feeling well, she screamed at him: "I want those damn kids to stop all that noise right this minute! Get over there and shut them up!" Her command, easily heard in our barracks, promptly broke up the party. By the time the commandant arrived, all was quiet. From that time on, care was taken to see that events quieted down when a three-bell rang in our barracks.

During my third hour of flight training, we flew to our area, which I now recognized. While reviewing turns and stalls the instructor suddenly pulled the throttle back. Without power, it was necessary to establish a glide and look for a place to land. I lowered the nose and set up a glide, then the throttle was reset by my instructor. We climbed back up did some steep 360-degree turns, coming out at the starting point, then reversing the turn. He again pulled the throttle back. This time I glided down to 500 feet above the ground before he reapplied power. I climbed back up to 2000 feet and leveled. I was sweating but enjoyed every minute. Before reaching Randolph Field I had not flown for some time and I was rusty. I flew home and set up in the pattern for a landing. I reduced power and when the field was clear made my approach turn. When we reached 200 feet, my instructor took the stick and landed. He told me to be more firm on the stick—let the airplane know who's boss. Again, he said: "Swivel your head more. It's very important to look around for other planes. They might not be looking."

That night the five of us got together to discuss our experiences. We were all doing about the same thing in the air, and getting the same comments. We agreed that if we weren't in too much trouble at this point, Lieutenant Gurr would soon solo all of us. We hoped.

After solo we practiced landings at auxiliary fields. One hot afternoon I was mentally droopy during one landing practice session at Davenport auxiliary. On one approach I checked the right side as I neared the fence. It was clear. A perfect approach, I thought. I looked to the left and saw I was rapidly coming down to a small tree just outside the boundary fence. I raised the left wing to avoid hitting the tree, then leveled for my landing. No one was at the instructor's shack and since I had neither felt nor heard any impact, I decided to take off and return to base. After landing at Randolph, I taxied in and parked. My crew chief wasn't in sight and I assumed he was at lunch. I made out the form and noted no problems. Then

I crawled out and took a look at the left wing. I had hit the tree all right. There was a dent in the lower wing about the size of a small plum. I left without saying anything or leaving a note. I thought it might be a routine type of bump encountered when moving the planes around or refueling. I was concerned that my poor judgment might be reason enough to wash me out. I would have reported it if the crew chief had been present. Overnight, I went through a lot of soul searching and decided to report it next morning. Upon arrival at the flight line, I walked to the airplane. The wing was already repaired. Attached to it with a piece of sealing tape was a message: "All cadets need a break, this is yours." I walked to the crew chief's shack and thanked him. He nodded, saying, "good luck!" It was a lesson I never forgot.

Figure-8s were a problem for me. These are maneuvers over a highway between two points with track over the ground forming the figure 8 while keeping the aircraft the same distances from the road during each turn. The purpose is to learn how different control pressures are needed under winds blowing from different directions. I made decent turns, but always overshot or undershot a pylon. Lieutenant Gurr just shook his head. At one meeting on the flight line, he spoke with us a few moments: "The BT-9 you will be flying is bigger, faster, more complicated than the PT-3. Study the differences and how they affect the control and flight. Study the new instruments and what they show you. Take your basic flying skills and apply them to the BT-9, it's a safe plane.

Our flights with Lieutenant Gurr on rechecks were mostly forced landing patterns and our selection of landing areas. He wanted to be sure we headed into the wind. It wasn't always easy to find the wind direction when surface winds were quiet. I would use the Randolph Field takeoff direction, and check to see if the plane was sliding sideways across a highway or railroad track for correction before landing. Lieutenant Gurr said little during the practice, but if there was a real screw up, like landing downwind, he had plenty to say when we got back on the ground. A tip off for us was after we had climbed back up to altitude. If the practice was poor he took over the controls and demonstrated the proper way. We all considered him an excellent instructor. Regardless of his warnings, however, we all screwed up at least once.

The evening of our last flying day with Lieutenant Gurr, the five of us made a social call at his quarters. We had chipped in for a small gift and thank-you card. He thanked us, but we could see it made him a little nervous. He was not the type of man who could easily accept appreciation in any form. After a few moments we left. On our way out he wished us success. As a credit to his teaching, all five of us passed on to Basic Stage and were graduated from Kelly Field. We didn't think about it too much until later, when we learned that almost 40 percent of our classmates had been washed out on Primary Stage. I dropped by Primary Stage early the next morning for a last look at the perky PT-3 I had grown to respect. I also stopped for a last visit with my good friend crew chief and we visited for a few moments. He told me it was the last class for the PT-3. The PT-13s were taking over. He thought it would be helpful for parts and maintenance. The PT-3 was introduced to Randolph Field in 1930 when 111 of them were flown from March Field by cadets and instructors. Whenever airplane trainers are mentioned, those who had the privilege of graduating say a silent "Thank you," in appreciation for the indestructible PT-3.

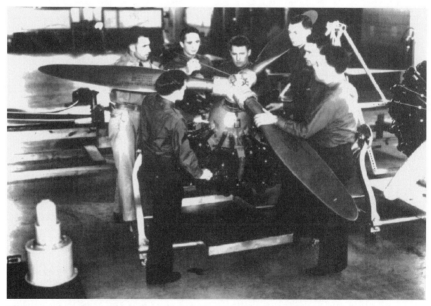

Flying Cadets from the class of 1938C listen as instructor (l. rear) points out carious mechanical functions of propeller's operating system used on the BT-9.

The move up to basic trainers

The Basic Trainers seemed more like a boxcar when compared to the PTs. As one enthralled Texas cadet commented: "That's a big dude!" It was more than that. The BT-9 had a huge instrument panel, adjustable propeller, flaps, radio, and big power plant. The landing gear was fixed in place. Although the cockpit change from a PT-3 to the BT-9 looked awesome, it was a surprisingly easy plane to control. The sliding hatch eliminated wind noise, making communication between instructor and student easy.

Flying Cadets with parachutes leg it to BT-9 trainers for afternoon session. Limited number of instructors (in shirt and slacks) indicate most cadets are flying solo. They would soon be flying fighters or bombers in action against highly qualified Japanese and German pilots.

Control in the air was positive and acrobatics uncomplicated. Landings and takeoffs from the small auxiliary fields, like Kruger and Zeule, were made positive by the quick response when engine power was suddenly needed. Night landings with Klieg lights created little difficulty for student pilots. If flaps were left down, they could be "milked" up gradually. Of course, it meant a down mark from the instructor. But, if a good job was done in milking them up the marks offset each other. Generally, most instructors used mistakes in a positive way to impress the student, but repeats were dealt with severely. Pilots who could meet the flying tests in the BT-9 were virtually assured of progressing to Kelly Field.

Flight with my new instructor almost led to serious trouble. We did a walk-around as he pointed out where checks should be made prior to takeoff. I flew in the rear cockpit for a transition check for my first ride. I was very pleased with the ride. The following day, I was seated in the front cockpit and flew for one hour doing turns, stalls, flaps and gear down, and the landing. I had flown a Waco before and the two were alike in size and equipment. On the next flight I again flew from the front cockpit. We did air work and two practice landings at an auxiliary field. I flew

Randolph Field BT-9s in tight formation demonstration flight by instructors.

back to Randolph, landed and taxied in. My instructor got out of the rear cockpit and motioned me to go up again, alone. I flew for an hour solo and returned. I was really stunned with the suddenness of being soloed. I didn't say anything about the solo that evening and it was a good thing.

The next morning, however, my instructor told me that the new rule required five hours of dual instruction before solo. He hadn't heard about it. It shouldn't have affected me, but it did and I had some trouble with my procedures that hadn't bothered me before.

I finished the dual time and was released again. I accumulated 25 hours with only two minor problems. My instructor scheduled night flying using Klieg lights. They were set up in a bank of lights shining down the landing area. A student would takeoff and when clear, another would land and so on. I made my first landing without difficulty. On my second landing, I taxied back, turned for takeoff and hit the throttle. I knew something was wrong because the airplane was sluggish. I realized immediately what had happened, or rather hadn't happened—I had left the flaps down. "How-in-hell did I do that?" I wondered as I slowly milked the flaps up flying straight and level. I finished the night landings without further mishap and taxied to the line. I was crestfallen. My instructor was displeased, too. He had been bragging about his great students when I pulled my trick. "Well, he advised, let it be a good lesson to remember."

We started our cross-country flying after the night landings. After a couple of daytime cross-countries, we were scheduled for a night round trip to Corpus Christi. Night flying is, and always will be, the best time fly. The air is smooth, city lights and highway traffic make it easy to navigate. One feels like king of the roost sitting up there flying a military plane. I contacted the tower at Corpus and gave my position report, made a circle around the town and started back. I was the last one in for landing and reported to my instructor. He seemed satisfied with my briefing and I left for some late chow.

Ground school was much more difficult than primary stage. We were in meteorology, advanced engines and propellers, theory of flight, telegraphy using Morse code, navigation, and military code of justice. Ground school lasted a full year, with one-third during primary, another third during basic and the final four months at Kelly Field. It was technical material, requiring a real effort to knuckle down and pass. Two in my class couldn't cut it and resigned. One of our classmates was killed in a flight accident and his roommate accompanied the casket home. It was a shock, as cadets become close friends as roommates.

One morning I was sitting on my 'chute waiting for a plane to return. Capt. Roger Ramey, the Stage Commander, walked up to me and asked what I was doing. I jumped up, saluted, and explained why I was waiting. "Take my plane," he said, "no use wasting your time."

I picked up my 'chute and legged it over to his plane. I had been having trouble with short field landings and was determined to do the short

The mess hall maintained the highest record of attendance by cadets, next to their bunks. There was a good reason. As one mess sergeant said: "I've never seen a flying cadet leave a doggy scrap or a dish not cleaned. Dishes are so clean they could be run through the hot water rinse. Of course we never do that, but it's amazing to see dishes come back almost as clean as when they're set." Food was always good, and when holidays came around, they somehow got even better. It's phenomenal what mess sergeants can do.

field technique right, even when using the commander's plane. I took off, circled the field, and set up my approach. I was determined to land within the first 200 feet. Cones marked a fence that surrounded the field. I knew I was coming in low, but I wanted to land in the first 200 feet. As I crossed over the fence I heard an odd noise but touched down within the 200-foot area. I taxied over to the instructor and crawled out. He was looking at the tail section of the plane. That odd noise came when I hit the top of a cone and ripped out a half inch of metal from the midsection to the tail. My instructor was not happy, especially when he learned whose plane I had. He determined there was no damage to the control lines in the tail section and we flew back. He did the flying.

I expected the worst when we advised Captain Ramey what had happened. He looked underneath the fuselage and asked my instructor if I had made a good landing. He said it was an excellent landing and the cone was partially hidden from sight by weeds. "Well," Captain Ramey

Flying Cadets meet in the briefing room to receive safety information and a discussion of the mission for the day. The flight commander leads the session with instructors taking part for any clarification. The cadets will meet with their instructors following the session and may ask for further comments. Briefing sessions are of great importance throughout the career of a pilot. Expressions on the pictured cadets mirror the intensity of their attention.

said, "I think the time was well spent and we're here to train these young flyers how to fly. There has to be mistakes, but one is usually all that's allowed. Good luck young fellow." My instructor excused me and I took off to the barracks for a fresh shower. I felt I had just escaped the worst of things that can happen. I never forgot Captain Ramey and his kindness to a frightened young cadet. Nor have I forgotten my instructor Lt. James C. "Bromo" Selser.

As upperclassmen we were more relaxed, especially with those 3-bells gone. Randolph Field was a beautiful place, more palatial than military. With the sun shining brightly in the fall air, the place took on an aura of peaceful pleasure, much in contrast with our reason for being there. We found it pleasant to drive in the clean and well-laid-out villages. This pleasure got me in trouble. There was a no fraternization rule with under classmen. I knew one from my hometown and borrowed his car to take a young lady for a ride on weekends. One of the "sneaks" empowered by

Pilots had to be in top physical condition. With all volunteers arriving during the 1930s, many came from economically depressed homes. It was only natural that the mess hall would be a popular place. Basic wholesome meals were on the menu Monday through Thursday, but on Friday the menu was Mexican food served with 3.1 beer. Cadets ate it all with liberal amounts of beer. Any cadet who couldn't pass the flab test, spent a few extra hours sweating it off in physical training.

the honor code in our class reported me. That was the end of my pleasant weekends for a month.

It was always a pleasure to visit San Antonio. We had a Cadet Club in one of the hotels, and cadets started gathering there by midday on Saturdays, following inspection and review. Although alcohol was not allowed, someone always sneaked in a bottle. That started trouble. Craps was a popular game and we had some erstwhile shooters. I noticed that after the first two hours, the same guys would win every time. I decided it was a game of knowledge, percentages, luck, and guts, Not being much of a gambler, I stayed out. But, sometimes, things could get a little ugly.

San Antonio was well populated with beautiful girls. It didn't take long for lonesome cadets to find dates. There was a great difference between the tension and constant pressure the cadet experienced during the week and the delightful aroma of sweet smelling, pleasant girls on the weekend. Many of those unions became permanent ties to San Antonio. After 23 classes passed through Randolph Field, the quaint village could certainly lay claim to being the mother-in-law of the cadets. In retrospect, it no

Inspection day on the ramp finds cadets in front of their PT-11s and PT-13s. A new class of cadets stand ready for review by the inspecting officer (located three hangars from the foreground). They were all volunteers with but one thought: make it to B-stage. Unfortunately, almost half would washout and return home in the first four months of training. "Washout" was a word that haunted the Training Command, but it could find no way to improve the system. The last class in 1939, under the three classes per year program, would be the end. A war was coming and pilots in larger numbers were needed. The 23 classes had produced 1700 officer/pilots from 1931 through 1939. Under the new system to prepare for war, that number of pilots would be produced in a few months.

longer exists as such, having now become a metropolis of busy people hardly knowledgeable about the Flying Cadets of the 1930s. The many class reunions held over the years, reveal this. It's safe to say that all classes held their 50th reunions there and cruised the romantic river that runs through the city. The people of San Antonio witnessed the classes of cadets that were the beginnings of the greatest air power that ever existed, the United States Air Force.

In the fall of 1937 the finishing touches were completed on the basic portion of training for the Flying Cadets. Their heads were now crammed with technology about engines, propellers, theory of flight, weather symbols of cold and warm fronts, code of justice, the pleasures of flying the BT-9, and much, much more. They were very different than the young men who had arrived eight months earlier—and much wiser. Now trained as pilots and soon-to-be officers, they were respected by their instructors. Many friendships created between teacher and student lasted into the coming years of warfare. I've heard time and time again about those "wonder" days of Randolph Field spoken softly, almost with reverence. It saddened me greatly when I learned that my instructor, Maj. Gen. James C. Seizer, had been killed in a bad-weather crash flying from Bolling Field during the years of WWII. He was a Lieutenant while my instructor, later becoming a Major General.

The class moves to Kelly Field

In October 1937, we packed our bags and said farewell to the Randolph Field, leaving behind our underclass. Now, they would be the upperclassmen. That's how it would go for another six classes as it had for the 16 classes before us. Then all would change because America would need thousands of pilots to operate its warplanes. Randolph Field continued training pilots but the program would be different from what it was for the original 23 classes set up for by the *Legends* of air power. Gone were the pleasant yesterdays when classes of 40 or 50 Flying Cadets lived in a closeness with their classmates. Unlike *Brigadoon*, it would never happen again, not in a hundred years.

Leaving Randolph Field with still four months to go on our training, our Flying Cadet class arrived at Kelly Field in November 1937. The differences, although subtle, were enormous. The hangars were World War One vintage. The barracks slept us in bays—old bays. It was cold. Texans called the winter winds sweeping down from Oklahoma "northerns" and we had them in November. The weather office advised us to expect many. Heat in the barracks covered only small areas where the space heating units were located. In comparison to Randolph, it was like leaving a fancy hotel to live in a boxcar. We had four months of it, to the end of February, which meant most of the winter. There awaited a real surprise—flying in the cold! After my first flight in an open cockpit, even the barracks felt warm. I was dressed for it, flight suit, leather-lined fur pants and jacket, fur-lined gloves, helmet, and boots. The airplanes were old. The Keystone and Martin bombers were inventions from the 1920s. They looked huge and cumbersome, but they flew. All cadets were required to fly at least five hours in every type plane. A large number of P-12s were lined up alongside A-12s, BT-8s and a few O-38s used for mapping. We came to realize that we were just plain spoiled from having the best at Randolph Field.

My first checkout by an instructor was in the P-12E. It was surprisingly easy to handle and could glide like a feather. Acrobatics were easy and positive, and it was excellent for formation flying. I put in a total of 10 hours on the P-12 series. The Seversky BT-8 was also an easy plane to fly, except on landing when it had a tendency to ground loop. A rumor persisted that some instructors had flown the BT-8s in a show formation, and when the lead plane landed it started a very slow ground loop. The rest of the planes followed like sheep, each ground looping after touchdown. The crowd cheered, thinking the team was continuing its performance on the ground.

After the P-12 and BT-8 transition, my instructor scheduled me to fly the Keystone B-4 bomber. He walked me around, indicating the important checkpoints. He told me to be careful with the brakes when taxiing. "Don't try to turn with the brakes, use the engine power. If you want to taxi to the left, increase the power on the right engine; to the right, use the left engine. That's something new for you, do you understand?" "Of course," I answered. That's easy to understand. He looked at me for a moment. "It might surprise you to know how many cadets can't figure that out and burn out the brakes. I'm going to take you for a turn around the field, then land it. Watch what I do and if you have any questions, ask." We filed through the cabin to the cockpit, sitting well out in front of the two wings. He fired up the left engine, and at his instruction I fired up the right engine. He taxied, showing me how to use the engines to turn into takeoff position. He pushed the throttles forward and the big plane started moving. At 80 mph we took off and slowly climbed up to 300 feet. He leveled off, but the airspeed remained at 80 mph. He entered the landing pattern and when it was our turn he turned on final and started down, still at 80 mph. He set up a glide—still at 80 mph—and when we reached the ground, he pulled back on the yoke and it settled onto the ground. It was an 80-mph airplane.

"Now, one other thing," he explained. "You have to pump gas from the lower tank to the upper tank in the wing for gravity feed to both engines. After one hour, carefully level the plane with the trim tabs, walk back to the cabin and wobble-pump gas to the upper tank, do you understand?" I nodded. "Now make one landing and she's yours for five hours." I followed his instructions and flew the bomber for two freezing hours, then landed. I followed instruction and pumped fuel into the upper tank. The two hours seemed like two eternities, but I had nothing else to do at that particular time. I thought I still have three more hours in this old crate, I'd better bring along my book on Tactics.

Ground school was less technical and concentrated more on planning and operations work. We also had several hours on theory, use of pursuit planes, and management of units in training. In addition, my instructor gave me a mapping project that would take 10 flying hours. I was selected to do the project with a foreign trainee, Major Travassos of Brazil. He spoke reasonably good English, and my instructor said he was a highly qualified pilot. We became very good friends, which was to be tested.

Our project required filming the railroad track north of San Antonio, cutting and joining the 6 x 8 pictures into a montage center display board for class study. To do the work an O-38 was equipped with an aerial camera in the aft cockpit, shooting straight down through a cutout in the floor. The flying had to be precisely on the course plotted along the air map we used. Otherwise the film wouldn't overlap the track properly when displayed. It sounded simple in the briefing. First, however, we had to check-out as pilots in the O-38. It was a single-engine plane used in 1934 to carry airmail and flew comparatively well through ice, sleet, and snow during bitterly cold nights. It had no de-icing equipment on wings, propeller, or windshield, and no cockpit heat. However, it was an easy and responsive plane to fly.

After flying five hours we started the mission. I soon learned that Major Travassos' English turned to Spanish when he became excited. One bitterly cold day, after checking for drift at the altitude we would fly, he started shooting film. The wind drift was excessive and I had difficulty holding course. Travassos had just started shooting when my map slipped to the floor. Watching my course carefully, I reached down to pick it up. For a moment my eyes strayed from the instrument panel and the nose moved, very slightly. It was enough, however, to throw off the photo line he was following. Naturally, the camera started shooting off-course film. He reached forward from his cockpit and gave me a whack that meant business. I knew I was in the wrong, but didn't think I deserved being whacked in the head. I turned, shook my head and went to work flying down line, then did a 180-degree turn reversing my direction, picking up the correct course. He immediately adjusted to the position and started shooting again. When we landed, he was beside himself with apologies. I told him what had happened and that it was my mistake. Despite this incident, we got good pictures. We had completed the mission for class study, received an A+, and maintained our friendship.

I completed my time on the Keystone bomber by flying due west for one hour and forty-five minutes from Kelly Field, then turning and flying back. With a tailwind, I hit my three hours exactly on the nose. On the way back, I trimmed the plane for straight and level flight and slipped out of the cockpit to pump the fuel. Just as I returned, I saw a P-12 flying away. The pilot probably reported a man overboard.

Major Travassos and I made a two-plane flight to Barksdale Field one weekend for our cross-country flight. While waiting for refueling, we watched the 20th Pursuit pilots flying P-26s. The planes were all painted up and the Major remarked that they reminded him of the Indian war dances with all the paint and feathers. As I recall, it was the 77th Pursuit Squadron. He snapped a picture of me leaning against the wing of a P-26.

My instructor at Kelly Field was Sammy Anderson. A very quiet man, he later became a four-star General. We received excellent treatment at Kelly Field from the instructors. If we made a flying mistake, the instructor discussed it with us as pilot to pilot and suggested methods to improve. Seldom were cadets harshly reprimanded. With our newly found liberty and acceptance, it seemed the instructors felt it was their responsibility to get us through alive and well. There are always some "hot shots" who couldn't seem to contain themselves. It's to the credit of the instructors that all in our class survived, only to have a few die in accidents during their first year of duty.

The last few weeks at Kelly Field were busy as preparations got underway for graduation day. We all frequented the uniform stores often. A

Flying Cadets attract Hollywood. Cadet Beirne Lay, graduate in the class of 1933B, and classmate Bernard Schriever wrote a book that was made into a motion picture. I Wanted Wings starred Bill Holden and Virginia Mayo, and much of the production took place at Randolph Field. This scene shows cadets approaching their aircraft for takeoff. The book and film proved to be an excellent public relations effort to attract cadets.

number of cadets planned weddings, requiring arrangements and accommodations for visiting relatives. We practiced for the big pass-in-review. A good pilot, Paul Tibbets, led ours and it came off without a hitch.

On graduation day we read with great anticipation the announcements on the bulletin board listing duty assignments. Most seemed satisfied with their assignments. The thought occurred that we would be going to our new bases as officers. As cadets at Kelly Field we were close to that, but not quite. While waiting for our schedules, we had time to visit with instructors. They treated us with courtesy and respect due an officer. This smoothed some of our rough spots and let us experience the relationship before putting on the uniform. We weren't dining with the instructors, but they were aware of the big jump from enlisted status to that of officer. We soon discovered how big a jump when salutes started coming our way. We had few concerns about saluting brother officers, but some senior officers played games with us at times, to our embarrassment. I'm satisfied it was all that way, and I don't recall having thoughts about changes.

Many cadets came to Randolph Field already commissioned through ROTC. A majority had taken ROTC during college days and wore the uniform of that activity. A few had been on active duty in ground force units. Several had served with ROTC units equipped with horses and were competent polo players. For example, one was Davy Jones, who later flew one of the bombers that Jimmy Doolittle led on the first raid over Tokyo.

Commencement without caps and gowns. These graduates wore helmets and parachutes as this class finished training at Kelly Field. The graduates pass the reviewing stands.

Those responsible for training us to become officer pilots at Randolph Field and Kelly Field could not know that in a short time war would be declared. What they accomplished would be the difference between our meeting huge obligations and making the correct decisions or failing our country and ourselves. We would suddenly be required to take command of squadrons whose officers and men depended on us to accomplish our missions. That responsibility would continue to grow as the Air Corps expanded into the Army Air Forces, growing to more than two million pilots and enlisted personnel. I know of no single incident where the former Flying Cadets, always in the front of things, did not meet the expectations of their commanders. As Lt. Gen. James Edmundson stated in his foreword of this historical review: *They were the very best, the cream of America's youth.*

The no-nonsense look on the faces of these Flying Cadets indicates the seriousness of their mission. They march toward a desperate time in United States history when a savage attack will be made from the air on Pearl Harbor.

3

Enlisted Personnel

IN THE MILITARY, the number of officers and enlisted personnel comprise the total strength of the organization. That arrangement has existed since *Hannibal*, (247 B.C. to 183 B.C.), the Carthaginian General, crossed the Alps to invade Italy during the Second Punic War. The tables of organization determine the number of officers and enlisted personnel for a unit, usually a squadron, group, and wing for the air force. Each lists the rank, duty, and assignment for all members. In effect, there is a reliance on each person to do the assigned job so well that the functioning of the entire unit is exemplary for the mission. In air force history, too little is said about the accomplishments of the enlisted corps. Yet, nothing would function without them: airplanes wouldn't fly, trucks wouldn't run, supplies wouldn't arrive, bugles wouldn't blow taps or reveille, and food wouldn't be served. Little would happen on a military base. This should indicate something about their importance.

Every pilot in combat knows success will depend on how well the engine functions, how straight the guns shoot, and how well the airplane responds during maneuvering. Failure caused by poor maintenance can place the pilot's life in jeopardy. Pilots understand this and in short time a bond develops between pilot and crewchief. This relates to flying in general, regardless of whether the mission is for proficiency, testing, or combat. It is no place for a rift or chasm, although there is a possibility of one occurring. However, in more than 40 years of military flying I have never had a bad relationship with crewchiefs or sergeant majors and have enjoyed professional friendships with many. They were all fine, competent soldiers.

Enlisted men learned that in wartime any roof is a good one. Sometime that meant the stars as a roof if the unit was on the move. This unit, in Italy, had at least four tents. The smoke indicates some kind of fuel was available.

The division line between officers and enlisted personnel usually occurs at the time of joining. With an equal interest in aviation, those fortunate enough to have completed school at a higher level might find it a qualifying factor to seek officer. Those with comparable interest but at a lessor educational level might seek the availability of schooling in aviation through the enlisted ranks. The air force has always offered opportunities for higher education through its own schools with a full array of subjects leading toward officer status. With service in the air force, enlisted personnel may take authorized steps to enter the USAF Academy where they receive a minimum four years college level education plus an officer's commission.

Advancement through training

Training programs offer instruction in special subjects. Among these are all types of aircraft engines, instruments, various systems that drive a multiple of accessories essential to instrument flying, gunnery, rocket firing, and processing incoming information from satellites for navigation and enemy search. Assistance is also provided to complete high school diplomas for those who might not have earned one. These are but a few examples of the vast array of training programs available.

Other important features such as medical care, food, clothing, barracks, and body conditioning are basic requirements. On-base features include movies, bowling, gym, swimming, base exchanges, places of worship, legal needs, recreation fields for track, baseball, tennis, football, and golf in some locations. It becomes obvious that personnel assigned to the important jobs of maintaining an air force are entitled to these and other benefits. Their mission in time of peace is to train and maintain a readiness for use on demand by the United States when faced with an enemy. Their mission then becomes one to help destroy that enemy with the training received. In time of conflict, enlisted personnel and officers leave a peacetime existence and start a Spartan type of life.

Paying their own way to serve

During the airmail crisis in 1934, when the Air Corps was ordered to deliver the mail, nothing could have been more Spartan than the life pressed on the enlisted men. Suddenly, they were ordered to leave their bases, which meant leaving the mess halls, the barracks, and medical services, all things essential to everyday basic life. They could only hastily pack a bag and leave for their assignments. In some cases they even had to pay for transportation to the municipal airport for duty. There was no money advanced to the Air Corps so it wasn't possible to request pay for food and lodging for the assignments. Leaving their bases meant leaving their basic existence needs. At the time, pay ran from $17 per month for privates to $90 for a master sergeant. The men were placed in a hard rock position of no funds and nowhere to turn.

The President and Congress knew of this situation but chose not to correct it. Using the military was a political issue in the first place, and the military personnel, who had no voice in the matter, were left out in the extreme cold to beg and borrow in the middle of winter. Near the New Orleans airport, as an example, the enlisted personnel lived in a grocery store, which did not have hot water. There was no bus or trolley into town, and a cab cost a prohibitive amount of $1.50 one way. There were no rooms at the airport. Mobile, Alabama, is another example. There were no hangar or repair facilities. Servicing fuel had to be hand pumped from drums, and the sergeant in charge lived in a barn on a nearby farm. He walked back and forth. Airmail pilot Lt. Curt LeMay, flying from Richmond, Virginia, noted his enlisted crew cooking homemade Mulligan stew in the corner of a hangar. It was a cold, wet, raw day and they were heating the thin gruel in an old stew pot over a plumber's flame. Their bed was a few wooden planks resting on saw horses with no protection except the hangar roof. In one instance a sergeant reported to LeMay that a nice elderly lady who had a hot dog stand gave them credit so they could eat and offered him a pillow to sleep on. She said she didn't need it. Nowhere in LeMay's report was any mention of a complaint about the situation. The sole purpose of these dedicated persons was to get the mail on the planes and keep it moving. In some cases, officers provided personal assistance. Ira Eaker borrowed $750 and gave it to the crews who were in need. At Burbank, he arranged with a restaurant and hotel to provide food and quarters. Lt. Eaker's pay was $170 per month.

In addition to lacking funds, an inspection showed the enlisted personnel were being overworked. Nor were they getting needed repair parts. As the army insisted on completed reports for all requisitions, everything was slowed down. In some cases, rather than stop delivery of the mail, pilots were asked by the enlisted mechanics if they could fly with parts they had repaired. Pilots would check their engines and if it responded all right, would takeoff if the condition wasn't too dangerous. Another problem facing the crews was the lack of tools. They had been ordered from their bases so fast it they had no time to pick up their toolboxes. They made do with borrowed pliers and screwdrivers.

There was little improvement from the beginning to the last delivery in late spring. Officers and enlisted personnel ended up in debt about $250,000 for lodging and food. The ground crews bore the brunt of poor living conditions without complaint, while the pilots flew aircraft ill designed to haul airmail. The response from all was a dedication to the Air Corps and getting the job done, a trait of their chief, General Foulois.

Fighting the elements as well as the enemy

The best opportunity to observe enlisted personnel is when they are under fire. Those of us shipped to Alaska before the war found conditions we had never before faced. Our airplanes were covered with Cosmoline to protect them from ocean salt water since we had to ship them by freighter. Cosmoline is a heavy grease and when the temperature goes below freezing, the stuff becomes hard as rock. In addition, they had been disassembled so it was necessary to reattach the wings. The planes were off-loaded at Seward port onto flat beds and taken by train to Anchorage. Trucks hauled them from the railroad to the hangar. The first sight to greet us the morning after arrival was 20 P-36 fighter planes, their wings folded beside the fuselage, and covered with

Enlisted crew is busy putting this A-20 to bed. Wherever missions were flown in cold climates, there was no time to waste brushing snow or scrapping ice off the airplanes. The design of wings, props, and tail assembly makes it essential that they function without disturbing the flow of air around them. Covering wings and motors, as these crewmembers are doing with the crew chief in charge, makes for a quick departure.

thick Cosmoline. One mechanic attempted to peel a strip off with a screwdriver. He couldn't dent the stuff.

The temperature was holding around 20 degrees Fahrenheit, and a cold wind dropped it to 10 degrees chill effect. The maintenance heads went into a huddle and decided they would need something like a blowtorch to loosen the Cosmoline. Situations like this is when American genius comes into its own. Unable to find a blowtorch, they scouted some mines that had been out of operation for years. In one they found an old steam jenny, once used to uncover deposits of gold ore. They cleaned it and put it back in running condition. It, together with a liberal amount of gasoline, slowly dissolved the Cosmoline. Many of the maintenance crew wondered if anyone at the depots, who packaged the planes for shipment, had any idea as to how that stuff could be removed in low temperature places like Alaska in wintertime. Regardless, it was self-reliance of the enlisted personnel that found the answer. Such resourcefulness was evident time and time again throughout the world during wartime. Whether facing ice, mud, sand, or water, they found ways to get their airplanes flyable.

Maintenance crews learned what it was all about when engines needed a change away from home. To meet this challenge, they rigged up a support with chain hoists and went to work. The sergeant in charge had two hopes: no rain and finding no left over screws or bolts when the job was finished.

There was never a thought about airworthiness when an airplane was marked "in commission" for flight. I claimed a first in 1941 when I taxied a P-36, cleaned of Cosmoline and reassembled, to a runway at Elmendorf Field and took off into a cold, clear sky over Anchorage, Alaska, for a test flight. I exercised the plane with a few rolls, loops, Immelmanns, and dives to be sure the wings stayed on tight. This was the first fighter plane assigned to the first fighter squadron to fly in Alaska. That unit, the 18th Pursuit Squadron, remained in operation in Alaska for 50 years, re-designated as the 18th Fighter Squadron.

In the first months of operation, everything the maintenance crews had readily available at their last base, Hamilton Field in California, was in short supply in Alaska. Spare parts were shipped to Alaska by freighters and train, a slow and difficult passage, and there was the lack of parts in stock. Airplanes aren't predictable. They present the unpredictable problem of different needs at odd times. Pilots learned early to respect and have a great reliance on the enlisted personnel. Not only was maintenance of the airplane critical for safe flights over the snow- and ice-covered mountainous areas, but the need for parachutes was equally important. This was a test of ingenuity as 'chutes had to be repacked periodically. To do it properly, they had to be strung up to full height for drying and inspection. Normally, with an enclosed warm hangar, a portion could be set aside for the parachute riggers. It wasn't that way during the early days at Elmendorf Field. After much investigation, a scheme was worked out with the recreation department to use a portion of the gymnasium part time. The parachute riggers, on their own, solved the problem and assured pilots that their 'chutes were inspected and safe if needed.

In Alaska, housing was the same for enlisted personnel and officers, with the exception of Ladd Field near Fairbanks. When war was declared, the Aleutian chain of islands became the first bastion for defense. Landing strips were constructed at Naknek, Kodiak, Cold Bay, Umnak, Adak, and the Rat Islands as bases for bombers and fighter units. If the enlisted crews thought life tough at Elmendorf Field, their comparison graph must have dropped below zero when they saw those bases in the Aleutian Chain. Strictly Spartan, pilots and enlisted personnel lived in tents, ate in tents, showered and shaved in tents, repaired and overhauled airplanes in tents, and cooked in tents. In the Rat Islands, where forward fighter units were based, winds blew 50 miles per hour in normal weather and up to 100 miles per hour in severe storms. Sand found its way into everything, tents, airplanes, shoes, food, eyes, anything it could get into as it blew through the air. When the wind gave a slight respite, hard driving rain, and sometimes sleet, came in gales, blowing first one way and then another. That particular area of the Aleutians is known in weather parlance as *frontogenesis,* or a place where two different atmospherically elements come together to create a front, bringing rain, snow, sleet, hail, blowing winds, and poor visibility. This condition caused by the icy-cold water flowing from the Bering Sea into the Pacific where it meets the Japanese warm water current flowing toward the east. It's a continuing phenomenon of nature. Enlisted personnel living under such conditions should have been rotated after one year, but the needs of war prevented it.

In the Philippines the situation was more than grim for enlisted personnel. Those in the 20th Pursuit Squadron were caught in the Japanese attack and had little hope of escaping. During the latter stages, after Japanese daily bombing had destroyed the P-40s and B-17s, a gradual retreat was ordered. Enlisted personnel and officers fought as infantry. Many from Air Corps units lost their lives or were captured. Other than the Bataan Death March, history records little of those men in the final days of struggle against the Japanese forces.

Following the attack on Pearl Harbor, Air Corps squadrons were soon ordered to Island warfare in the South Pacific to fight entrenched Japanese forces. Many facilities were constructed to accommodate air units, but it was not possible to control fever, dysentery, and other diseases associated with living in temporary conditions. Although efforts were made to bring diseases under control, they became effective after the original personnel were transferred.

Enlisted personnel went to all parts of the world during WWII. Those assigned to the early forces faced great difficulty wherever they were sent. In England, enlisted personnel assigned to B-17 crews who made the first daylight raids into Germany suffered tremendous losses from German fighters. Without fighter escort they were at the mercy of the German Luftwaffe that waited to attack until the short-ranged American fighters

These four mechanics check every tube, bolt, screw, pump, motor, hinge—anything that gets loose, wears out, or requires replacement. In the process, they will fight mud, mud, mud. They will have mud in their shoes, their clothes, even in their hair. There will be no overtime pay, but this Lightning will run like a clock for its pilot.

During the early morning hours before the mission, Cpl. Pete Javis and Sgt. John McClennon check the ordnance needed. Enlisted personnel were the silent weapons of the war. When missions were scheduled, they were up for hours before departure, checking ordnance, pre-flighting the airplane, running checklists of equipment needed, checking all systems, loading the guns and bomb racks. Only then did they hit the mess hall for a hurried bite of breakfast before rushing back to the flight line to stand by for takeoff. They got little rest. During the day they had required duties, then a wait for the planes to return to check for needed repairs and prepare their charges for the next day. They were the unsung heroes, modest with no horns to blow.

had to turn back. It would be 1943 before the first P-51 Mustang group—the 354th—arrived to take the B-17 crews all the way to the target and back home again. Then the huge loss of crews decreased dramatically as the P-51 pilots attacked and destroyed German fighters.

Bases in England brought some pleasure for pilots and crews. This young woman is doing her bit to make life just a little easier for the sweaty "go-boys." The smiling Red Cross girls were always a waiting pleasure after a mission, with home-baked delicious donuts.

During the period from 1940 to 1945 the Air Corps trained 400,000 crews, which included gunners, flight engineers, radio operators, and other specialists. For every person in the air, there were seven ground-crew members and four ground technical specialists. They weren't there for the money: privates were paid $50 a month, staff sergeants received $96 and master sergeants earned $138 per month. A four-star General, responsible for the lives of more than two million persons in the command made $666 per month. Congress could never be accused of overpaying its fighting force.

Enlisted personnel made up a large part of the force that fought and won WWII. It will always be thus as long as the United States remains free and controls its own destiny. Those who rely on the military forces for protection against enemies of a free America should always consider their support for the enlisted personnel. Without it there might be little to support.

P-51 crew chief wedges his way into Rolls Royce Merlin engine for essential maintenance. Swastika symbols on side of plane mark the number of German fighters shot down. The swastika symbol represented the Nazi party in Germany prior to and during WWII. It was a hate symbol of anti-Semitism.

A crew puts finishing touches on B-17 engine repair. Crude and dangerous foot supports for mechanic on ladder were allowed only away from home during warfare. Not long after repairs, B-17s from the 100th Bomb Group made a run to Berlin. It turned out to be a massacre. Many planes did not return. The Squadron commander became the Group commander the next day. One gunner reported he was living in the spare gunner's hut, and for 15 days after the raid he was alone. Everyone was either killed or taken prisoner. In less than two months after joining the Group, he became the senior gunner in the outfit—he was 17 years old.

B-29 passes over a six-man enlisted crew as they head for the maintenance shack. They carry the special kits essential to check out equipment on the B-29. These are the young men of America whose job it was to help keep the big birds ready for missions, flying from island bases in the South Pacific. The B-29 carried the final weapons to Japan that ended the war.

4

Combat

THE QUESTION of battlefield doctrine had not been settled when American forces went on the offensive in North Africa during WWII. Ground commanders and air commanders held differing views about control of air power and there was no clear delineation between the two while conducting the desert conflict against Rommel's forces. Conclusion of the battle came at Tunisia. It was the first great victory of the western allies in the European Theater during WWII. The American estimate of prisoners taken was 275,000 between April 22 and May 16. German aircraft shot down totaled 273, with 600 abandoned near Tunis, Bizerta, and Cape Bon[1].

The Tunisian campaign made it clear that air force commanders were not going to relinquish the concept of equality between air and ground commanders. Air officers continued efforts to change the practice of army commanders to require troop cover. This, they said, disregarded the essential steps to air superiority for the entire campaign. Gen. George C. Marshall, Chief of Staff, GHQ, took steps to codify new principles of air power. This had the support and approval of General Eisenhower. As a result, a new manual—FM 100-20—was issued on the "command and employment of air power." It characterized air power and land power as co-equal and established that gaining air superiority is the first requirement for success of any major land operation. It further stated that air forces must be employed—primarily—against enemy air forces until air

---

[1] Air Superiority, B.F. Cooling, pg. 260

superiority is gained. It established command of air forces under air commanders and further confirmed that if an air force might be attached to
other friendly forces it would be only under other air commanders.

For the first time in actual combat, air officers and ground officers
would identify air superiority for the battle area. All that Billy Mitchell,
Benny Foulois, Hap Arnold, Tooey Spaatz, Frank Andrews, Ira Eaker, and
many other air power supporters had fought for become a reality. Air
power had been recognized at the highest level of the army. FM 100-200
declared what could and would be done concerning air superiority and
who would command air units. The following is quoted from FM 100-20:

> The primary aim of the tactical air force is to obtain and maintain air superiority
> in the theater. The first prerequisite for the attainment of air superiority is the es-
> tablishment of a fighter defense and offense, including radar equipment essential
> to the detection of enemy aircraft and control of our own. While air superiority is
> maintained, both the ground forces and the air force can fight the battle with lit-
> tle interference by the enemy air. Without this air superiority, the initiative passes
> to the enemy. Air superiority is best obtained by attack on hostile airdromes, the
> destruction of aircraft at rest, and by fighter action in the air. This is much more
> effective than any attempt to furnish an umbrella of fighter aviation over our own
> troops. At most, an umbrella is prohibitively expensive and could be provided
> only over a small area for a brief period of time during daylight and in good
> weather.

Publication resulted in mixed reactions. All air officers received copies.
Army ground forces generally considered the manual an air force
"Declaration of Independence," and officers expressed varying degree of
dismay. With few exceptions, the manual cleared the air for future battles
concerning air power.

Air superiority means control of the aerial battlefield. According to Gen.
William Momyer, former commander of the Tactical Air Command and
Flying Cadet, class of February 1939: "No battle can be won if air superiority is not achieved." According to his beliefs, the best pilot, best airplane,
and the freedom to utilize them is the essential combination. WWII is an
example of United States forces eventually putting these three requirements together and acquiring air superiority over the European Theater of
Operations. It did not come easily.

Air superiority was not possible during the early part of air force action
over Europe. The German Me.109 and FW.190 aircraft were potent in
numbers and flown by well-trained, combat-competent pilots. Allied
forces did not have fighter airplanes—including the RAF Spitfires and
Hurricanes—in sufficient numbers, nor with ranges long enough to escort

Skinner

The Spitfire Mk. IX was flown by American fighter pilots in the 31st Fighter Group. The group and its Squadrons were organized with American pilots who flew with the Royal Air Force for experience, then formed up its own squadrons with the 31st. When American pilots asked about the restrictions on the Spitfire, they were advised that they had a fighter plane without restrictions; do anything you want, straight down full throttle, then pull the stick straight back. Short ranged, the Spitfire was a better tactical fighter than escort.

bombers. The P-40, P-47, and P-38 had certain advantages and disadvantages. The P-40 had speed and guns but was short on range and maneuverability; the P-47 was a "man of iron" with guns but unable to maneuver with the Me.109 and had only a short range. The P-38 had range and guns but was not designed for close combat maneuvering. Even with these deficiencies, the air force could fend off German fighters during escort, but their short range dictated a return to base before bombers reached the target. Thus, the B-17s were left to the mercy of the Germans fighters.

Strategic bombing required long flights from bases in England. Without escort it was necessary for the plane's gunners to defend themselves. Although later B-17 models carried six positions of guns—tail, nose, both sides, and top and bottom fuselage—it still was difficult to defend against attackers from several directions and in swarms. Consequently, they suffered heavy losses. Even many B-17s that were able to return to base arrived nearly destroyed from gunfire. B-17 gunners gave a good ac-

Crew Chief Don Firoved and armorer Ralph Francis, part of the 31st Fighter Group, have their British Spitfire ready. In addition to Spitfires, the American pilots flew Hurricanes with the British units. These American pilots were authorized to wear British wings on one side of their tunics and Air Corps wings on the other.

count of themselves by shooting down a substantial number of attacking fighters but it was insufficient to support the losses.

Long-range fighters arrive

In November 1943, the 354th Fighter Group, commanded by Col. Kenneth Martin, Flying Cadet class of March 1938, arrived in England. The group was equipped with the Mustang P-51. Within two weeks it was ready for combat. This new fighter had speed, range, and could maneuver with the best.

Fortunately, six months earlier the Germans made a decision that might have changed the balance of air power had it been made differently. On May 23, 1943, German Fighter Gen. Adolph Galland strapped himself into a test model of the Me-262 twinjet fighter. After his flight he was convinced the plane would guarantee the Luftwaffe air superiority. It left the ground at 120 mph and made 520 mph in level flight. Galland landed with great excitement over the prospects of utilizing this new fighter in combat against the B-17s. He reported his findings to Field Marshall Milch, head of procurement, and to Field Marshal Goering. All three recommended an immediate speed-up of production. Hitler crushed the idea immediately. He was angry with Goering for other failed promises and saw no reason to approve the rush to build the jet.

During the first six weeks of operations, the 354th Mustangs escorted 14 long-range missions, destroying 41 German fighters while losing six P-51s. On February 20th a sustained bombing attack began, which included the RAF night bombers. More than 3800 bombers participated in the attacks over a five-day period. Losses included 226 bombers and 28 fighters. It cost the Germans 600 fighters. The raids resulted in damage to 75 percent of the German aircraft industry, a disastrous loss for the Germans.

Air superiority gained

In March 1944, General Spaatz decided to draw the German fighters into combat. To do this he scheduled raids against Berlin, and instructed that the fighters leave their escort positions and attack the Germans. General Galland, who commanded the German fighters, later admitted that was when air superiority of the American fighters came into its own. "They attacked us from everywhere, when we landed, when we took off, in the air flying formation, approaching their bombers . . . we weren't free of them."

When the invasion of France was made on June 6, 1944, the German air force was not in evidence. The weight of Allied power was thrown full force at ground targets. The Ninth Air Force and the RAF 2nd Tactical Air Force destroyed 551 locomotives in June, leaving the Commander of the 2nd Panzer Division to complain: "The Allies have total air supremacy." Still, as bomber attacks continued, German air production remained high, and a reported 3013 planes were produced in June, mostly fighters. This was accomplished by spreading all aircraft production into small locations and assembling the planes in remote areas. Galland reported later that parts of plants were located in tunnels, caves, and old mines. Some were hidden in the forests, ravines, and villages, all well camouflaged. General Spaatz believed the only way to stop the German Luftwaffe would be to destroy the oil supply to the Germans. A continued bombing of the German oil industry by the VIII Bomber Command resulted in reducing the 160,000 gallons of aviation fuel required per month to the availability of only 18,000 gallons. With the fuel shortage, German fighters remained on the ground during raids on the Ruhr industrial valley. Losses from combat declined for the allies as air power continued to grow. By the fall of 1944, the combined total of Anglo-American air power stood at 14,700 aircraft.

The question is, of course, how would the battle have gone if Hitler had listened to his air Generals and permitted the building of the jet fighter? German jet aircraft would have sorely tested the P-51, and might have required the speedup in production of our own jet. This would have taken time, and only guesswork and imagination can determine the results of a fleet of Me262 fighter-bombers attacking our bombers and fighters. Fortunately, it will never be known.

The Americans had established air superiority over Europe. The best fighter available was the P-51. All three elements: best pilots, best airplane, and best use of air power had come together and the enemy was defeated. It was a long and expensive war in terms of young lives lost and in dollar cost. Little was gained and much of Europe had to be reconstructed. The unanswered question was whether civilization could withstand such losses and survive.

5

Theaters of War

South Pacific

At 7:55 in the morning of December 7, 1941, Lt. Akira Sakamoto, carrier pilot with the Imperial Japanese Navy, arrived at the point of attack. He pushed the stick forward and the nose of the Aichi 99 dive bomber dropped on its run toward Hickam Field. He released the first bomb to fall on Pearl Harbor, pulled up, and then dropped low to the ground to start strafing runs. He was virtually unopposed, flying one of 190 Japanese fighters, dive-bombers, and torpedo planes to strafe the island for more than an hour. As the damage was being inflicted by Akira and fellow pilots, another wave of 170 planes was preparing for takeoff from their carrier bases. The pilots were handpicked for the task and highly experienced. The U.S. Navy ships at anchor were sitting ducks and heavily damaged.

Enough U.S. P-40s and heroic pilots were on the Hawaiian Island to blunt, to some extent, the surprise Japanese attack, and help to protect the naval ships in Pearl Harbor and those tied up at some of the smaller islands. However, the aircraft were bunched together on the airfields to be safer from sabotage, and there was no advance warning for pilots to scramble into action. The planes were easy targets for attackers. The damage was done and the great naval base was virtually demolished, with many of it capital ships blasted out of action. Investigations followed as everyone from Hawaii to Washington wanted the monkey on someone else's back. The result could have been worse—much worse. Why did a Japanese naval force of that size not include a landing force of Marines? Capturing Midway would have added gigantic problems for the United States, tying up retaliation for years. Fortunately, it did not happen.

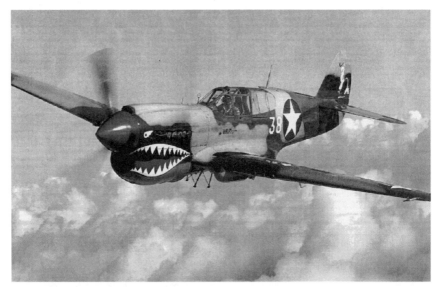

The P-40 was a workhorse and the first real combat fighter of WWII. It was utilized in many theaters of war, always recognized in the China-Burma-India theater by its open Flying Tiger mouth. The first American combat, however took place in the Philippine Islands following the Japanese attack on Pearl Harbor. On one occasion, (April 4, 1942) Lt. "Benny" Putnam responded to a report of a Japanese convoy in the Straight of Cebu. With six gun belts full of .50 caliber ammo, he attacked and destroyed the main troop ship and two Japanese float Zeros. He returned to refuel and had 73 bullet holes in his plane. He was recommended for the Medal of Honor, but turned down by General MacArthur— typical of army treatment.

In the wake of the Pearl Harbor attack, the civilian ranks exerted frantic efforts to move war plants into high gear production. For the Air Corps, it was expansion speed up: more pilots, more units, more airplanes, more mechanics, more of everything. Fortunately, the visionary thinking of those responsible for establishing a flying center at Randolph Field and Kelly Field had provided a pool of young officer pilots. Before air battle could be considered however, squadrons, groups, and wings had to be staffed, equipped, trained, and capable of successfully destroying the enemy.

The making of a combat pilot is a selective process. They must meet required standards, be selected, and sent to flight training school. Of those, approximately 40 percent will qualify and earn their wings. They are then ready for assignment to field units for tactical and combat training. From inception, two to three years are spent on these processes. When Japanese pilot Akira Sakamoto accomplished his mission at Pearl Harbor, a pool of 1700 Flying Cadets had been trained from 1931 through 1939, and most were still on duty. A few had been killed in training, some had resigned, and some were flying for the airlines. From those remaining would come the commanders and staff officers to help build the Air Corps with a capability to destroy the enemies in the Pacific and across the Atlantic.

In the Flying Cadet Personal Reflections section of this book, a number of these officer/pilots provide a first-hand look at their assignments following the Pearl Harbor attack. Without the availability of this pool of pilots, years would have been required to develop even the core of air power. After 1939, it was necessary to create a huge pilot pool for expansion, and the training program was changed. But the increase of squadrons, groups, and staffs necessitated cadres of command, engineering, supply, and personnel officers around which a squadron or group could be created. This process provided these units for all theaters of war: South Pacific, Europe, North Africa, Alaska, China, and Hawaii.

Air power delivers devastating blows

As the war progressed in the South Pacific and more units became available, Lt. Gen. George C. Kenney, Commanding General of the 5th Air Force operating from his base in New Guinea, saw his air strength increase in February to 207 bombers and 127 fighters. Kenney had altered his B-25s by removing the Plexiglas in the nose and installing eight .50 caliber machine guns. Also, his pilots learned skip-bombing, a technique of dropping bombs to have them skip over the surface of water to their targets. These and other changes were designed to be more effective in attacking Japanese ships bringing supplies to the Japanese forces. On March 3, Kenney's pilots attacked seven transports carrying 6000 infantry reinforcements for New Guinea. The B-25s went after them, flying at wave level and firing a strafing sweep at deck level with all eight guns spraying bullets. Anything they hit was knocked down or overboard, leaving the decks filled with bodies and debris. Then B-25s came in with their skip-bombs blasting the sides of the ships, leaving huge gaping holes. As water poured into the guts of a ship and hit the hot boilers, the ship exploded and started to sink. Wave after wave of attacks continued until the entire convoy and regiment of infantry was wiped out with all ships at the bottom of the Bismarck Sea.

Shortly after U.S. air power delivered this loss on the Japanese, another different type of loss was inflicted. A high level Japanese message, intercepted by the U.S. Navy, revealed the plans of Admiral Isoruko

Yamamoto to visit Japanese troops in the Solomon Islands. Unknown to the Japanese, Americans had cracked the code. A fighter Group of P-38s on Henderson Field Guadalcanal, was alerted and given the Japanese Admiral's itinerary and instructions to attack and destroy the bomber carrying the Admiral. The high level purpose was to disrupt the Japanese command and inflict a loss of morale among Japanese troops. At 6 A.M., April 18, Yamamoto was tracked leaving Rabaul for Ballale, near Bouganville. A second bomber followed carrying the Admiral's staff. Six Zero fighters were escort.

At 9:34 A.M., a pilot flying in Maj. John Mitchell's group made contact and reported "Bogies, 10 o'clock high." As previously briefed, the cover flight broke and climbed to altitude. The four attacking P-38s, led by Capt. Thomas Lanphier, dropped wing tanks. Lanphier's wingman, Rex Barker, zeroed in on one of the bombers and Lanphier took on the other one. Both Japanese bombers went down with Admiral Yamamoto in one of them. The bomber's starboard engine and wing caught fire, crashed in the jungle and blew up in a blazing inferno. Lanphier and Barker shared the credits. Strike one Japanese Admiral.

As American and Australian forces fought through the New Guinea jungles and Marines with army infantry took one island after another in the Solomons, Kenney's 5th Air Force attacked the Japanese with maximum-effort strikes daily, destroying 175 enemy planes at Wewak alone. The 5th Air Force's top fighter pilot during the air battles raging over that part of the Pacific was Maj. Richard Bong. At age 23 he quit college and joined the Flying Cadets, successfully completing the course. Bong had crossed Kenney's path in the states for looping the Golden Gate Bridge in a P-38. Kenney believed he could use that sort of bravado fighting Japanese pilots. The judgment was well placed. Bong knew the P-38 and how to fight with it against the more agile Zeros. In 146 missions he shot down 28 Zeros. He was ordered back home to teach other pilots his methods but returned to the Pacific eight months later and gunned down another 12 Zeros, bringing his total to 40 destroyed Japanese Zeros.

The Japanese made serious mistakes in their planning to manage and supply their far-flung island outposts in the South Pacific. Their long lines of supply, stretching across the Pacific to various islands, created a military empire. They had no support for such a military force. Their merchant marine was a third that of the British Empire. They provided no convoy protection and no carrier escort. Consequently, those long lines could be attacked from the air and by submarines. The overall mission became that of destroying the supply lines throughout the South Pacific,

Crew is handling paper drop-tanks for fighters that were lighter and less expensive than metal ones. They could joke even in wartime. "Look, here's one made in Japan," says Sgt. Mike Moran to S/Sgt. Bob Keich, standing by tank, and Cpl. Howard Middlemans.

leaving their ground troops to whither on the vine, and ground the air forces from lack of fuel and parts. American submarines concentrated on Japanese shipping in what some historians called a "massacre." In 1943, U.S. subs sank 296 Japanese ships totaling 1.335 million tons. In just one month—October 1944—that number increased by 321,000 tons. In that same year, air forces in the Pacific sank a million tons of shipping, both military and merchant. The effects of supply starvation were deadly to Japanese operations.

The Japanese used primitive methods to clear the jungles for buildings and runways while the U.S. used heavy machinery to move or carve away rock for runways. As a result, the U.S. placed new bases in operation quickly. Also, the Japanese poor medical practices caused debilitating health problems for personnel. Commander Kofumada of the Japanese navy commented: "It became evident our military and government leaders had never really understood the meaning of total war."

As air strength grew in the South Pacific, so did supplies, troops, and guns for General MacArthur's forces. With training completed, the island-hopping strategy was started by leap-frogging his forces, leaving Japanese garrisons stranded in the jungles to starve and be forgotten by the Japanese command, making these forces no longer of military importance. Hundreds of U.S. planes bombed and strafed the important Japanese base at Rabaul day and night. High flying bombers inundated their camps at night with bombs, giving them no time for rest or sleep. On February 20, 1944, what was left of Japan's 2nd Carrier Division was withdrawn from Rabaul and moved to Truk. Rabaul had become useless as a military base, conquered by air power. Considering Truk strongly defended, the U.S. by-passed it.

The U.S. made a tragic mistake attacking the Gilbert Islands. The joint chiefs ordered it taken. According to Marine Corps Maj. Gen. Holland "Howlin' Mad," Smith, Tarawa had no strategic importance or value as a base. The Japanese were deeply entrenched on the tiny island and predictions by the navy of bombarding it into submission were overstated. The first wave of Marines went ashore at 9:00 A.M. The heavy fire from defense positions quickly revealed that the 37mm antiboat guns, machine-gun nests, rifle pits, and blockhouses were intact and active. The attacking force of 15,000 Marines slugged it out with 5000 elite Japanese troops. After 76 hours, 1000 Marines lay dead and many more wounded; 17 Japanese were captured. The others had been killed by the fighting or had committed suicide. More accurate bombardment by navy and air force on the later attack against Kwajalein in the Marshall Islands, resulted in 373 losses of ground troops, much improved after the casualties of Tarawa.

B29s arrive

After initial problems with their engines were solved, the new B-29 super-bombers began air bombardment of Japanese factories. General Arnold, who organized the 20th Air Force in a highly unusual command arrangement, called on Gen. Curtis LeMay to lead strikes against Japan. The B-29 had been designed for the singular purpose of taking the war to the Japanese homeland. The big plane could range 1600 miles from base, carrying a load of seven tons of bombs. Before leaving for the Pacific, LeMay insisted on being checked out on the B-29. He found it full of problems. The big ship turned out to be a maintenance nightmare. Anything that could go wrong seemed to happen to the B-29. As time went by more and more of the problems were solved.

As this was going on, a fight of great intensity for control of the Marianas was underway. Not only were large numbers of Marines involved, but also the navy and Japanese fleets. On D-day, Marines went in with a backup of 12 escort carriers, 5 battleships, and 11 cruisers. The 5th fleet appeared the next day with 7 more battleships, 21 cruisers and 69 destroyers. Standing by were 4 carrier groups—a total of 15 carriers

USAF

B-29s were first sent to China June 5, 1944, and the first mission was to bomb Bangkok. One June 15, raids were made against Yawata, Japan's steel-making plant. The bases in China were expensive and difficult to supply with fuel and bombs. With the capture of the Marianas, B-29 operations could become more effective. The attempt at high altitude bombing of Japan failed due to weather and the high velocity winds at altitude. General LeMay came up with a more effective type of bombing: incendiary at low altitude. It was devastating and totally effective. The 678th B-29 Bomb Squadron, 444th Group was commanded by Winton R. Close, based in the Marianas. He was a graduate of the class of 1939, retiring with the rank of Major General.

and 956 aircraft. While the battle raged for the island, a sea battle developed between U.S. and Japanese fleets. The Japanese lost 346 carrier planes while the U.S. lost but 15. The second round began with the U.S. fleet chasing the Japanese. At the end of the day, 3 Japanese carriers were at the bottom along with nearly 500 of their aircraft. The Americans lost 130 planes. Many of the pilots were recovered after ditching in the ocean after running out of fuel.

The back of the Japanese naval air power was broken, eliminating interference with the ground campaign. Tinian was secured on July 30. Sufficient air bases were now available for the air attack on Tokyo. On November 24, 1944, a force of 111 B-29s was briefed for the first attack on an aircraft plant north of Tokyo. Ninety-nine made it to the target and dropped bombs from an altitude of 5 to 6 miles with poor result. One bomber was lost when a Jap fighter rammed it. Additional high altitude flights were made with no improvement in results. Finally, the pentagon placed the program under General LeMay. Top command fears were that without success from the strategic bombing, a landing attack would be necessary to defeat Japan, with a huge loss of ground troops. For LeMay it was a must-do situation.

Fire-bombing of Japan

After considerable study and with the knowledge that the heavy winds at high altitude over Tokyo made strategic bombing too difficult, LeMay decided to bomb from 5000 feet using firebombs. All crewmembers except the pilots, engineer and tail gunner as observer, were taken off the crew ready list. The first mass raid on Tokyo was launched late in the afternoon on March 29, 1945, when 325 fully loaded B-29s took off from Saipan, Tinian, and Guam for the 6-hour flight to Tokyo. The first two bombers arrived early and laid down timed strings of incendiaries. They blazed up, making a huge X for the target. At 15 minutes past midnight, a cascade of thermite, magnesium, and napalm bombs began raining down on the center of Tokyo. Two thousand tons of firebombs were broadcast over the city. Within 30 minutes the roaring inferno was completely out of control.

Flames leaped from building to building chasing the oxygen in the air. An inferno was created from which there was no escape. Temperatures reached 2000 degrees Fahrenheit. The tail observer in one B-29 reported seeing the red glow from more than 150 miles to sea. Sixteen square miles of Tokyo were completely destroyed. A later count revealed that 261,171 buildings, factories, homes, business offices, municipal buildings, schools, and hospitals were gone. Maximum number of dead was estimated at 130,000 with another 40,000 burned or badly injured. Fourteen bombers were lost from flak and ditching in the ocean. Nagoya burned on March 11, and Osaka on March 13. Kobe was flamed on March 16, and three days later 290 bombers unloaded another 1900 tons of incendiaries on Nagoya. The first fire blitz lasted 10 days, at the end of which 32 square miles had been destroyed.

The B-29s were diverted from their bombing of the Japanese mainland to assist Admiral Nimitz on tactical targets located on Okinawa, scheduled for invasion on April 1. On April 13, they returned to Tokyo with 2000 tons of incendiaries, burning out another 11 square miles of the city. Tokyo was hit again two days later, along with Yokohama and Kawaski. With P-51s from Iwo Jima flying escort, the bomber command started daytime bombing along with the night attacks. It was too difficult to determine accurately all the bombing effect because of the terrible state of chaos to which Japan had been reduced by August 1945. LeMay advised Hap Arnold they would be running out of targets in September, with only the railway system to attack. Still, the Japanese refused to surrender!

Dropping the A-bomb

At 8:15 A.M. on August 6, 1945, the B-29 *Enola Gay* of the 509th Composite Group, made a planned bombing run over the city of Hiroshima, which had not been firebombed, and loosed a single bomb. The pilot, Col. Paul W. Tibbets, a Flying Cadet graduate from the class of 1938A, banked away to observe. The bomb, a black, ugly shape, fell from 31,600 feet, detonating 43 seconds later at 600 yards above the city. Hiroshima felt an explosive force of 20,000 tons of TNT loosed in a millisecond. The fireball generated a second of heat equivalent to 300,000 degrees Fahrenheit. The B-29 headed back to Tinian. Still there was no surrender.

On August 9, the B-29 *Bock's Car* loaded with an atomic bomb "Fat Man" prepared to make its bombing run against the city of Kokura. The city was obscured, and after the second run pilot Maj. Charles Sweeney called a "no drop" and set a course for the secondary target, Nagasaki. The mission by then had become urgent from a shortage of fuel. The bomb was dropped on the first run and Sweeney wheeled the big plane around and headed for Okinawa, unable to reach Iwo Jima. The bomb destroyed Nagasaki, killing and injuring more than 76,000 Japanese. Radiation would cause additional deaths.

In addition to the destruction of Nagasaki, Japanese territory was also invaded by Russian soldiers: one million were pouring across the

Col. Paul Tibbets prepares to depart in the B-29 Enola Gay *for Hiroshima, Japan with the first atomic bomb.*

The crew of the Enola Gay. *Back row, (l. to r.) Maj. Tom Ferebee, Bombardier; Capt. T.J. "Dutch" Van Kirk, Navigator; Col. Paul Tibbets, Pilot; Capt. Bob Lewis, Co-pilot. Front row, (l. to r.) Sgt. Bob Caron, Tail Gunner; Sgt. Joe Striborik, Radar Operator; M/Sgt. Wyatt Duzenbury, Flight Engineer; Cpl. Richard Nelson, Radio Operator; T/Sgt. Robert Shummard, Asst. Flight Engineer.*

Manchurian border. There would be no agreement for a negotiated peace, instead the demand was for unconditional surrender. At a cabinet meeting to discuss the ending of the war, a majority of Japanese generals and admirals would not listen to talk of surrender. They would fight to the last Japanese person alive using bamboo spears if necessary. These were the men who had come into power in 1930 when the military decided to capture Manchuria and fight China. They were the men who bombed Pearl Harbor without warning, and they were the men who condoned the capture and torture of men, women, and children wherever they seized control during five years of war. Now, they had brought war and destruction to the doorsteps of their own people and were determined to see them die. Fortunately, Emperor Hirohito made his appearance and announced the war must end. "My people have had enough."

The final mission of the 21st Bomber Command was carried out at Kumagaya on August 14, 1945. On August 15 Hirohito's message was heard, bringing an end to the war. Still, ever cruel and evil, a B-29 crew captured by Japanese people, was taken to a small patch of woods on the island of Kyushu where they were stripped and beheaded, one by one.

Flying the "Hump"

The China-Burma-India (CBI) Theater was basically a supply route. With the fall of Singapore in the spring of 1942, and with Burma, Rangoon and Myitkyina overrun, there were no landlines open to supply China. Everything from rifle bullets to high-octane fuel had to be flown over the Himalaya Mountains, whose peaks rise to 18,000 feet along the route. The route flown by the "Hump" pilots took them from bases in the vicinity of Chablis in northeast India and across the mountains of northern Burma to Kunming, China. Air Corps pilots flew them to supply Chiang Kai-shek's Chinese Nationalist Army. They flew unarmed two- and four-engine cargo planes through some of the worst weather in the world. More than 1000 men and nearly 400 planes were lost during a four-year period. They flew C-46s and C-47s, affectionately named "Commandos" and "Gooney birds." These aircraft had been designed originally as passenger planes. They were never intended for high-altitude work, having inadequate engines and unpressurized cabins. The Himalayas rise higher than peaks of the Rocky Mountains in the United States with Mt. Everest—located between India and Tibet—rising to more than 29,000 feet. In most places there were no navigation aids and pilots navigated by guess and by prayer, with a good eye as to what mountain could be recognized and matched up with the map. Pilots refer to it as pilotage or

Flying the Hump in the China, Burma, India Theater was the route to supply the Chinese effort during WWII because there were no land routes that were not under control of the Japanese. Hump pilots flew everything from rifle bullets to drums of high-octane fuel, food of all kinds, airplane parts, medical supplies, army mules, cannons, shells, and people, The route was from Chabua, India, across Burma and the Himalayan peaks into Kunming, China. Flying C-47s and C-46s, they daily threaded their way around peaks that rose to 29,000 feet. Navigation was purely look and see with flight limited maps and often facing high winds and huge storms. They flew unarmed aircraft and more than 400 planes and in excess of 1000 crewmen were lost during the four-year period.

A reluctant "passenger" is forced into an airplane, which will take it over the Hump to supply commandos that landed behind Japanese lines.

dead reckoning. The problem with mountains is they look entirely different in the morning than at night. This fools the eye, much the same as flying over water during a cloudy day when every shadow on the water looks like an island. Usually, these conditions diminish when good navigation aids are available and pilots are more confident of their positions.

A pilot carried a wide variety of cargo before going home on rotation. One who flew 100 missions might make the following runs, for example: 37 trips with 100-octane gasoline in 55 gallon drums; 18 loads of gasoline pipeline; 11 loads of mixed ammunition including 2 loads of grenades; 2 loads of jeeps; 2 loads of Chinese soldiers; 3 loads of trailers and trucks; 2 loads of canned tomatoes and canned beans; 18 loads of mortar shells; 3 loads of 100-pound demolition, and 2 loads of spare parts and aircraft engines. Most flights carried enough flammables and explosives to blow peaks off mountains. One young pilot described his "Hump" flying this way: "It was like a trip into and out of the 'guts of hell' on rough days, then it got worse."

Overcoming weather and Zeros

Weather was a constant problem caused by the warm, moist monsoons from India colliding with frigid air from central Asia moving southward, with winds sometimes at speeds exceeding 100 miles per hour. It was strong enough to flip a plane on its back, send it upward like an elevator several thousand feet, then thrust it back down faster. Icing was a constant problem according to the season, with an average icing level over the "Hump" from 10,000 to 20,000 feet. On many flights, pilots encountered these conditions throughout the trip, including the return flight home. Carburetor icing was the most common cause of engine failure.

Sometimes a Zero would appear causing pilots to immediately dive for shelter within a nearby cumulus cloud. Inside the cloud, a plane would be bumped around until the pilot decided to take a peek after 20 minutes or so. Fortunately, pilots saw the Zeros less and less frequently as they were required at home for defense or for action in the Pacific. At night the storms could produce St. Elmo's fire (a discharge of electricity) that jumped around from windshield to the instrument panel, and even to the nose or ear of a crewmember. Ball lightening was even worse. A blue fireball could bounce around the flight deck scaring everyone. Sometimes a buzzard would explode through the windshield, knocking out the pilot. So many pilots found it necessary to jump at one time or another that they didn't bother mentioning it. Their stories of flights through the Himalayas were occasionally funny and frequently stretched the imagination.

The 14th Air Force, commanded by tough Maj. Gen. Claire L. Chennault, was created on March 10, 1943, from units of the China Air Task Force, including some of the famous Flying Tigers of the American Volunteer Group. The medium bombers of the 14th blasted targets at Hankow and Canton in China, Haiphong and Hanoi in Indochina, and struck heavily at oil storage dumps in the vicinity of Hong Kong. When Chennault received heavy bombers, Formosa and Hainan came within range.

The "Hump" operation started in 1942, and the atom bombs over Hiroshima and Nagasaki ended the need for it in 1945. During its operation, the military purpose was to keep China supplied and fighting, while an all-out effort was being made to help get General MacArthur organized and equipped to keep his promise and return to the Philippines. This kept the Japanese fighting on two fronts, draining their resources and slowing movement of supplies to bases in the South Pacific. As in so many other battlefields of the war, the "Hump" operation was very expensive in manpower lost and equipment destroyed. It was caused by a lack of proper aircraft and the difficult flying weather that surrounds the Himalayas. Today, jet aircraft operate thousands of feet above the jagged peaks that extend from Nepal to Kunming. However, in the days when flying over the Himalayas was so essential, no greater tribute could be paid those fearless pilots who risked their lives almost daily with great honor and courage than being called a "Hump" pilot. It was a genuine badge of distinction, worn only by

UPI/Bettman

The Japanese attacked China in Manchuria in the 1930s. China could offer little more than its masses of people and their hard labor in the war effort. Its people were used in a variety of ways, one being the building of airports. Fairly level ground would be selected and then cleared of big rocks by hand and leveled with a stone roller pulled by men. A Chinese officer is shown at the rear of the right side. Work details were made up of young men on the one side and old men on the other. Not pleasant work with only a pocket full of rice for the day. Symbolizing the past and the present, a B-24 is landing on the runway as it is being extended.

those who earned it. They accomplished their part of the worldwide mission with great bravery and determination to get the supplies through, regardless of weather and other dangers flying the Himalayas. Their success marked another essential victory over the Japanese in a part of the world far removed from Kansas, Georgia or New Jersey.

European Theater of Operations

Declaration of war against Germany in 1941 surfaced the problem that had dogged the leaders of the Air Corps during the 1930s: fighting a war against well-trained combat pilots flying the best fighter aircraft of the day. Gone were the days of scholarly discussion about tactics and recommendations for their implementation. The embarrassing truth was: United States military aircraft could not compete and its pilots were totally lacking in combat experience. The one bright spot in this weakness was the ally Great Britain and its Royal Air Force. Destined to become the strategic power against Germany, the 8th Air Force was to be based in England. Under the plan worked out by planners with the RAF, B-17s and B-24s would conduct daylight precision bombing against industrial plants, and RAF bombers would continue their night raids.

A rude shock awaited Brig. Gen. Ira Eaker when he arrived in England. He reported to Maj.Gen. James E. Chaney, commanding the Army Special Observer Group, who had arrived much earlier to observe RAF operations against the Luftwaffe. Chaney, an air officer, headed a staff of 35 officers of which all but 4 were ground army types. In their meetings, Eaker soon learned that only a few supported air operations against German cities while the rest were indifferent or antagonistic toward any Air Corps operations. When Eaker requested a HQ office for Gen. Carl Spaatz who would command the 8th Air Force, he was informed Spaatz would not be coming and there would be no Air Force HQ. This matter was settled by organizing the 8th Air Force in Washington and transferring it to England. Chaney and his group of army ground officers were ordered home.

Spitfires protected early B-17 bomb runs. General Eaker flying the *Yankee Doodle* led the first. He took the B-17 to 23,000 feet over a railroad switching yard. The flight attracted little attention, probably to the great relief of the Spitfires flying cover. The photos revealed hits causing damage and destruction to rolling stock, sheds, and sidings. Although it was a minimal raid it was impressive to the press and British people. It had been common knowledge that the RAF believed greater success would be achieved if B-17s were assigned to their night mission program.

Air Corps and RAF differ on bombing techniques

The theory of strategic bombing was based on selecting and destroying the infrastructure of the enemy's factories, munitions, transportation, and flying resources. The U.S. commanders believed methodical bombing would cause the enemy to be unable to continue supplying the necessary support for warfare. The British, on the other hand, believed that by dis-

B-25s were outstanding and thoroughly dependable medium bombers during WWII. They gained fame when Jimmy Doolittle led his volunteers off the Carrier Hornet on the first raid on Tokyo, Japan. Davy Jones, Flying Cadet class of 1938B, bombed targets in Tokyo but missed connections after the raid and crashed in China.

rupting the cities using night area bombing, poor working conditions and damage would ultimately bring production to a standstill. It was not General Eaker's position to argue the point. Instead, he was able to support his cause by suggesting a 24-hour program of day and night bombing. This, of course, greatly appealed to the British who had suffered under the night bombing by Hitler.

The initial arguments against day bombing were dropped as American B-17s began to arrive, although the early bombing mission losses were devastating. As Americans began to grasp the mentality of warfare, a better understanding of their English counterparts evolved. Also, the British better understood the American point of view, knowing the Yanks were coming.

Germany's path to war

The treaty of Versailles after WWI prohibited Germany from building military aircraft or engaging in military activity. Yet, in only 18 years that nation made a formidable rise in air power. Step one occurred in 1922. Noted aces from WWI were assigned the duty of organizing veteran combat pilots into reserve units. They developed glider units and gave instruction to German boys. It appealed to German youth and in a short time gliding became a national sport. Transferring to powered flight was but a step away. By another move, Germany made a secret pact with Russia to establish a military flying school to train German pilots in Russia. German aircraft plants were building commercial aircraft for Lufthansa Airlines and a method was devised to convert transports into bombers. Germany developed fighters under the guise of sport planes, and a factory built in Russia developed the combat aircraft flown by German pilots. As with other military dictators who developed forces by stealth, Hitler created his Luftwaffe.

In 1935, Hitler denounced the Versailles Treaty and unveiled his Luftwaffe to the world. Wasting no time, in 1936 Germany sided with Gen. Francisco Franco and sent its planes to fight the inferior Republican planes in Spain. With Franco triumphant and the German forces trained, Hitler returned his Luftwaffe to Germany in 1939. In September of that year he struck at defenseless Poland after Poland denied Germany access across the Danzig corridor to East Prussia. Britain and France had guaranteed Poland's freedom and these countries declared war on Germany. The French held a secure belief for the touted Maginot Line, a system of heavily fortified pillboxes and tank traps constructed on the eastern frontier of France and believed impregnable. The Germans quickly rendered it useless. After that, the only French resistance was volunteers in England and the underground at home. Hitler came to his next target, England. It would be his greatest prize of all. Field Marshal Goering convinced Hitler that his Luftwaffe would bring England to its knees without a ground fight. Instead, the Spitfires and Hurricanes, flown by valiant members of the RAF, destroyed Hitler's timetable. Although London was heavily bombed, the Luftwaffe was stopped cold during the daylight in the Battle of Britain. Well before the time set for victory, Goering admitted to Hitler that his Luftwaffe had failed.

The first B-17 arrived in England on July 1, 1942, flying a route from Presque Isle to Goose Bay in Canada, then across the Atlantic to Greenland and Iceland. From there they flew to Prestwick, Scotland, a total distance of 3264 miles, much of it over water. The flight was accompanied by P-38s whose range was 1420 miles. On July 4, 1942, a celebration flight of six American crews flew with RAF crews on a strike against German airfields in Holland using A-20 light bombers. The flak was intense and two American A-20s were shot down along with one from the RAF. The first European Theater of Operations *Distinguished Flying Cross* was awarded to Capt. Charles C. Kegelman, a graduate Flying Cadet,

Nixon/Galloway

An artist's work depicts Capt. Charles Kegelman flying an A-20 with right propeller blown off by German ack ack and the engine of his plane Boston II *on fire. It was the first bombing mission flown by U.S. pilots in light bombers on July 4 1942. Damage caused Kegelman's plane to strike the ground and bounce back into the air. He gave full power to the good engine and kept flying. A flack tower was trained on him, but he adjusted the plane's position and destroyed the tower with nose guns. He flew the damaged plane back to England. A graduate of the Flying Cadet class of 1937, Kegelman received the Distinguished Flying Cross for his outstanding flying under fire.*

class of June 1937. Kegelman earned it when his damaged A-20, with one engine out, hit and bounced off the ground in front of a flak tower. He calmly shot up the flak tower, destroyed it, and headed for home across the Channel on one engine powering a badly damaged A-20.

The RAF (Royal Air Force) had forged ahead in face of Hitler's threat to capture the Island Kingdom. Spitfire and Hurricane fighters had been developed to meet in combat with the Luftwaffe fighters and they were successful in defense. However, in the role of escort for the British bombers, they were short in range. For this reason, all bombing by the RAF was done during darkness, and was not too successful. While waiting for development and production of American fighter aircraft, select Air Corps pilots were sent to England. They flew with RAF squadrons, learning combat tactics and gaining valuable experience. In time, enough were qualified to form an American unit, the 31st Eagle Group. Flying Spitfires and Hurricanes, they became very effective in combat.

The deplorable situation faced by the United States is best described as a total failure by its leaders to provide for the defense, highlighted by the inability of the State Department to recognize the magnitude of the German threat. However, two items contributed to this dilemma: the Great Depression, and reliance on the two-ocean theory of defense, eagerly accepted by a public dominated by isolationist dogma from the aftermath of WWI. Only one bright light existed in the Air Corps' arsenal: the B-17. It was there by reason of one far-visioned proponent, Maj. Gen. Frank M. Andrews. Although he, like Billy Mitchell, had been rudely ordered away from Washington by army brass, Andrews had insisted on including B-17 procurement orders in the budget. For that reason alone, 17 B-17s were on order before December 7, 1941.

B-17—an unprotected delivery system

Appearance of the B-17 in combat over Europe brought home the rude awakening that although it could carry a load of bombs to German bases of production, without fighter escort the losses were too high during daylight hours. In addition, it had poor defensive machine gun fire forward with which to fend off a frontal attack. Part of the strategy behind protection of the Flying Fortress, as the B-17 was called, from fighter attack was the cross fire gun support from within the formation. With its twelve .50 caliber machine guns, the B-17E was the latest production model and thought to be better armed with two power turrets mounting twin .50-caliber machine guns, one on topside aft of the pilot's compartment, and was calculated to be a successful beginning. This was welcomed news as the British views concerning daylight bombing had not been favorable. On October 9, 1943, 115 bombers including 24 B-24s, escorted by 156 RAF and 8th Fighter Command Spitfires and P-38s, struck at steel plants in the industrial city of Lille. Thirty-three bombers aborted before reaching the target, and three B-17s and one B-24 were shot down.

In early 1943, the P-51 Mustang began to reach units in England. Although the P-51 was in short supply, it was considered a much better escort plane than the P-47 or P-38. The 51 could tangle successfully with the German Me-109. P-51s took over on longer escorts. The tactic surprised the Germans who were waiting to pounce on unescorted B-17s, and instead found P-51s on their tails. Still, at the end of 1943, not enough P-51s had arrived to establish air superiority. The 9th Air Force Fighter Command had five groups assigned. Of them, three groups had not yet received airplanes, a fourth had only 10 P-47s, and one P-51 group was in

USAFA

The P-51 was a pilot's dreamboat in the sky. It could do any maneuver with no strain. After the war they were scrapped except for a few turned over to the Air National Guard for training. When Korea heated up, the air force federalized the Guard squadrons and sent P-51s and pilots into action over Korea. It was a tough chore when Russian Migs entered the fight and many Guard pilots didn't make it back. It was the beginning scenario in the United States: get into a war, build up military strength, win the war, junk the airplanes, get into another war, etc. etc.

combat. To cause more worries, operation Overlord—code name for the channel crossing attack—was scheduled to begin in approximately five months, and the 9th Air Force had received only 40 percent of its authorized aircraft strength. General Quesada was not a happy warrior.

Nevertheless, in October 1943, a bomber offensive involving the 8th Air Force and 9th Air Force got underway. Its mission was to attack all manufacturing plants making aircraft, ball bearings, steel, aluminum, chemicals, rubber, and other war material. Its code name was Argument. The first attack hit the ball bearing plants at Schweinfurt. Although 315 bombers reached the target area, more than 100 were badly damaged. The loss ratio was too high. In addition, the plants were either quickly replaced or moved, and losses of that magnitude could not be maintained. Part of the solution would be better weather reports. More important was an urgent increase in long-range fighters. Winter weather promised no relief and it appeared the timetable for the mission might be compromised. However, things improved with the increase in new bombers and fighters.

On February 20, 1944, escorted to the targets by 832 fighters, 1000 bombers hit manufacturing plants in central Germany. Losses were 25 bombers and four fighters. Germany, however, lost 153 fighters. The fol-

USAFA

A P-47 pilot gets ready to roll. The P-47 had difficulties in taxiing because of limited forward vision. It required pilots to constantly swivel to prevent cutting off the tail of the plane ahead or jamming on the brakes and nosing the plane into the ground. One P-47 pilot, turning into final approach, lost speed and crashed into a concrete culvert. The big R-2800 engine protected the pilot. Any "bolt" pilot will tell you that no fighter plane gave more protection to the pilot than the venerable "Thunderbolt."

lowing day a second strike went off with 924 bombers and 679 fighters, but weather caused a diversion to targets of opportunity with losses of 19 bombers and 5 fighters. A third strike was set for February 22, when 605 bombers struck aircraft plants at Bernburg, Halberstadt and Aschersleben, including industrial plants and German fighter bases. The 15th Air Force also sent 400 B-24 bombers from Foggia, Italy, to bomb Regensburg. However, the weather was poor and many of the targets were obscured. Losses included 43 bombers and 11 fighters, with 110 German fighters destroyed.

The Luftwaffe changes tactics

Losses caused the Luftwaffe to change tactics from the earlier attacks when their fighters attacked in *schwarms*—flights of four or five aircraft.

USAF

Many U.S. units were based near the food-producing farms that dotted England. Here, the 322nd Bomb Group's Marauders nestle next to Bacon Farm, Stebbing. The group was the first to fly B-26s from Britain, beginning in May 1943.

NASM

The 357th Fighter Group at Hamilton Field received orders to join the 8th Air Force in England in July 1943. Group CO Col. Edwin S. Chickering's Aircobra P-39 is hand cranked by ground crew. Chickering graduated from Randolph Field and Kelly Field in 1937.

USAF

Cpls. Larry Roth and Wally Merquardt are busy bringing in B-24s from active runway at Mendlesham. Radio control Jeep was a big help moving traffic on and off the runway, especially when the 34th Bomb Group moved out in force.

With the larger sorties by 8th Air Force, the Luftwaffe countered with larger attacking groups called "mass against mass." The larger assaults by 50 fighters at first caught the Americans by surprise. Soon, however, the sheer numbers of bombers and fighter assaults overwhelmed the weakened and decimated Luftwaffe, now flying with inexperienced youngsters.

The raids had destroyed the once invincible and proud aerial warriors. The Allies claimed air superiority.

Gen. George Marshall, United States Army Chief of Staff, developed two plans for quickly carrying the war to Germany. The British didn't like either one. Marshall wanted to build up forces in England and strike across the English Channel into continental Europe without hesitation. His plan, "Sledgehammer" was based on using a large-scale strike force whose purpose would be to drain German troops from the Russian front and lure the Luftwaffe into battle with the covering Royal Air Force. A follow-up would be a full-scale invasion to be launched in 1943. The British were leery, wanting a peripheral attack that bypassed Germany's main strength. They suggested an invasion of North Africa. Marshall disagreed but reluctantly accepted it as the least harmful plan. He designated Gen. Dwight Eisenhower to command the invasion.

Battle for North Africa

The initial plan called for an American force to land on the Atlantic coast of Africa. This was increased to include an Anglo-American operation to land on both the Atlantic and Mediterranean coasts. Winston Churchill named it "Torch." It would light the way for the allied force's return to Europe. Pressure to get the plan into action came from the effort to stop Field Marshall Rommel from reaching Tunis, and by the Allies taking that city to shut off any route of escape for the German desert forces.

There were many snafu's. The French were thought to be friendly but in the Oran Harbor, French warships blew the American cutter *Walney* apart and set the *Hartland* afire. This was only one of many problems to be overcome by an untried plan using untested troops. However, within two days, the invasion had secured bases on the African coast at Sari, Pedals, Casablanca, and Port Luautey in Morocco on the Atlantic, and Oran, and Algiers on the Mediterranean Sea. The plan called for the Western Task Force to land in French Morocco; the Center Task Force at Oran; and the Eastern Task Force at Algiers. The forces covered an area of 750 miles, landed on November 8, 1942, then headed east for the real battle with the Germans at Kasserine. The Allies had lost the race to Tunis because of bad weather and good defense by the Germans. This set up the battle for Kasserine Pass.

Air support was furnished by the Middle East Air Force commanded by Maj. Gen. Lewis Brereton. His force started with B-24s commanded by Col. Harry Halverson, whose original orders were to attack Japan from China, but this order was changed and he was to take his force to Egypt.

He landed there with 23 B-24s on June 2, 1942. They started flying missions 10 days after arrival against oil refineries in Rumania and the Black Seaport of Constanza. On July 24 the 57th fighter group flew its P-40s off the flight deck of the U.S.S. *Ranger*. The 12th Air Force commanded by Gen. Jimmy Doolittle, and the 9th Air Force joined with Brereton's force with B-25s and B-26s, plus American pilots flying British Spitfires. It was a substantial force and flew 1366 sorties, destroying 45 German and Italian planes. Thousand of tons of enemy shipping were destroyed, and burned out tanks and trucks littered the desert.

Rommel forces became the next air targets. The 8th Air Force sent four fighter and two heavy bomber groups to bomb ships, harbors, and supply dumps to choke off Rommel's supply lines, and fighters made sweeps

The B-24 was the workhorse of four-engine bombers. It flew in the South Pacific area, China, North Africa, Europe, and the Aleutians. It was easy on maintenance and consequently usually available. In July 1943, Col. John Kane commanded the 98th Bomb Group equipped with B-24s operating out of North Africa. He and four other group commanders were briefed on bombing Ploesti oil refineries. It was to be a low-level hit—below 200 feet. However, bad intelligence on defense of the area and bad weather, plus bad timing, caused the mission to fall apart. Losses were severe, but with determination and effort the raid produced significant damage. Colonel Kane, Flying Cadet class of 1932, was one of five to receive the Medal of Honor for bravery under extreme fire.

against his mechanized forces and troop dispositions. On November 28, German airfields and docks at Bizerte were hit by 37 B-17s. They encountered resistance from FW.190s and Me.109s, losing two B-17s and costing the Germans 10 fighters. In answer to more attacks on shipping at Bizerte and Tunis, Rommel ordered additional flak guns and more German fighters directed by radar. Medium bomber losses caused a switch to the B-17s with P-38 escorts. B-17s also bombed a major Italian base at Castel Benito near Tripoli, on January 12, 1943, and again six days later with excellent results and few losses. On January 23, B-17s and P-38s hit Bizerte, sinking ships, setting oil tanks aflame, destroying hangars, and shooting down 12 fighters. Raids were extended across the Mediterranean to hit German bases at Sardinia and docks at Sicily. Targets of opportunity at sea caught carrying goods for Rommel were hunted down and destroyed. Within 30 days, 20 ships were sunk and 26 others damaged. On April 10, the heavy cruiser *Trieste* was sent to the bottom with one salvo of bombs.

With shipping being knocked out, the Germans resorted to flying their Ju.52s at sea level carrying badly needed cargo. On Palm Sunday April 1943, 46 P-40s from the 57th Fighter Group, escorted by RAF Spitfires flying top cover, jumped a large formation of Ju.52s flying low in V formation headed for Tunisia. Fifty Me.109s and Me.110s flew escort for the Ju.52s. The Allies bagged 58 of the Ju.52s and 18 fighters. It was called the Palm Sunday Massacre. In the next 17 days, 195 additional German transports were shot down and 21 of the large six-engine Me.323s destroyed. Rommel had gone back to Germany and Gen. Jurgen von Arnim surrendered himself and 266,000 German officers and soldiers to the British 8th Army. The battle for North Africa was finished. The allies shared the credit but the real winners were the American troops. They went into battle raw and cocky; they came out combat smart and resolute. It also firmly establishment General Eisenhower as the leader of all Allied forces.

European Theater Battle Resumed

The next target after Tunisia was Pantelleria, 42 miles of rocky coastline and deep ravines. In an effort to pressure the Italian unit to surrender, General Brereton ordered bombing missions around the clock to deny sleep or rest and terrify the defenders. The raids began on May 30 with medium bombers and fighter-bombers. On June 1, the B-17s flew 700 sorties, unloading 1300 tons of high explosives. The attack reached a high point on June 10, when 1100 bombers and fighter-bombers smashed the island with 1500 tons of bombs in a day-long assault. When British forces went ashore there was little to no resistance, and the defeat was recorded as an air attack surrender with minor ground support. On July 10, British and American divisions stormed ashore at Sicily to begin a 38-day campaign ending with a race for Messina, won by Gen. George S. Patton.

In 1943, oil became the number one target priority. During the summer, a study of the industrial complex revealed that about 35 percent of oil required for the Luftwaffe was being produced at Ploesti, Rumania. Because no previous raids had been made to that site, it was believed that a low level heavy-bomber attack with B-24s from Benghazi would catch them by surprise. Five groups of B-24s were selected to make the attack, which was named Tidalwave. The plan called for a low-level "on the ground" final approach after hitting the initial point (IP). The 178 Liberators were divided into five groups led by Cols. John R Kane, Addison Baker, Leon Johnson, Keith K. Compton, and Jack Wood. Fifty-percent losses were expected. Because no raids had been made to that location it was difficult to assess the security ground support. Air support was expected to be intense.

It was difficult to get the plane commanders to fly their B-24s low to the ground. None had done it before. Vortex forces from the propellers and wingtips when flying that low could be dangerous for the bombers flying close behind. The five commanders were assigned to make bomb runs from different initial points to get maximum coverage over the spread-out area of the target. Bomb loads varied and delayed fuses were used in accordance with the scheduled times of attack. This would prevent the later planes from being blasted by bombs dropped by earlier waves. General Brereton was assigned the command task.

Preparations were meticulous with scale models created of the facility for pilot study. Crews flew practice missions daily with commanders being urged to fly low. After three intensive weeks of flying daily practice missions, General Brereton gave the word to proceed. He was not permitted to fly the lead by order of General Arnold. In his place, Gen. Uzal Ent, second-in-command, took the lead. On takeoff, each B-24 far exceeded the maximum gross weight, which included extra fuel to make the 2700-mile round trip. Each ship had completed the takeoff and sluggish climb to altitude until one, named the Kickapoo, rolled down the runway. It made its takeoff, then lost an engine to fire, slammed back to earth, and hit a telephone pole. The plane broke into flames and blew up. Two survived. It set up the ill-timed fate that would continue to effect the mission as it progressed to the target.

Ten planes aborted and the lead plane, for no apparent reason, suddenly veered and plunged out of control into the sea. As the lead elements hit the coast, huge clouds appeared that towered over a range of mountains, which were 11,000 feet high. The two lead groups climbed through the clouds, topping out at 16,000 feet. The other three groups climbed through, but were now 60 miles behind. The carefully planned timing was compromised. After seven and one-half hours flying time, the first group hit its first initial point at Pitesto, 65 miles from Ploesti. The two groups dropped down to low level and spread out in attack formation. When they reached the second initial point, Targoviste, the lead group changed course heading for Bucharest. The navigator had mistaken the IP. The second group flew to the third IP and started its run on Ploesti.

Lt. John Palm, pilot, nosed down to 20 feet above the ground making 200 mph. He aimed his plane straight at the smokestacks as he approached the refineries. Flak hit from all sides and an explosion blew the nose apart, killing the navigator and bombardier. More blasts hit. Two engines caught fire and a third blew up. A shell hit the cockpit and Palm's right leg. A Me.109 flew low and finished off the bomber. The co-pilot, Bill Love, guided the bomber onto the ground, wheels up. Seven survived, including Palm, who lost his leg below the knee in a POW hospital.

The 93rd and 376th Groups, realizing they missed the IP, turned back, flying a course 90-degrees different from that briefed. The 93rd went in first. To their surprise they met heavy flak. An exploding shell hit the cabin of one plane and set it afire. The pilot, now at 300 feet, jettisoned his bombs and continued to the refineries. Engulfed in flames, some of the crew bailed out as the plane fell off, crashed, and exploded. Other crews were being fired on by guns hidden in haystacks and 20mm guns fired from a moving train. Other B-24s were running into cables tied to balloons, and heavy prop-wash caused several to crash. All the planning and briefings were forgotten as pilots fought through the fire, smoke, and explosions. Of the 34 B-24s over the target area, only half survived. General Ent ordered the 376th Group to hit targets wherever they could find them. It would have been impossible to form them up for the planned attack.

It was a confusing situation with bombers flying wildly, trying to avoid each other and locate targets they could hit. One refinery was missed, while several were hit twice. John Kane's group hit their IP and raced on to bomb the refineries. He had mounted a pair of .50 caliber machine guns on the nose of his B-24 and went in with guns blazing. He was so low the heat singed his arm as the plane passed through the violent eruption of flaming oil and dropped its bombs. Kane led 41 B-24s into the attack, but only 19 came through, close to the expected 50-percent loss. He landed at night on Cyprus. The 389th Group split up into three elements and made their runs from different IPs. Savage ground fire hit them all. Those surviving the fire and explosions limped away, only to be harried by German and Rumanian fighters. Only 87 B-24s survived and returned to their bases. In all, 54 failed to return, and 310 airmen were known to be killed or missing. Those reaching Libya, Turkey, Cyprus, Sicily, and Malta brought back 54 wounded. Seventy-five were in Rumanian hospitals.

Five earned the *Medal of Honor* for bravery in action, but others, equally brave, were not so honored. This decision was reached because "chaos over the target made it impossible to furnish proper information." That decision stretches the imagination. Colonel Kane commented later: "It was as deserving of immortality as the *Charge of the light Brigade.*"

The 8th Air Force, crippled from the decision to attack North Africa, had continued with the concept of strategic "precision" bombing. That concept was almost dumped when Winston Churchill, Great Britain's Prime Minister, made it known he wanted the B-17s to join the RAF in night bombing. When Ira Eaker heard about it, he strongly protested and requested audience with Churchill. Eaker presented to Churchill a single sheet of typed lines supporting daylight bombing. Among them was a phrase: "We give them no rest, they will be bombed around the clock." Churchill liked the idea, saying he would give the Americans their chance. At the meeting in Casablanca in January 1942, between Roosevelt, Churchill, and the Joint Chiefs, the directive regarding air ordered the progressive destruction and dislocation of the German military, industrial, and economic system. The last few words pleased Gen. Ira Eaker very much. He was now assured that strategic, precision bombing would have its day.

Few problems were more difficult in personnel matters than replacing airplane commanders killed in combat. Bomber crews arrived from the United States as a team. The skipper was the captain of his ship and guarded all members of the crew while aloft. However, in some cases, crewmembers had to be switched to other airplanes. Capt. William W. Spain arrived in England, after ferrying a B-17 across the Atlantic, and suddenly found himself assigned to a base to fill the boots of a pilot who had been killed. As a total stranger, he hoped for a little time to meet his crew. It didn't happen. The next day, on takeoff, he felt the eyes of all nine crewmen boring into the back of his head. Also, they were giving him the

R. Sand

P-38 Lightnings roll into position for takeoff. They did effective work as escort for B-17s in Europe, but lack of range forced them back when needed most. They were a welcome sight in the Aleutians and could make the trip to Kiska, attack and return with ample fuel. Before their arrival, P-40s and P-39s struggled to make the flight and many didn't make it, forced to ditch in the icy water from the Bering Sea. Maj. Dick Watt, Flying Cadet class of 1938, and Lt. Robert Dickinson from Colorado were only two of many who lost their lives in the Aleutian area.

"Yes sirs" and answering queries with a "sir" at the end. After the bomb run, he found himself out of position and couldn't catch up. That meant catching it from FW.109s after the flak stopped. The tail gunner reported jammed guns. Spain told him to keep moving the guns back and forth to fool the German pilot. The answer came back, "Thanks, skipper." They caught hell then and holes were showing up all over the fuselage. Spain wanted to bring the plane home for the crew. The top-turret gunner slumped down with blood running down his chest. He couldn't bail out and Spain knew he had to keep flying. The bombardier climbed up into the top turret and began returning the German's fire. One of the waist gunners called out to Spain: "Keep up the good work skipper!" It pleased him to hear something without the "sir." At that moment, the German fighter turned away and Spain realized they were near the Channel. He felt much better as the RAF Spits nestled in beside him, something like a police escort. Spain set the B-17 Fortress down on the nearest field. They crashed through a fence, and rolled through a patch of Brussels sprouts. Spain kicked the rudder to guide the plane into a haystack. They were all taken to the hospital and in a few days were ready to fly again. Spain knew in a few moments that he was on the team. No one called him anything but Bill.

During 1943, losses were heavy in the 8th Bomber Command. Its commanders were concerned about slow replacements and damage reported on raids. Actually, they were doing much better than they thought. If they could have listened in on some of the problems facing German Gen. Adolf

Galland, life would have been a little easier. Charged with the fighter defenses, Galland had two bosses: Adolph Hitler and Hermann Goering. He
couldn't please either. They demanded that he move his fighters back to
protect the people and not the strategically important plants. Galland
warned that soon the B-17 bombers would have long-range fighter escort.
He was right, but Goering told Hitler it wasn't possible.

*The flight surgeon (in leather jacket) and medics wait with the "meat wagon" for
injured coming in on B-17. Pilots fired two red flares indicating wounded aboard.
It was normal procedure at any wartime base when planes were returning from
missions. Immediate care of wounded could often mean getting injured crewmen
back early. Medics look nonchalant, but when that plane rolls to a stop they will be
ready. Medics aren't always appreciated because they appear immune to suffering.
That isn't true. They deal with pain and death each day and must find personal
ways to cope with it.*

On August 17, 1943, a raid on Schweinfurt resulted in the loss of 24
Fortresses. The bombers also struck at the Messerschmitt plant at
Regensburg, losing 36 B-17s. A maximum effort was being set up to once
more bomb Schweinfurt on October 14. A combined total of 383 B-17s and
B-24s were scheduled with P-47 Thunderbolts providing cover, but their

range was short, causing them to leave when needed the most. The 60 B-24s took off, but the weather prevented their joining up and they returned to base. The B-17s took off on instruments 30 seconds apart, climbed thorough the overcast and started the climb. Mechanical or electrical problems forced many to return to base. The strike force was reduced to 291 bombers. At the German border, the P-47s pealed off and returned to England. In a few moments the bedlam started. The FW.190s and Me109s formed up in waves in front of the bombers, then turned in *schwarms* of six to eight fighters to attack. They opened up at maximum range with their 20mm cannon and continued firing as they passed through the mission, head-on, at 500 mph. Then they did a half-roll toward the ground and formed up for another attack. Fighters, sitting out on the flank, swept in on individual runs. Twin-engine Ju88s, Me110s and 210s started firing eight-inch rockets from 1000 yards out, beyond the effective range of the B-17 gunners. By the time the mission reached Schweinfurt, 28 B-17s had been shot down. From the IP to the target, the fighters pressed the attack and another 11 B-17s went down. With all bombs gone, the remaining Fortresses turned and headed for the Channel, followed by attacking waves of fighters until reaching the White Cliffs at Dover. Sixty B-17s were lost, including 600 men in one afternoon.

Appearance of the P-51 Mustangs changed the picture. In the first six weeks of operations, the 354th Fighter Group escorted B-17 bombers on 14 long range missions, destroying 41German fighters, while losing six of their own to flak. When the 354th escorted the 1000 bombers to Leipzig and back, a distance of 1100 miles, the longest fighter-escort mission to that date, only 21 heavy bombers were lost, or two percent of the force. When General Spaatz took stock on the profit and loss sheet, he had:

Bombers engaged: 3800	Bombers lost: 226
Tonnage dropped: 10,000	Casualties: 2600 killed, wounded
Fighters lost: 28	or missing

The six-percent loss figure for the bombers was well within the acceptable ratio, and somewhat below the percentage loss sustained by the RAF. The loss to the Germans was so great that Albert Speer, on behalf of Hitler, handed down an order to disperse all German aviation industry. Approximately 75 percent of the industry's plants had been damaged or destroyed. It marked the waning moments before the surrender, having proved to the world the value of strategic bombing with fighter escort.

Mission is over and here comes the gang. At the hot coffee and donut stop, officers and enlisted personnel alike line up for the goodies. The Red Cross workers had but one command: Come and get it!

The Aleutian Chain

The Aleutians, a part of Alaska, is made up of groups of small islands with its furthermost island, Attu, at the west end. The islands form a barrier between the Bering Sea to the north and the Pacific Ocean on the south. William H. Seward, while Secretary of State, bought Alaska from the Russian government. Because of its location, cold climate, lack of industry capability, and difficulty of travel to and within its borders, it was named "Seward's Folly." That was changed when oil was discovered in the arctic area and a long pipeline was built to transport it to the south. The amount of oil remains unknown, and it is difficult to extract because of the extreme frigid conditions.

In 1934, Henry "Hap" Arnold, then a Major, led a formation of ten B-10 bombers to Fairbanks, and returned safely. He prepared a complete military study for the War Department. It was widely believed that Alaska was of strategic importance. World War Two, however, did not support that claim, the only action being the Japanese occupation of Kiska and Attu, and an aborted effort to bomb a naval base. The purpose of these actions was never defined, either by the United States or the Japanese, other than creating a diversion for the expansion of Japan's forces in the

South Pacific. If Japan had not occupied Kiska and Attu, it's doubtful that so many bases would have been constructed on the Aleutian Islands.

The bases of consequence on the chain were Kodiak Naval Air Station, Cold Bay on the Bristol Bay side of the chain, Umnak, Adak, and Attu. Only first and second echelons of airplane maintenance could be performed on those island bases, necessitating that all planes be returned to Elmendorf Field for heavy repairs. This was a difficult way to run a war when a shot-up P-38, P-39, P-40, B-17, or B-24 aircraft had to be flown 1000 miles for repairs and 1000 miles back to base after repair.

After the aborted effort to bomb Dutch Harbor, the Japanese Carrier fleet off-loaded soldiers at Kiska, who were soon building a runway. Major Eareckson, in command of a composite group, flew from Umnak in

USAF

B-24s were utilized for missions through the world during WWII. Though not as proclaimed as the B-17, it became a highly efficient fighting four-engine bomber, destroying many targets. In 1944, Col. Jack Randolph, Flying Cadet class of 1933, was assigned as Group Commander of the 463rd Bomb Group. On June 26 the group led a strategic mission against the aircraft factory at Schewechat, Austria. Direct hits were received from antiaircraft during the initial run, knocking out fuel lines and instruments. Fire broke out in the nose and tail turrets. One gunner was killed and another badly wounded. Holding position, the Group cleared the area. The lead plane was badly damaged, forcing a landing on an emergency strip.

a B-18 with bombs and dropped them on the Kiska camp. Work had already begun to scrape out a runway, and Zeroes on floats were present in the bay. The distance was a prohibitive range for the antiquated B-18. Its only purpose had been as a training plane. Eventually, B-17s and B-24s replaced it.

When the Adak base opened, it greatly decreased the round-trip distance to Kiska. However, the long over-water flights, and combat against float-equipped Zeros, were back-breaking for a squadron of P-39 fighters. Capt. Wilbur Miller, Flying Cadet class of October 1937, received hits and had to ditch his aircraft before reaching Adak. Other pilots flew down and saw him fighting to get his dingy inflated, but survival time in cold water was only eight minutes until hypothermia set in to claim its victim. He was lost.

When the P-38s first arrived, pilots were having difficulties in attacking the Zeros. Maj. James R. Watt, Flying Cadet class of 1938A, flying P-38s in Hawaii, was temporarily transferred to Adak to demonstrate the correct method of attack. Watt told the pilots to never attempt dog-fighting with Zeros. Hit and run is the only way. In short order, all Zeros on Kiska were eliminated. The story should have had a good ending, but Watt and his commanding officer were killed on a flight before leaving the Aleutians.

In early 1943, troops who had been training in the desert, were sent to attack the dug-in Japanese on Attu. It was a difficult and bloody fight for the infantry. The Japanese, already accustomed to the wintry cold, ice, and snow, fought effectively. They wore white coats, making it extremely difficult to know where they were. Many of the American infantry suffered from frostbite, frozen toes and fingers. The cold did help to stop bleeding wounds by rapid coagulation. The wounded and dead count was too high for the purpose. Naval action utilizing submarines and patrol boats could have isolated them, making their position unimportant.

Of interest to many fighter pilots on Adak, was the action by a bomber pilot to employ fighter tactics during an attack on Kiska. In the Flying Cadet personal reflections section, Maj. Don Dunlap, Flying Cadet class of 1935B, relates how he flew his B-17 much the same way a fighter pilot flying a P-38 would have done it. A very effective and positive attack was successfully completed, showing that a B-17 bomber pilot could adapt to use the tactics from the fighter pilot's arsenal of tricks and make it work with a B-17 bomber.

The Alaskan airport situation had improved only slightly since the Arnold flight with B-10s in 1934. In 1941, when Air Corps units were ordered to Alaska, a newer and longer runway was added at Nome, and the navy added a short runway on Kodiak Island. The Cold Bay airport was in process of development as the first on the chain. Short-range aircraft still could not fly from Vancouver to Anchorage. This improved when the Canadian base at Metlakatla Island on the coast south of Juneau and a new runway at Yakutat, were completed. The P-40s, P-36s and C-4Ss could now fly from Seattle to Anchorage, having a landing field or strip every 500 miles.

The soil of most islands in the Aleutians is a mixture of ash and soil from old volcanoes, sand, and degradation (erosion) of rock it creates. The Alaska Corps of Engineers' officer-in-charge during WWII in Alaska was Col. B. B. Talley. Demands for air facilities to support air plans after the Japanese attack required 24-hour work days.

Colonel Talley had difficulty locating island bases where the 11th Air Force wanted them. Few islands were a fit. Either there wasn't enough flat area, or heavy rains would flood it. He and his Air Corps pilot and assistant, Maj. Joe Schneider, worked around these problems, rapidly developing many landing strips, except at Adak. It was a highly desirable location but a small lake prevented clearing for a strip. They had almost given up when an old trapper came down from the hills and told them the lake would drain between heavy rains. Colonel Talley took a fresh look at the problem, noting the drainage flowed to the sea at the south end, and incoming tides flooded the area. He developed a pumping station to empty water when the area flooded or came in with the tide. Once finished, he determined it would work, and Adak Air Base was developed.

In the summer of 1943, final action was taken against the Kiska garrison. After a suitable air bombardment and naval shelling, troops went in during the short period of darkness. It was anticipated that the remaining Japanese troops would surrender. However, they had already departed aboard ships that had maneuvered during bad weather to pick up the survivors. No one remained on the Island to surrender. Many injuries occurred when Americans shot each other by mistake in the dark. The battle for the Aleutions had ended, but bomb runs to the Kurile Islands continued with limited success.

USAF

B-17 crew receive ditching instructions, or how to get out if forced down over water. Thousands of crews received similar instruction. Knowing how saved many crews enabling them to dry off and fight again. Generally, the first step was to make the landing without submerging the aircraft immediately. Every occupant had to know how to leave the airplane; once clear, dinghy's had to be inflated quickly, especially in the cold waters off the Aleutians and of the English Channel. Fighter pilots wore the dinghy attached to the parachute.

6

Strategic Air Power

IN OCTOBER 1924, General Billy Mitchell addressed the National Aeronautic Convention as representative of President Coolidge. His subject was strategic bombardment and its effect on an adversary's ability to produce implements of war. It was the first time an American officer had discussed the theory publicly. Mitchell argued that, if it was properly planned, aerial bombardment could make it unnecessary to fight on a battlefield. It caused great controversy. (And still does as this book is written.)

In 1933 and 34, then Major Hap Arnold was in command of March Field. His mission was to improve the training of bomber pilots, and to do so he was in dire need of a suitable bomb range. If bombers were to do their job they had to be accurate over the target. This required practice. He happened onto a dry lake range near Muroc, California. It was a vast, uninhabited area. A check of ownership showed the land belonged to the federal government. Quietly, to avoid land speculation, he had a reconnaissance made of the entire area. The military was able to acquire the land and at last had a suitable area for bombing targets. The Muroc range became one of the finest bomb and gunnery ranges in the world.

The theory of delivering bombs on centers of industry far behind the actual lines of battle prompted many discussions among military and civilian defense leaders. Nothing existed in theory that had been tested, nor had there been studies made of it. In 1933, the Materiel Division, under Conger Pratt with Jan Howard as the principal engineer, undertook such a study. The purpose was to produce a feasibility study on the question of the maximum range of a four-engine bomber carrying a bomb load of up to 2000 pounds. They arrived at an answer: 5000 miles at 200 miles per hour. Their proposal to build such a plane was turned down. Funds would be used, instead, to purchase B-10s. The 1933 study, however, had set up the trail leading to a bomber that could meet the specifications described. During the early 1930s, Claire Egtvedt of the Boeing Company, became active in the design of multi-engine bomber aircraft. In 1931, Boeing designed and built the B-9, a twin-engine bomber. It was the first effort to build a bomber not designed for army battlefield support. The airplane had design problems. Later Boeing rectified these in the model 247, a modern passenger transport aircraft. Arguments at the time that bombers would not be able to cope with fighters, were laid to rest when altitudes above 20,000 feet were reached. With Boeing Company operating in the red, a decision was reached to design and construct Model 299, and the company committed all its assets to the project. The plane was ready for shipment on July 1, 1935, to Boeing Field for its trial runs. After viewing the plane in motion, the press dubbed it the Flying Fortress.

On August 20, test pilot Les Tower, took off on a non-stop 2000-mile flight from Seattle, Washington, to Dayton, Ohio. Nine hours later he brought the plane—to be officially named the B-17—in for a landing after an averaged speed of 235 mph. No welcoming committee was on hand, as it was assumed it would take at least 10 hours for the flight. The result was pure music to the ears of Hap Arnold, Frank Andrews, and other supporters of strategic bombing. However, there would be heartbreaks along the way. On October 30, 1935, while making his first takeoff in the new bomber, Pilot Pete Hill ran down his checklist, and started the takeoff roll. The big plane broke ground and suddenly nosed up, stalled and crashed. The elevator control lock had not been removed. It was a problem then and became one of the worst to deal with in the service. All was not lost, however, and in the next procurement, 17 B-17s were placed on order.

The most promising role for a future strategic force came with the appointment of Frank M. Andrews to head the GHQ Air Force. It is important to realize that the advent of the GHQ Air Force was strongly supported by Gen. Douglas MacArthur, Army GHQ. His views, however, weren't calculated to support autonomy for a separate air force. They were more the realization that future wars would require the input of all services: army, navy and air. It is clear that General Andrews recognized this position and worked within the parameters so as not to harm his GHQ Air Force. Although treated harshly for his views and reduced in rank after his term at GHQ Air Force, he was later recalled to Washington. In later years he gained further recognition when Andrews Air Force Base, outside Washington, DC, was named in his honor.

Strategic bombing begins

Strategic warfare in Europe began with the British RAF flying night missions over enemy targets. They concluded daylight missions would be doomed to destruction by the Luftwaffe fighters. Their efforts, however, were not sufficiently productive, basically because the bombing was a general area type, not to precision-selected targets. When United States General Eaker, who would initially command the 8th Air Force, arrived in England, the RAF personnel provided excellent assistance. The RAF had been in a shooting war more than 46 months and Eaker considered them to be experts. He wrote a note to General Spaatz, in Washington awaiting his transfer to England, noting that the RAF had just sent more than 1000 bombers over Cologne in an all-night strike. He added, "I've been here for six months without receiving one B-17."

He would receive it on July 1, 1942. The long circuitous route of more than 3000 miles, flying over cold, deserted stretches of land and icy ocean from the United States to England, had been established. Before the end of that month, 47 B-17s, 74 P-38s, and 52 C-47 cargo planes were available for duty. The beginning of strategic, daylight bombing would soon be underway.

The B-17 had been designed and constructed as a bomber capable of defending itself against fighter aircraft. Air force plans for strategic bombing—selected targets by precision bombing—was based on that concept. It was, therefore, of great surprise and concern when it was found that it would not work without fighter escort. The tactics employed by the Luftwaffe fighters simply overpowered the gunners in a B-17, attacking in swarms of five or more Me109s and FW190s. During the early raids, when escorted only a partial distance by the P-47s and P-38s, losses were high as the escorts had to return to base when reaching the maximum of their range.

An essential task of the 8th Air Force was to convince the RAF and the English people that strategic warfare, using daylight precision bombing, would shorten the war. The British people had witnessed the efforts of the Luftwaffe to end the war by destroying London, and saw the failure when RAF fighters eliminated the threat. The RAF believed the Americans should assist them in the nighttime operations. The Americans were determined to destroy German resources and its ability to supply the materials of war. Public opinion gradually swung the American way. As the B-29 pilots bombing Japan learned, however, bombing from high altitudes was almost eliminated by extreme wind currents, making it impossible for bombsights to accurately compute drops on targets. This eventually led to fire bombing in Japan, devised by General LeMay, as a sure way to eliminate the ability or will to continue the war. Even this became suspect as the Japanese refused to surrender when city after city had been burned to the ground.

The theory of strategic bombing was proven over Germany. Bombing of factories and manufacturing centers, as well as communication and shipping facilities, ultimately destroyed the ability to support military aircraft with fuel, parts, and better equipment. It also destroyed the will to carry on and fight, an effective part of strategic bombing. When it was over, those two friendly air force ghosts, Billy Mitchell and Frank Andrews—who suffered hell's damnation for their views on strategic bombers—surely shared a chuckle, turned to each other, and said: "That's what we tried to tell them."

Air Superiority

Air superiority means control of the aerial battlefield. According to Gen. William Momyer, former commander of Tactical Air Command, and Flying Cadet class of February 1939: "No battle can be won if air superiority is not achieved." According to his beliefs, the best pilot, best airplane, and the freedom to utilize them are the essential combination. World War II is an example of United States forces eventually putting all three requirements together and acquiring air superiority over the European Theater of Operations. It had not come easily. Heavy losses, bickering with the British, fighters with ranges too short for full escort, and other difficulties, were overcome by new aircraft, determination, daring, experience, and, often, brilliant planning.

Book Three

7

Flying Cadet
Personal Reflections

EVERY PERSON in every war could relate many stories of duty, daring, and danger. To select snapshots of time in any life requires putting aside many equally momentous events. These Flying Cadets have done just that. Perhaps these brief accounts, however, will illustrate the meaning of "Beyond duty—honor."

Col. Robert G. Emmens, USAF-Ret.
Flying Cadet Class of 1938A

I graduated from Kelly Field in 1938. From that time until February 1942, I was busy flying the military aircraft assigned to our outfit. The B-25 was the first really modern medium bomber assigned to us. It exceeded my expectations and pleasure. In February 1942, I volunteered for a highly classified mission. When all the pilots got together we decided it was probably submarine patrol duty along the East Coast. I asked one of the pilots, Davy Jones, what the scoop was. His answer was that the mission would be dangerous, and anyone could chuck it now. Otherwise, stay to the finish. From Minneapolis, where the B-25s were modified for auxiliary fuel tanks, we flew to a base near Columbia, South Carolina. There, we were introduced to Col. Jimmy Doolittle. He also informed us it would be a volunteer and dangerous mission. Some might not return. He asked if anyone would care to drop out, with no questions asked. No one did. Afterward we were briefed to fly to Eglin Field in Florida. There, more modifications were made in power, weight, and armament for the mission. While they were being made, Colonel Doolittle commuted often from Washington to Eglin. When the B-25s were ready, the Colonel advised that we would start a specialized flying program. During the next three weeks, a navy pilot was assigned to observe as we practiced short-field takeoffs. Most of us believed the mission would be involved with a navy aircraft carrier.

During the last week of March we flew to McClelland Field in California for some final adjustments. The 16 planes were loaded onto the aircraft carrier *Hornet*. On the second day at sea, we learned from the ship's speakers that we would bomb Tokyo. Our rather cool reception from the navy hands, up to then, completely changed and they freely offered their help and cigarettes to our crews.

The plan was to take us within 400 miles of Japan, where we would take off. The plan was altered on April 18 when a Japanese patrol boat sighted us. Although it was quickly sunk, it was believed a warning radio message had been sent to Tokyo. An order was sounded through the ship's speakers to "man our planes." We left our breakfast below decks and ran for our night bags. Captain "Ski" York, our pilot, and I got aboard our plane with the rest of the crew and completed a fast preflight check. The flight deck of the *Hornet* carrier was pitching and rolling as the gusting wind of 20 knots kicked up white caps. As York and I settled into the cockpit, we noticed our air speed was already registering a bouncing 45 to 50 miles per hour. It was a combination of the carrier's speed and the wind, a big boost for takeoff. Ahead of us we saw the navy starter hold up his arm as Colonel Doolittle's engines were revved up, then the arm came down and in seconds, the Colonel was in the air. When our turn came, York held the brakes hard as we did a quick check of the instruments. When the engines reached maximum output, the starter's arm came down and we were off. With full flaps and full throttles, the B-25 jumped forward as the yoke was pulled full back, and we were in the air. We immediately reduced power to save fuel and set course for Tokyo. Because of the early takeoff we had to fly much further than originally intended. When we sighted the Japanese coast we realized we couldn't reach our landing destination at Chusien in China. Nolan Henderson, our navigator, calculated we could reach Vladivostok after dropping our bombs. After the drop, we turned to a heading of 300 degrees for Russia. In near darkness we flew over a small sod airport near Vladivostok. "Ski" took a run over the airport, then made a final approach and smooth landing. We were about 40 miles from Vladivostok. When the Russians showed up, we identified ourselves and were confined under arrest by the Russians. We had thought they might release us, but it was 13 months later before we escaped into Persia and returned to United States control.

B-25s were used early after the attack on Pearl Harbor to patrol coastlines for Japanese submarines. Bob Emmens, Flying Cadet class of 1938A, volunteered to fly with Jimmy Doolittle's B-25s on the Tokyo raid. The flight left the carrier Hornet early, but made it to Tokyo and bombed targets. Emmens was low on fuel and flew to Russia. The Russians held him until he escaped after 13 months.

Lt. Gen. Marvin L. McNickle, USAF-Ret.
Flying Cadet Class of 1937C

I completed flying school at Kelly Field in September 1937, and was assigned to the 94th squadron, 1st Pursuit Group at Selfridge Field, Michigan. A split-off was made soon after with a cadre of personnel forming up the 31st Group. My assignment was operations officer to the 39th Pursuit Squadron. Two months later I became the squadron CO. We were assigned P-35s, P-36s, P-40s and finally, P-39s, in that order. Following December 7, 1941, many rapid changes were made as more units were being formed up for the huge expansion underway.

The Group was ordered to Bellingham, Washington, where we flew submarine patrol along the Pacific Coast. Shortly afterwards, the 39th, 40th, and 41st squadrons were transferred as cadres to form the 35th Pursuit Group in the Far East. My assignment was to the 307th squadron of the 31st Group. We received P-39s and, after an intense period of long range operations using auxiliary tanks, received orders for our unit to prepare to fly to an overseas base. General Arnold countermanded this and directed that the 31st Group would be the spearhead for U.S. fighter units in the European Theater. Our unit was transported by ship to England, then on to Atcham RAF Base to fly Spitfire MK Vs with full U.S. markings.

I started flying with various RAF/RCAF squadrons on scheduled missions to gain experience. On August 1, the 307th squadron was moved to Beggin Hill RAF Base where my pilots flew regular scheduled missions with British and Canadian Fighter units. On August 19, the full squadron joined in the Dieppe raid, a port in north France on the English Channel. We flew in excess of 50 sorties. On August 25, we moved to Merston RAF Base in southern England to fly escort missions for B-17s and fighter sweeps.

U.S. Combat aircraft weren't on a par with the Luftwaffe ME109s and FW190s when America entered the war against Germany. Early on, General Arnold ordered some of the fighter pilots to fly with the British RAF to gain experience against the Germans while waiting for new American fighters to arrive. The Mk V Spitfire was a late model. It could hold its own in a dogfight with the German pilots.

In September I headed a team of selected pilots from the 31st and 52nd Groups plus 10 experienced RAF pilots. The mission was to assemble, test, and make ready new Spitfires and Hurricanes for the 31st and 52nd Groups. The team was also given the additional mission of air defense for Gibralter. We completed our work and all fighters were fully operational when we departed for North Africa.

I joined the 31st group at La Senia, Algeria, in February 1943, as Deputy Group Commander. When the group commander of the 350th was shot down I was reassigned as its CO. We were based near Algiers. In August 1943, I was switched to command the 52nd Group at Palermo, Sicily. In November, I moved the outfit to Corsica, assigning one squadron to Calvi on the north coast, with Headquarters and two squadrons at Borgo on the

East Coast, opposite the Island of Elba, Napoleon's first place of exile. We outflanked the Luftwaffe units, which proved very costly for them.

In July 1944, I received orders to return to Washington for assignment, concluding two years of combat duty throughout the European and North Africa Theaters. After serving in various staff and command assignments of the air force, I retired in August 1972 following 35 years of active duty since my graduation from Kelly Field.

Col. John R. Kane, USAF Ret.
Flying Cadet Class of 1932B

In July 1943, I commanded the 98th Bomb Group flying B-24 bombers. Toward the end of the month, more than unusual interest in our bombing practice became apparent. Also, the condition report of our B-24s and those requiring parts had maintenance working late at night. It was easy to sense that something big was under way. During the last week of July, other Group COs and I were called to a secret briefing. I was right about something big. We were going to bomb the Ploesti oil refineries. The round trip would exceed 2400 miles. My group would join up as the third element of the mass, low-level attack. I briefed my pilots and crews for takeoff on the morning of August 1. I told them it would take an entire army a year to fight its way up there and smash this target. We are going to do it in a couple of minutes with fewer than 2000 men.

As we approached the mountains, cumulous clouds and heavy rain required maneuvering and I was separated from the rest of the flight. It would disrupt the plan for the attack, but I decided to continue with my bombers to the target. As we approached Ploesti the sky was dark with what I thought was a thunderstorm. I thought it would cut visibility to the target. I picked out the two tall stacks at White Four, the target. Suddenly, everything but the kitchen sink began to rise from the ground at us. I dived behind a row of trees and told the men in the nose to stand clear. We had to shoot our way in. I lifted over the trees and opened up with the fixed front guns. My tracer streams glanced off the ground a mile ahead. I saw natural-looking haystacks unfold like daises, with guns spouting fire at us. On our right, a flak train moved full speed down the track with guns belching black puffs at us. They were shooting eighty-eights like shotguns, with shells set to go off immediately after they left the gun barrels. My nose guns jammed, and I yelled at Normen Whalen, "Clear the guns!" He yelled back saying I shot up all the ammo. That was 2400 rounds through the guns in less than two minutes. I could see now that it wasn't clouds over Ploesti, but smoke. The flak train hit my wingman, but he stayed with us. I took my flight down so low the flames singed the hair off my left arm. My co-pilot, John Young, yelled that number four engine was hit. I feathered the prop and increased power on the other three engines. The bombs were dropped on the target and I decided to call the other planes—low on fuel—and advise them to head for Turkey. After dropping our bombs, I turned away and headed into the German fighters. I felt like a crippled fish fleeing from the sharks. My co-pilot reduced power and I yelled why? "We have to save the engines," he said. "We'll save them after they save us," I yelled back. With full power, I could only make 185 mph. I couldn't hear anything from the turret gunner. My bombardier, Ray Hubbard, reported that he had shot all his rounds and was oiling his guns. Both Hubbard and I started laughing like crazy. It beats me why men will laugh under those circumstances, but, by glory, they do. The other gunners were busy with attacking fighters and I took five hits on the inboard engine and the underside of the right wing. The fighters were hanging on us like snails on a log. I decided to head south away from the high mountains and Libya was too far away. I got a heading for Cyprus and took three of the damaged ships along. I thought we could clear the lower passes of the Balkans. I still had to nurse it to 6600 feet so I told the men to throw everything overboard except the 'chutes. I learned later that we had destroyed half the productive capacity at Ploesti, but we lost 22 ships and crews. That made it costly.

Maj. Gen. Walter B. Putnam, USAF Ret.
Flying Cadet Class of 1938B

I completed military fight training at Randolph Field and Kelly Field in June 1938. In October 1940, the 20th Pursuit Squadron was ordered to the Philippines. I was operations officer and upon arrival at Nichols Field, learned the squadron would be equipped with P-26 planes. This was a definite set-back as this was a trainer type plane I flew at Barksdale Field two years earlier. In early 1941, the squadron received its first new P-35A planes, a decided improvement over the P-26, but not capable of close encounters with the Jap Zero. I was busy with my headquarters squadron and training flights with the lesser experienced pilots as new airfields were being created and older ones expanded. My first prewar contact with Jap planes occurred in mid-November 1941. I was making a flight over the harbor at Corregidor. As I circled a ship, I detected sunlight flashes above me. I immediately climbed to 10,000 feet, and identified nine Jap "Betty" bombers. With full throttle on, the P-35A couldn't catch them. On

December 6, 1941, General MacArthur placed all units on full alert. On December 8, the Japs attacked the Philippines. In the first day, a third of our fighters and half of the B-17s were destroyed. In the next few days, Clark Field was hit 33 times by Japanese bombers and fighters. On April 10, word reached us that a convoy of Japanese troop transports was sailing through the Strait of Cebu. I took a P-40E out for a look. It was a clear day and I spotted the main convoy steaming north. Off to the left I saw a plume of black smoke rising into the clear sky. I headed for it and saw a 10,000-ton troop transport with a dozen landing barges off-loading troops. I circled the ship and identified the Rising Sun flag. I turned and flew out a few miles as if leaving. I was under orders not to attack as the P-40 was required for reconnaissance. I also realized this would probably be my only chance to repay them for killing my friends, the sneak attack on Pearl Harbor, killing and torturing POWs, and other atrocities. I decided to attack and circled for a gunnery run on the transport and barges. I had six .50 caliber machine guns ready to fire and opened up with all guns firing on my first pass over the transport. I could see the tracers fly into the ship's hull. I pulled the P-40 around for a second pass and raked it thoroughly from the opposite side. As I pulled off, a motor launch headed from shore to the ship. I gave it a two-second burst. It split into pieces and sank. Since no serious return fire was coming back I decided to go after the barges. I lined up so any misses and ricochets would hit the ship. I dropped down low on the water and as I got in close, the guns were actually shooting into the barges and up into the ship. I could see the destroyers and escort cruisers moving in at top speed. As my fuel was low, and I was almost out of ammunition, I returned to refuel and reload at the Santa Barbara airport. I got an American mechanic to help me refuel and reload the guns. Then I took off and headed back to the convoy. The last troopship in a line of four looked like a luxury liner swarming with Jap troops. At 4000 feet, I turned out of the sun and dove in with all six guns firing. The troops were running around like chickens in a coop. I could see them shooting rifles and revolvers at me, but they just disappeared as my guns sprayed the deck. As I pulled up, the air was suddenly filled with black puffs and tracers, and I realized the cruisers and destroyers were in range. The concussion from bursting shells flipped me over and my ears were ringing. I stayed low for the next run with the troopship between the firing ships and me. I pulled up but dropped back down low over the wave tops. The armor piercing shells had destroyed the hull and the incendiaries started fires. I made one more pass and as I pulled up the ship exploded. I circled back around, raking the decks once more. As I pulled up two Jap float planes scattered, jettisoned their bombs and climbed for altitude. Then they turned and headed directly for me. I sighted one and gave it a direct burst, catching it dead center. It caught fire and started down out of control. The second plane turned tail and ran for the cruisers. I followed him and at 50 feet over the water gave a burst that set him on fire and he crashed into the sea. I pulled up and started one more pass on the troopship but my guns froze up so I returned to Santa Barbara. After landing we found 73 holes, but no artillery shell hits on the plane. That night I learned that two American naval officers had witnessed the attack and reported the ship went down and the two planes crashed. I knew I would probably get a "dressing down" but I gave the Japs a little of what we had been catching. My military training had taught me to destroy the enemy. This was a target of opportunity. I couldn't pass it by.

Brig. Gen. William R. Yancey, USAF Ret.
Flying Cadet Class of 1938B

In 1955 I was assigned to the Air War College Evaluation Staff, having just completed the school course. Shortly thereafter my old boss, General LeMay, called, instructing me to report to him at SAC headquarters. I arrived the next day. In his brusque manner he instructed me to report to the Air Staff in the Pentagon for a briefing; obtain a secret security clearance and return. After I complied, General LeMay assigned me to command a group of five hand-picked pilots, a navigator and a few logistic and maintenance personnel. We were based at March Field AFB. However, our "work area" was to be on a tightly secured dry lake bed several miles north of Las Vegas. Our mission was as follows: Test the U-2 aircraft and its reconnaissance equipment, determine its total capability and effectiveness as claimed by CIA Project Director Dick Bissell and Kelly Johnson, Lockheed company. Concurrently, train 45 pilots for CIA U-2 duty and, finally, train 15 additional pilots to fly U-2s for the air force. The U-2 was developed to fly over Russia, observe their development of a nuclear bomb, its delivery system, and type of ICBM under construction. Development of the U-2 aircraft came about because of the inability to penetrate Russian security. Requirements for the plane were: that it be subsonic, fly above 75,000 feet unarmed, single seat without ejection, and transport 700 pounds of payload. At that altitude it was believed the plane would be safe from current Russian jets and ground-to-air missiles. My job was finished by April 1956. The U-2 had proved its capabilities, and the pilot training was completed. I made my report to General LeMay and we flew to Washington to brief the Air Force Chief of

Staff and the National Security Council on the status of the program. Their recommendation to President Eisenhower led to the fly-over of Russia, starting in late 1956. On May 1, 1960, CIA pilot Francis Gary Powers was shot down, presumably by a surface-to-air missile, which detonated close by. The U-2 had been flown for three years and one month with impunity. Flights over China and other areas continued. The U-2 program was built in secrecy, trained in secrecy, and flown in secrecy. During the testing and training period of 18 months, we flew widely-spread coast-to-coast missions over the United States, unintercepted by the Air Defense Command. There is little doubt that development of the U-2 airplane by Kelly Johnson and his fabled Lockheed "Skunk Works" for use during the Cold War will continue to astound all who research its accomplishments.

Lockheed

The U-2 reconnaissance plane gave the U.S. vital photos of the Soviet Union during the Cold War period. Developed to fly above 75,000 feet, the U-2 flew at the edge of space above the range of antiaircraft fire. Brig. Gen. Bill Yancey, Flying Cadet class of 1938B, was in charge of evaluating the plane and training of 45 pilots for the CIA and 15 for the air force.

Col. Wayne Thurman, USAF-Ret.
Flying Cadet Class of 1938C

My advanced training at Kelly Field in 1938 was in pursuit. By graduation we had been trained and qualified to fly all types of military aircraft. I was assigned to the 9th Bomb Group at Mitchel Field, equipped with B-18s.

From there I received orders to the aerial photographic school at Lowry Field. After graduation, orders took me to North Africa as CO of the 15th Photo Mapping Squadron. Completing my assignment to map an air route across Africa in B-17s, I was assigned to the 99th Bomb Group flying B-17s in North Africa. On November 2, 1943, at a mission briefing, my group was assigned to participate in bombing the enemy aircraft factory at Wiener Neustadt, Austria. On arrival at the rendezvous point, the lead Group had not appeared and several other Groups plus 50 fighters were circling. It was a long flight through an area of intense enemy aircraft and ground fire. Sensing indecision, and burning needed fuel, my group assumed control of the mission and proceeded on course with the 98 bombers and 50 fighters. The defense was intense but the bombers held their positions during bombing runs, and the fighters were superb in disrupting enemy fighter attacks. Later, we learned that the mission destroyed 50 percent of the plant's productive capacity of enemy fighters. Maj. Gen. Twining, Commanding General 15th Air Force, had kind words for the mission's crews, especially the bombardiers. On March 1,1944, I completed 50 combat missions and was rotated back to the States. I experienced mixed emotions on leaving, but departed with a great deal of pride and admiration for my outfit. Only those who have experienced it know the emotions entwined between combat crewmembers.

Just two days after my arrival, orders were received to report immediately to the Pentagon. I was assigned to the European Intelligence Section in the War Department General Staff. Ten months later, I was detailed as air officer to Gen. Thomas T. Handy, Deputy Chief of Staff, directly under Gen. George C. Marshall, Chief of Staff. The Pentagon was a pressure cooker that never cooled down from the time of arrival until the end of day. One either learned to deal with it or moved on. At the end of my tour, I was selected to attend the Armed Forces Staff College, then stationed briefly at Chanute Field. The Pentagon reached for me once again, and I was assigned as Secretary of the Air Staff under General Vandenberg, Chief of Staff to the new separate USAF. I remained for three years and was selected to attend the Navy War College. Then came a stint of two years as Chief Advisor to the South Korean Air Force. My final assignment was to the 4th Air Force as Inspector General. I retired from active service April 1, 1968.

This is a brief capsulated picture of one Flying Cadet. As a group of special people, we were privileged to serve our nation in the United States Air Force. In the annals of military history, I believe it fair to say that in the contribution to Air Power, our accomplishments have been truly remarkable.

USAF

Flack and fighters attack B-17s en route to a German target. On November 2, 1943, Wayne Thurman, of the 99th Bomb Group, was assigned to bomb an aircraft factory at Weiner Neustadt, Austria. Going was rough. On arrival at the rendezvous point, the lead group didn't appear so Thurman's group took control of 98 bombers and 50 fighters and proceeded on course. With excellent fighter cover, the bombers stayed on course and made the bombing runs over the target. Reconnaissance showed about 50 percent of the plant's production was destroyed. Thurman was a graduate of the Flying Cadet class of 1938C.

Col. Kenneth R Martin, USAF-Ret.
Flying Cadet Class of 1938A

During WWII, while leading my Group of P-51 Mustangs over Germany, I collided head on with a German Me-109 and was badly injured but managed to open my 'chute. I hit the ground hard and crumpled into a heap. Local farmers found me and took me to a small German hospital. The doctor did what he could with limited equipment and medicine. He set the broken arm and leg in plaster casts and sewed up the head wound.

He was unable to operate on the damaged foot, as it needed special equipment requiring a larger hospital. The burns on my face from being sprayed with hot engine oil were treated. After the anesthetic wore off, the pain was severe. It was difficult to converse with the German nurses and I could only point to where pain occurred. There was very little painkiller available, and the sedative given for sleep was ineffective. Later, they transferred me on a stretcher to Dulag Luft, the Interrogation Center at Frankfurt. It was winter, and I had to wait outside for transfers to other trains. Although the weather was cold and windy, it acted to reduce the pain I felt constantly in my neck and foot. The vertebra just below my neck was painful to touch and probably injured. They finally loaded me on a stretcher into a baggage car behind the locomotive. The train made numerous stops and starts and the jerking was painful. Piles of baggage were stacked around me, threatening to fall at every stop.

At Frankfurt, an ambulance moved me to the interrogation center. I was placed on a small narrow bed in a cell-like room, and the doors were locked leaving me alone. I had received very little nourishing food since the crash and felt weak and exhausted. My first real taste of nourishment came when an orderly opened the door and gave me a warm chocolate drink. It tasted good and warmed me inside. When morning came, a breakfast of ersatz coffee and two slices of dark brown bread arrived, as it would each morning for the next two weeks. It was difficult to swallow the dry bread, but if I didn't feed myself there would be little chance of leaving there alive. In addition to my injuries I was very weak and had lost considerable weight.

The first interrogator, a German sergeant, came in to question me. I was so sleepy it was difficult to follow his questions, and I finally fell off to sleep. I know it must have disgusted him because he left. During the day, my food consisted of a bowl of thin soup and a slice of dark bread for lunch and another cup of bitter coffee and slice of bread in the afternoon. The evening meal was a small bowl of solid food, cooked oatmeal with prunes, or boiled potato, peas or cabbage. I worked at eating the stuff, but I had no appetite. When I was finally released from solitary, my weight must have dropped 30 pounds. After several days, a doctor visited. I complained about pain and told him I didn't think the bones had been set properly. They appeared to be at an angle above the casts. I also told him about the constant pain and lack of nourishing food I needed to recover. He said nothing about the bones, but agreed to change the diet. It was changed that day: white bread was substituted for the dark bread, but it was easier to eat. On the 12th day following my arrival, they took me to a large hospital in Frankfurt. I felt extremely weak, and my vitality was at it lowest ebb. They X-rayed me, and when I got off the table I fainted. When consciousness returned, I was on an operating table with two doctors and a third man, whom I instinctively did not like. They gave me an injection and told me to count to 15. As I counted, I urged my brain not to answer questions about my outfit or its location. I could hear the third man asking me military questions. At the count of eight I felt myself slipping into unconsciousness, but repeated to myself "don't tell, don't tell!"

I don't believe I told them anything, as the interrogation later covered the same questions I had been asked before. After returned to my room— more like a cell—the effects of the anesthetic wore off. The doctor had re-set the bone in my arm, and there was less pain. The doctor came in after the operation and asked if he could help me. I requested a Bible and shortly after he left, a Red Cross Bible was handed to me. I turned to words I knew: *I am the Resurrection and the Life. He who believes in Me shall never die. He who believes in Me and lives in Me, though he be dead, yet shall he live.*

I read the verse several times, then slipped it under my pillow and went to sleep. The Bible was the first English written document I had seen, and the only thing to break the solitude I lived in. I decided nothing is fur-nished a POW except the bare essentials in the hope he can be broken and furnish information. I was promised better medical attention, good food, release from solitary confinement to join the other airmen, writing paper for letters to my wife, and incoming mail. I wouldn't accept any of these bribes for information. They also tried threats. A tough-talking man visited one day and advised I would be turned over to the Gestapo. He said they could do this because the Red Cross had not been notified of my capture. I was still an MIA (Missing In Action). I believed him. He was smoking and blowing the smoke toward my face. It struck me he was try-ing to tempt me, and for the first time, I started to laugh and laugh. I laughed so hard the tears ran down my cheek. I know he thought I was losing my mind, so he left. I could expect him back later. I stopped laugh-ing as I looked at the ceiling. Then the thought struck me again: he was trying to bribe me with cigarettes, and I never smoked tobacco in my life.

I decided to keep my mind busy, and set up a mental schedule. I re-viewed the different periods of my life. I thought about the decisions I had made and their outcome. I thought about my parents and my boyhood days, my wife when we were classmates. I thought about TWA and Ted Weed, and my year at Randolph and Kelly, my friends in those days, and wondered where they were now. With the lessening of pain in my healing arm and leg, my appetite returned.

Occasionally, a medical orderly smuggled an extra piece of bread to me, and I allowed no crumb to fall. The long nights were nightmares, as the British bombers were constantly hitting Frankfurt with 2000- and 4000-pound demolition and incendiary explosives. The hospital was emptied, as the staff took to the bomb shelters, leaving the POWs behind barred windows. The shattering concussion of exploding bombs shook the interrogation center on its foundation. I wanted to hide, but there was no place in that small cell. I knew that no report had been made of my capture.

Once the Red Cross was notified, they sent a weekly food package to each POW. It contained concentrated food, chocolate, coffee, one-quarter pound of sugar, a box of K2 biscuits, a can of Spam or bully beef, a can of fish, cereal and a can of dried milk, two other food items and cigarettes. Another Red Cross package contained pajamas, underwear, three pairs of socks, shoe trees, slippers, a pull-over sweater, toothbrush and powder, comb, razor, a pipe and tobacco, and a box of vitamin tablets. A pair of shoes and a GI overcoat were included. One day, a visitor was let in, and in excellent English expressed amazement I had not received my packages. He offered to get them if I would sign a small form. I couldn't read it and told him no thanks.

The orderly left his scissors on the table one day, and I hid them. I was thinking of trying to escape, and the scissors might help open the locks. I knew it was doubtful, but if I remained without food, I would die anyway. The orderly came in, and, as he was leaving, left the door open. He motioned me to follow. I thought this is it. Instead, he took me to a room on the third floor. I was finally released from solitary confinement and joined the other POWs.

Lt. Col. Jesse A Tobler, USAF-Ret.
Flying Cadet Class of 1938A

On the 10th of November 1942, the 60th Troop Carrier Group flew a mission of 1500 miles direct from Lands End, England, to Oran, French North Africa. I commanded the 12th Troop Carrier Squadron. The mission was to transport the 2nd Battalion of the 503rd Parachute Infantry direct to Oran. I was the lead flight with 12 C-47 transports. The mission of the paratroops was to take the airport at Oran, which was under French and German control.

During training, I was unaware of the mission purpose or destination. We trained in England, making short-field takeoff flights with full load. Our 12 planes were fitted with extra 150-gallon tanks, which were secured in the cabin. It would be the longest paratroop mission in military

K. Martin

In early 1943 Col. Ken Martin's 354th Fighter Group arrived in England with the new P51 Mustangs. They had the capability to escort bombers all the way to a target and back. This escort ability reduced bomber losses substantially. Martin, Flying Cadet of 1938A class, survived a mid-air collision with a German fighter, but was taken prisoner.

history. We were briefed the day prior to the mission as to its purpose, our route of flight, and whether the paratroops would be dropped or carried to a landing. If the airport at Oran was secure when we arrived, we were to land there. If not, we were to land on the dry lake bed at Sebcrat de Oran. The flight would be made under cover of darkness and, we all hoped, away from German air patrols. Weather en route was reported to be satisfactory for formation flight. Radio silence was maintained during the flight.

We took off and formed up proceeding on course to the target. At 2:00 A.M. I passed over Madrid and the city was all lit up. We did not expect interference with the flight over Spain. On arrival, I was advised the armored division had not yet secured the airport. I led the formation to a landing on the dry lake. Later, I was notified the airport was secure and to bring the paratroops in. On landing, we were fired on and waved off the

Toliver Collection

The C-47 flew missions virtually all over the world, hauling all descriptions of essential items to fight a global war. Jessie Tobler, Flying Cadet of the class of 1938, participated in an early mission carrying hundreds of paratroopers to North Africa. The 1500-mile flight was the longest undertaken by the C-47s. Supposedly the airport for landing had been cleared of French Foreign Legion troops, but planes were fired on while landing.

runway. I was told a unit of the French Foreign Legion was making an attack on us with old 1918 armament, and a battery of French 75s fired at us. The armored division eventually secured the area.

I learned later that we were a part of the North Africa Operation, Code Name TORCH. It started a military action in the North Africa area November 8, 1942. General Mark Clark made the first negotiations. He was brought into the area via submarine and landed at Algiers for protocol discussions.

Capt. Paul S. Wooley, Senior Airline Chief Pilot
Flying Cadet Class of 1932B

I was a member of the historic first class of Flying Cadets to complete basic training at Randolph Field in 1931. I was then transferred to Kelly Field for advanced flying, and graduated on July 28,1932. I was assigned to the 99th Observation Squadron, Mitchel Field, for one-year reserve duty. I skimped through the depression years of 1933 and 1934, finding work wherever I could. I was recalled to active duty at Barksdale Field and assigned to the 79th Pursuit Squadron, and later to the 90th Attack Squadron. One flight I've always remembered was demonstrating our attack with low-level parachute bombs against infantry troops before a large group of Japanese officers. In 1936, I applied for regular commission but was medically disqualified for hay fever.

I applied for pilot duty with Eastern Air Lines and was accepted as copilot. In June 1942, EAL started flying freight from Miami to San Antonio. Through a series of route shifts, I left Miami and ended up in Fairbanks, Alaska. The Japanese had made an attack on Dutch Harbor, and Alaska was declared a war zone. This meant all planes were, in effect, confiscated for military use. Through some fast-talking, I was able to get permission to fly back to Chicago to get the airplane winterized and, then to return. However, the night before returning, EAL had been given the South American run. I was assigned to Miami for the flight to Natal, Brazil, and remained on that run, flying C-46s, until 1945. I continued flying for EAL until 1956. I joined on with Seven Seas Airlines flying the Atlantic and Pacific runs, and living in Amsterdam and Luxembourg. Later I signed on as Chief Pilot for Panama Aeronautics, and delivered a Constellation to Buenos Aires. I made two cattle trips between Buenos Aires and Vichey, France. After checking out the crews, I signed on with a Flying Club, operating a Constellation as Chief Pilot for the next two years. We made exotic trips to Europe, Japan, Hong Kong, Panama, Peru, and Canada, taking my wife with me. In 1968 and 1969, I flew as Chief Pilot for a cargo company, transporting cattle to South America. One route was to Rabat, Morocco, and non-stop to Miami. It was almost a 17-hour flight. In the Connie it was an easy flight, a fabulous plane, reliable and easy to handle. My flying career was concluded flight testing a guidance system for ICBM missiles. It combined radar and laser beams that could drop them on a dime. My last flying was completed in 1974, with no regrets, except I've always missed military flying. The reason for disqualifying me for hay fever was unfortunate. It certainly never bothered me during the next 38 years of flying throughout the world under all conditions.

Col. William J. Feallock, USAF-Ret.
Flying Cadet Class of 1938A

I departed the United States for duty in the Philippines, arriving on December 5, 1940. I was a member of the 17th Pursuit Squadron, flying

P-40s. Our outfit was stationed at Nichols Field, Manila, approximately 40 miles south of Clark Field. After we got our planes, it took sometime to get them cleaned up from the ocean trip. The machine guns had been covered with Cosmoline, a heavy protective petroleum coating that was very difficult to remove. A dogfight with Japanese Zeros, after they attacked the Islands, almost cost me my life.

Before the Japanese attack on the Philippines, fighter units there were equipped with P-40 aircraft like this. On that day, fighter pilots were on patrol or waiting for takeoff. Their planes had been shipped from the States to Philippine bases aboard ship and their guns covered with Cosmoline to protect them from seawater. Difficult to remove, the Cosmoline caused Bill Feallock's guns to misfire when he had a bead on the Japanese Zero leader. Two other Zeros jumped Feallock, Flying Cadet class of 1938, who fortunately managed to bail out and return to base.

I was on a patrol flight over Nichols and Camite when we encountered eight of them. I had the leader in my sights ready to fire but the guns were jammed from the Cosmoline. I was jumped and started maneuvering by diving to a lower altitude, hoping the warmer air might free up the guns, but it didn't. I could see bullet holes all over the plane and more coming in. I heard them smack against the protective armor plate. The next thing I knew the plane was on fire. I opened the canopy, but that made the fire worse, and I closed it. I decided it was time to bail out or blow up with the plane. I jumped, but there wasn't enough altitude for the chute to open. My P-40 went down ahead of me and blew up. The blast of air opened my streaming 'chute and saved my life. I had been hit and my ankles were injured. After they patched me up, I returned to duty on crutches and was assigned to duty with General Southerland, General MacArthur's chief of staff. Just before Bataan fell to the Japanese I was assigned a seat on a LB-30 (B-24 type) plane departing for Australia. I was on it.

Maj. Gen. George Benjamin Greene, Jr. USAF-Ret.
Flying Cadet Class of 1938A

I was graduated from Randolph Field and Kelly Field in 1938, received my wings, and was appointed a 2nd Lieutenant in the Air Corps. After Pearl Harbor was bombed, I was assigned as squadron commander of the 35th Fighter Squadron, flying P-39 fighters. My squadron was soon ordered to the South Pacific. We were transported via the freighter *Maui* to Australia, a distance of more than 4000 miles. Our planes had been crated and shipped to Australia. It was a long trip, and we were on the constant look-out for submarines. Below decks, it was smelly of oil odors and garbage. Refrigeration was limited, and we ate dried vegetables, canned Spam and powdered eggs. After arrival, we were stationed in Australia and operated under the Australian Air Command. It was a very confusing situation, eventually straightened out by the arrival of senior American officers. A combat problem for us was the .37mm cannon on our planes. It would fire only three or four shells, then quit firing. This was unworkable against the Jap Zero. It was solved when we were equipped with the P-400, a P-39 type with the .20mm cannon. It would fire until we hit the target. The .20mm shell had enough power to destroy the Zero. We moved to a base on the south end of New Guinea to attack the Japanese bases on the west side of the island. I quickly learned that we could not maneuver with the Zero. Our tactics were to get above them and dive, picking up speed to pull back up for another shot. It was effective and we got our share of enemy Zeroes.

Constant rain drenched us. Slogging through the mud from tent to mess tent to the operations tent to the makeshift latrine kept our feet wet and our spirits low. The rain grounded us often. The growing number of Zeros, and their increasing attacks on our base concerned us. The Japanese intended to take Port Moresby and control shipping to and from Australia. The big battle over Port Moresby took place in the Coral Sea. It was a battle of American and Jap Carriers. The Japanese hope to use Port Moresby as a naval air base was eliminated. It marked the beginning of defeat for Japan. Using the .20 mm cannons against the Jap Zeros was successful, and our forward bases in New Guinea were growing. This substantially limited the hope of the Japanese to prevent Australia's efforts to assist General MacArthur. I was ordered back at the end of my tour. I wanted to stay but I was underweight and suffering from fever.

Bell

The advanced P-39 "Aircobra" became the P-63 "Kingcobra." In the P-39, a 37mm cannon was fired through the hollow crankshaft. Its gun would stick after firing a few rounds. A new version, the P-400, fired 20mm rounds with more success. Maj. Gen. George Green, Flying Cadet class of 1938, commanded a P-39 squadron in New Guinea.

Maj. Gen. H.A. Hanes, USAF Ret.
Flying Cadet Class of 1939C

I was assigned as Director of Flight Test Center at Edwards Air Force Base, California, in 1953. It was an opportunity to test-fly the latest air force combat fighters, bombers, and cargo aircraft. I test-flew all century series fighters from the F-100 through the F-106. The bombers test-flown included the B-52, B-57 and B-66. Cargo types tested included the C-23, C-130 and C-133. Test flight was made to ascertain the aircraft system's functions and reliability when placed under stress, and response of the controls and maneuverability of the aircraft in high G-load conditions. We also conducted special testing of isolated systems. In the final analysis, the purpose of flight test was to determine the ability of the aircraft to meet the demands and requirements of its mission. In addition to the assigned test work, I took advantage of the opportunity to fly two experimental aircraft, the Bell X-1B and the X-5. It was an adventure into the future. I established the first supersonic speed record on a measured course in the F-100C. In 1955, I was honored to receive both the Thompson trophy and the Mackay Trophy.

Bell Lab

Loading research aircraft required a method of positioning it into the mother plane. Here, a method utilizes hydraulic lifts to raise the EB-50A above the smaller Bell X-1B and move it into a secure position. In 1953, H.A. Hanes, Flying Cadet class of 1939C, was director of the Flight Test Center at Edwards Air Force Base

Maj. Gen. Marvin C. Demler, USAF-Ret.
Flying Cadet Class of 1932A

After completing engineering courses at New York University School of Aeronautics in July 1931, my appointment as a Flying Cadet was in the first class to graduate from Randolph Field. Our arrival at Randolph Field marked the beginning of a flying training program that had been on the agenda of the Air Corps since Billy Mitchell first set the direction for air power and strategic bombing. From Randolph Field I was sent to Kelly Field for advanced training. On graduation, I received my wings and commission in the army air corps. It was a distinct honor to have been a member of that first Randolph Field class. Receiving my wings fulfilled a goal I worked hard to achieve.

During WWII, I was involved in two programs that I believe had great importance for the development of future combat aircraft and the conclusion of the war. During the period from 1942 to 1944 I was assigned as the Project Officer in HQ army air forces, for the development of the first American jet engine. It was used in the P-59A fighter aircraft to produce the first American jet aircraft. It antiquated the reciprocating engine. We were aware of the advancement in jet engines by the Germans and the

British. I continued my work in developing gas turbines for future air force aircraft. In 1944, Col. R C. Wilson and I were sent to the highly classified Los Alamos Laboratory of the Manhattan Project where we were briefed on the atomic bomb development. We were then directed to establish and monitor the secret Silver Plate Project for delivery of two atomic weapons by the 509th Bomb Group (B-29). The highlight of my career was overseeing the air force laboratories during 1962 to 1967, while commanding the Research and Technology Division of air force systems command. I was proud to be honored by presentation of the newly authorized Air Force Distinguished Service Medal on November 14, 1967. Technology developed by the 8th Air Force Laboratories under my command assisted the rapid and sound improvements in existing weapon systems and provided a sound basis for future weapon systems. In 1969, I was assigned as Assistant to the Chairman, Joint Chiefs of Staff for Arms Control, until my retirement on November 1, 1971.

Capt. John Sidney Templeton, AAL
Flying Cadet Class 1934A

I started my aviation career in 1928 working for the Swallow Airplane Company and TravelAir Company. In 1930, I entered Purdue University

USAF

In 1944, the highly classified Los Alamos Laboratory of the Manhattan Project was a part of the development of the atomic bomb, which at the same time saw development of the secret "Silver Plate" Project of the 509th Bomb Group to prepare for delivery of the bombs. Delivery would be by two B-29 aircraft and crews trained to carry one bomb each. Marvin C. Demler, Flying Cadet class of 1932, got the assignment for "Silver Plate."

and graduated with a degree in Civil Engineering. I entered the army flying program at Randolph Field in 1933, graduating from Kelly Field in
1934. My assignment was to the 2nd Bomb Group at Langley Field. In
1936, I made application for regular commission and was physically disqualified. The army doctor said I had tuberculosis and a short career.
Later that year, I applied for a job with American Airlines, was accepted,
and made my first flight as co-pilot in a DC-2. In 1940, I was promoted to
Captain and in 1942 started military contract flights for Air Transport
Command. The route was from New York to Natal, Brazil, across the
South Atlantic via Ascension Island to the Gold Coast Colony in Africa,
Flying C-87s (B-24). From there we carried military personnel and mater-
ial across central Africa via Kano, Maiduguri, and Khartoum to Aden,
then Masira Island and Karachi across central India to eastern Assam
Province. During latter stages of WWII, I flew C-54s from New York,
transporting personnel and cargo via Newfoundland and the Azores to
Paris and Scotland. When the Korean conflict began in 1950, I was assigned to fly DC-4s via Honolulu, Wake Island, Kwajalein, Guam, and
Midway, transporting war cargo once again. I returned to domestic flying
on DC-6s, DC-7s, and in 1959, checked out in 707s. Back to military air
transport in 1966 flying personnel and cargo to Viet Nam. I retired in
1969, having spent 30,000 hours in the air, much of it for my country during war conflict. I hope that doctor who kicked me out of the army air
corps in 1936 reads this.

Lt. Gen. Joseph H. Moore, USAF-Ret.
Flying Cadet Class of 1938B

On December 8, 1941, I was sitting in the cockpit of a P-40B at Clark
Field in the Philippines. I commanded the 20th Pursuit Squadron and my
pilots were sitting in their cockpits awaiting orders to take off. The
Japanese made their attack on us around 1230 Hours with a mass attack
by bombers and Zeros. I immediately signaled my pilots to take off. My
two wingmen followed me into the air to attack departing bombers.
Instead, we encountered nine Zeros and began maneuvering in a dogfight. My wingman shot down the first Zero to be downed in the
Philippines. I got two others. We quickly learned a hard lesson: the P-40
could outgun and outrun the Zero, but could not dogfight with it. Later, as
the invasion grew and our air power was spent, my squadron became infantry troops and was ordered to defend a section of the Bataan Coast on
the China Sea. The Jap forces were attempting a landing behind our front
lines. Assigned and designated as the 71st Provisional Infantry Battalion,
my squadron manned that beach position, fighting as infantry troops for

six weeks. We were then relieved and sent to operate the landing strip at Mariveles. Although the attack date on the Philippines was December 8, 1941, it was the same day as the attack on Pearl Harbor. Time of the attack was varied because a fog over Formosa grounded the Jap planes.

On the day the Japanese attacked the Philippines, Joseph Moore, Flying Cadet class of 1938, waited in his P-40 and when the attack came he got into the air and shot down two of their planes.

Brig. Gen. Dorr E. Newton, Jr. USAF Ret.
Flying Cadet Class of June, 1939

I was graduated from Kelly Field in 1939 and assigned to the 19th Squadron, 18th Pursuit Group, in Hawaii for a tour of duty. In October 1941, I completed that tour and returned to the States. I was the last Air Corps officer to leave Hawaii before Pearl Harbor was attacked. Those remaining were either frozen in place or sent to the Philippines with B-17 units. My new assignment was Luke Air Force Base in Arizona. In August 1942, I was given secret orders to proceed to England on the Queen Mary. On my arrival in England, I reported for duty with the 12th Air Force Headquarters. My assignment was in the A-3 (plans and operations) section to assist in the preparation for the invasion of North Africa. I participated in the invasion, assigned to 12th AF operations.

Upon completion, I was assigned to the 27th Fighter-Bomber Group as deputy commander and subsequently as commander. We were equipped with A-36s, then P-40s and P-47s. I flew 92 combat missions over North Africa, Sicily, and Italy. While on patrol over Anzio, we attacked a

Luftwaffe ME 109 unit. During the ensuing battle I shot down two ME 109s. I was promoted to Colonel in 1943 and given a short leave in the States. I returned to Italy as A-3 for the 12th Tactical Air Command, directing the air activity of four Fighter Groups; 2 Light Bomber Groups and the French Air Force, for the invasion of southern France and Germany. At the conclusion of the war I took the surrender of German Fighter Gen. Adolf Galland, commander of the Luftwaffe's English Channel coast fighter command. Galland had been promoted to General of the Fighter Arm at the age of 29. I made plans with his liaison officer for his pilots to fly their two squadrons of the ME-262 jets from Austria to Frankfort where we could hold them, but the liaison officer was shot down flying back over U.S. lines. The jets were then destroyed. After the war, I continued my service until retirement in 1967.

USAF

The P-47 Thunderbolt operated in Europe, North Africa, and the Pacific. The 27th Fighter-Bomber Group was equipped with Thunderbolts and based in North Africa, Sicily, and Italy. The wings and fuselage of this P-47 have the black and white marking of the English Channel invasion force. At end of WWII, Dorr Newton, Jr., Flying Cadet of class of 1939, accepted the surrender of German Fighter General Adolph Galland.

Capt. Peter Wiltjer, United AirLines
Flying Cadet Class of 1939A

I was graduated from Kelly Field in 1939 and stationed at Scott Field. That year the Air Corps offered permanent commissions in the regular army. I was disqualified physically. I made application with United Air Lines and was hired as co-pilot. In 1942, a selection of 50 pilots from all airlines was made to form a Special Air Mission, stationed at West Palm Beach on June 1, 1942. I was selected by UAL as a Captain for the mission and transferred to St. Joseph, Missouri, to train ferry crews flying the overseas route. After a year, orders came in transferring me to National Airport, Washington, DC. During 1942 and 1943 I flew short-haul missions assigned by the military, some of them for Vice President Wallace and other dignitaries. During the next 18 months, I was stationed at Casablanca. Supplies from incoming ships were flown to Algiers, Cairo, Tehran, and Delhi, India. As injuries increased from the war, we were assigned to fly hospital ships using the C-87 and C-54s to transport the casualties for medical evacuation.

During this time, a mission named Triangular Bombing was set up. It called for flying from London to the target, then to Russia for landing and refueling. A second bombing target would be hit and the flight then continued to Italy for servicing. From Italy a third bombing target would be hit and the planes returned to London. Unfortunately, the eager Russians, seeking to please, parked the B-24s in one long line on their airport. The Luftwaffe observed the operation and, when the planes were in perfect alignment, destroyed 40 of the bombers in a single strike on the Russian Base. That type of bombing was concluded by mutual agreement with all countries involved. We received orders to pick up the ground crews from the Russian and Italian bases. With the proper controls, the idea of bombing and continuing on to a closer base could have eased the fueling problems of long-range missions.

In early 1945, we received orders to prepare for the Crimea Conference with Roosevelt, Stalin, and Churchill. In February the three men met at Yalta, a town on the Black Sea in Russia. Our unit set up flight operations to notify the Russians when the official flights were expected to arrive. Also, a large number of support flights arrived to bring the essential equipment for security needed for the meeting. Equipment had to be moved from the airport to the small town of Yalta. It was a significant event. The three most powerful men in the world on that day met together in a face-to-face conference. Afterwards, many believed Stalin had been given too much with respect to the Russian war contribution. The

J. Wilson

The B-24 flew in many capacities, including carrying cargo and as a medical evacuation plane. Peter Wiltjer, Flying Cadet of the class of 1939, was disqualified from military service on medical reasons but assumed a job with United Airlines. When WWII broke out, Wiltjer and many other airline pilots were called on to fly various missions. While in North Africa he flew the C-87 hospital version of the B-24.

arrangements and support given by our operations section enhanced the conference in a location ill-equipped for the historic meeting. At the conclusion of the conference our operations section was ordered back to Casablanca. On V day, I took off my Major's leaves and returned to my United Air Lines uniform. I continued to fly DC-4s, the DC-6, and then jets. I retired in 1974 as an active Captain. Having suffered no physical problem during my career with United, I've often wondered about the decision of that doctor who denied me a regular commission in the military service in 1939. However, in reviewing the activities during the war years, I believe my contributions were helpful and supportive.

Col. Ancil D. Baker, USAF Ret.
Flying Cadet Class of 1937B

The Cold Weather Test program was set up by Wright Field to determine the effects of cold weather operations on military aircraft. In places where warfare might take place, problems of engine lubricants congealing without the support of sheltered heat could degrade both attack and defense efforts. It was essential that units be able to meet mission requirements with their assigned aircraft regardless of where they might operate. All components, including power systems, engines, instruments, heaters, navigation and communications, would be tested for their ability to provide normal operations during extreme cold weather conditions. Much was learned from Bush pilots and airline operators. Their system was the obvious: drain oil after flights, remove batteries, and pre-heat engines before starting. During our study of seals and hoses, we found the neoprene superior during cold temperatures. Rubber hoses would become stiff and snap like kindling wood. Our first heater units were plumber torches, which were gradually improved to become sophisticated diesel-burning units. Some of the work was a trial and error mode, eliminating what wouldn't work. Wright Field engineers flew in now and then with projects for research. All this, of course, required reams of paper work describing test work and results in detail. As our work progressed, so did the load.

With war declared, we received B-17s, B-24s, B-25s, C-54s, P-40s and P-38s. My work became specialized in four-engine testing, although I

36th B Sq

Cold weather test programs called on the skills of Ancil Baker, Flying Cadet class of 1937. Started at Wright Field, the project moved to Ladd Field in Alaska at the start of WWII where it included B-24s, B-17s, B-25s, C-54s, P-40s, and P-38s. It was essential to examine and test the effects of cold weather on all instruments, accessories, and armament as well as aircraft.

kept my hand in on the smaller types. In 1947, I was transferred to Eglin Field to command the Climatic Hangar Squadron. It provided sophisticated test instrumentation for gathering and recording test data at any selected temperature. The early work concerning operation of military aircraft under cold conditions provided much assistance to units stationed in cold zones during the war. It was not my choice of wartime duty but essential to help solve the problems of cold weather operations for those responsible for mission performance.

Col. Marvin S. Zipp, USAF-Ret.
Flying Cadet Class of 1938A

During the Cold War, when an attack by the Soviet Union seemed a distinct possibility, it was determined that some type of early warning system of any such activity should be provided. This led to establishing warning stations across Alaska, Canada, and Greenland. Obviously, this was not an easy requirement in consideration of the vast terrain—some unexplored—and the extreme cold weather conditions.

Five radar stations would be built between Sondrestrom Air Base and Angmagsalik on the east coast of Greenland. The U.S. Army proposed to tunnel the Greenland Ice Cap, lay rails, and transport freight with electric trains to build the radar stations. The plan was to utilize a Swiss Tunnel Borer, acquired by army transportation corps. The borer was already there, having been shipped by freighter to Thule Air Base to build huge storage caves in the ice cap. The army had been successful in that project. The radar stations were to be located at sites above 10,000 feet, and manned by personnel of the Danish government.

The high altitude requirement posed questions about moving the building materials to the locations. Prior to this development, the Air Corps had been making ski landings on the ice cap with C-47 aircraft, assisted by Berndt Balchen and other pilots. When the Army announced the plan in 1955, I suggested to my commander, Gen. Glenn Barcus, that the Air Corps could provide the airlift. I outlined my methods for the project and it was approved. I was detailed to organize and actively determine the feasibility of my proposal.

Orders were sent to Narsarsawak Air Base rescue squadron to transfer a ski-equipped C-47 to Sondrestrom Air Base. There, the C-47 was equipped with a JATO (jet assist takeoff) bottle in case it was needed at the high altitude for takeoff. Polyethelene coatings were ironed on the skis to reduce friction drag. The JATO bottle was attached and used in a practice takeoff with excellent results. Five landings were made, starting at lower altitudes on the cap. The final landing and takeoff were at the high-

82nd AB

The C-47 was the camel of the desert, a workhorse over water, and a cargo and paratrooper carrier throughout the world in WWII. When an early-warning radar system was needed during the Cold War, Marvin Zipp, Flying Cadet class of 1938, used the venerable C-47 to lift equipment into high, snow-covered areas above the 10,000-foot levels.

est elevation of 10,000 feet. All were successful. I was able to take off in the C-47 without jet assist. The Danish Liaison officer planted the Danish flag in a ceremonious declaration and thanked the United States for the assistance rendered. Subsequently, 18 battle-weary "gooney birds" were provided with skis and experienced crews. Air lift of the radar stations in pieces and parts were soon assembled at the 10,000 levels and placed in operation. The DEW line (Distance Early Warning) was established to provide radar early warning of aircraft approaching the United States coming from Russia during the Cold War.

Col. Robert N. Maupin, USAF-Ret.
Flying Cadet Class of 1938A

When WWII started I was stationed at Hamilton Air Base (California) in January 1941 as operations officer with the 18th Pursuit Squadron, 35th Group. Orders transferred the outfit to Elemendorf Field, Anchorage, Alaska. Our P-36 planes were flown to Sacramento Air Depot and prepared for sea shipment because we didn't have sufficient flying range to fly them there. The wings were taken off and loaded on sleds with the fuselage, then a very liberal coating of Cosmoline was applied to protect the metal from sea salt. They were then shipped to the San Francisco docks and loaded onto the freighter *Chirikof*. The squadron personnel embarked and we sailed under the Golden Gate Bridge, bound for Seward, Alaska.

As a member of the Flying Cadet class or 1938, I flew cross-country to Barksdale Field, Louisiana, home base for the 20th Pursuit Group and posed nonchalantly on a P-26 Boeing pursuit fighter.

We arrived several days later and disembarked during a snowstorm at Seward. Our P-36 planes were unloaded and placed on flat railway cars. Pilots and other personnel were loaded into the passenger cars and proceeded to Anchorage. We arrived several hours later, in a driving snowstorm with temperatures of 10 degrees. It was the first pursuit (fighter) squadron to be stationed in Alaska. The next morning, we took a look at the airfield. One runway had been completed, the hangar was a skeleton with a dirt floor, no glass in the doors, and no heater. The Cosmoline was frozen and hard like a rock. Mechanics used a mixture of steam from a resurrected steam jenny and gasoline to clean off the Cosmoline. Five days after our arrival I flew the first P-36 into the frigid skies over Alaska. It was still winter, and daylight lasted for only about 3-to-4 hours. We soon learned that Alaska was neither friendly nor forgiving to careless pilots.

Col. Joe G. Schneider, USAF-Ret
Flying Cadet Class of 1934B

In the months preceding the Japanese attack on Pearl Harbor, I was assigned to the 73rd Bomb Squadron, stationed near Seattle. In early 1941, the squadron was ordered to Elmendorf Field, Anchorage, Alaska. On February 18, 1941, I flew to Elmendorf Field in advance of the squadron.

At that time, no coastal air route existed between Seattle and Anchorage to provide necessary refueling stops. The inland route required flying from Great Falls, Montana, to Calgary, Fort St. John, Watson Lake, White Horse, and into Fairbanks. It was a very difficult route, requiring weather and visibility conditions for VFR (visual flight rules) because it lacked necessary navigational aid. The squadron was equipped with B-18 medium bombers. This aircraft had been the mainstay of the Air Corps in the midthirties but worthy only as a training plane, not capable of combat.

When I arrived at Elmendorf Field, the runway was 5000 feet long and 60 feet wide. There were no hangars ready. The only facility was a hangar shell without doors or windows and no heat. It was snowing and the temperature hovered near the low 20s. A few buildings had been erected near what would become the hangar line. They could house essential hangar facilities for the time being. No control tower had yet been erected. The only other facility was the municipal airport, which was for small aircraft. A low-frequency range was the only navigation aid available. It was very clear that the big job ahead would be to build up the facilities for use, not only at Elmendorf but throughout Alaska, including the Aleutian Chain. Very little possibility existed that units could be ready for combat until facilities were constructed and equipped. Fortunately, I had completed three years with the airlines before going on active duty with the Air Corps. As such I had some knowledge of the latest equipment, weather phenomena, and instrument flying.

Preparation for flying activity got underway at a fairly rapid rate, considering the cold weather. The Canadian government was completing a military-type airport on Annette Island (also called Metlakatla), south of Juneau. The Corps of Engineers was constructing an airport at Yakatat. Both facilities were located on the west coast of Canada and staged at intervals of 500 miles. Thus, short-range fighters and other types could fly to Alaska via the coastal route. The building of airports along the Aleutian Chain would prove to be very difficult. Many of the islands are formed from extinct volcanoes, and the surface material is porous, volcano ash, sand, or tundra. The engineers solved much of the problem using pierced-plank steel matting, interlocked and laid over the base. At Adak, they constructed a tide gate and used huge pumps to minimize flooding runways. However, during the rainy season, water covered the main runway. I was active in providing aircraft to the engineering crews during much of the airport construction and admired the speed of completion for needed facilities. As a pilot I could appreciate their professional work.

USAFA

This B-17, named the "Dutchman" is in for a complete check and no one praised the work of the ground crews more than the pilots who flew the planes. Joe Schneider, Flying Cadet class of 1934, called the B-17 "excellent for bombing and bad weather flights" that he flew against the Japanese.

Col. Raymond F. Toliver, USAF-Ret.
Flying Cadet Class of 1938C

Although my advanced course had been in pursuit, after completing the military pilot course at Randolph and Kelly Fields I was assigned to the 9th Bomb Group, Mitchel Field. The limited military budget made a drastic cut in flight time to four hours per month. I didn't believe I could learn much or maintain credible flight proficiency. Flying was my future, so when TWA airline offered a job, I considered it an opportunity to build flying time and gain valuable instrument-flying experience. I began logging about 75 hours per month flying DC-3 and the four-engine Boeing Stratoliners as First Officer (co-pilot). My crew Captain was a high-time pilot who gave me the benefit of his experience. In 1941, TWA was forced to cut back its flight operations and that meant less pay and reduced flying hours. The lend-lease program to help England with supplies became law. Canadian Pacific Railroad Air Service (later to be the Atlantic Ferry Organization) was hiring experienced pilots to ferry Lockheed Hudson planes across the Atlantic for military use by Great Britain. Pilots would be paid $1000 per month. The New York agent took my application and sent me to Montreal. It wasn't a soft job. The Atlantic route from Montreal to Gander, Newfoundland, then to Prestwick, Scotland, nonstop took about 11 flying hours. During winter, heavy storms and icing weather occurred in that area. Navigational ground aids were scarce and instrument equipment in the planes was limited. We were required to have a navigator in the crew. However, at that time, they had limited experience. I decided to take the course in celestial navigation and use a co-pilot in place of the navigator. I made two trips without difficulty. On the third flight, bad weather forced a one-week delay at Gander. Finally, the flight was scheduled for takeoff at five-minute intervals. The forecaster recommended we fly at 10,000 feet where we would have a 30-knot tailwind. A 60-knot tailwind, however, was reported at 14,000 feet. A little clear ice was forecast at the mid-point of flight on to Prestwick. My training with TWA led me to doubt a "little" clear ice. I made out my flight clearance at 14,000 feet. This was objected to but I pointed out the difference in tail wind and I was the pilot and accepted responsibility. The other two pilots accepted the lower level as recommended. At 14,000 feet I was in the clear. The other planes, at 10,000 feet, were on instruments in the soup. Although I suggested they join me, it was ignored. Five hours into the flight, a full moon appeared. Moments later a shimmering vapor mist appeared in the moonlight, falling from an absolutely clear sky. It appeared to fill the sky between me and the moon. It was a warning of clear ice. I notified the crew and worked the props back and forth to get hot oil into the prop domes, and set them at climb rpm. Power was increased by six or seven inches of mercury increasing airspeed about 40 mph. At that moment we slammed into clear-ice, encountering violent turbulence. It lasted a short time, but we lost about 60 mph of airspeed. Then it became calm. The windows and fuselage were iced over. Wind friction began to melt the ice on the side window and I shined the Aldis Lamp onto the left engine and wing. I was amazed to see solid ice extending from the fuselage to the engine. Ice covered the cowling and extended out on the arc made by the prop. The plane was carrying a heavy load of ice. Soon friction started to melt the ice and huge chunks began breaking off, some striking the tail. It could do serious damage to the tail, but nothing happened. I instructed the radio operator to notify the other two planes to climb above the clouds as we had passed through the ice. There was no response, but a message was intercepted from one pilot advising both engines were dead, forcing him to ditch the plane in the ocean below. Then another message was heard from the other pilot with the same problem. Both planes and crews were lost. In March 1942, I returned to duty in the Army Air Corps.

Maj. Gen. Winton R. Close, USAF Ret.
Flying Cadet Class of 39C

On December 7, 1941, I was flying a B-18 en route from Miami to my home base at Boringquen Field, Puerto Rico, and listening to the music from a commercial radio station. It was suddenly interrupted as the station announcer informed his audience that the Japanese had bombed Pearl Harbor. One month later I was in Cairo, Egypt, passing through on a survey mission for the Atlantic Ferry Command. After that, I returned to heavy bombers and all my future assignments were, in some manner, connected to bomber planes. In the period 1943 to 1945, I commanded a B-29 squadron in India, China, and the Mariannas. We were engaged primarily in missions over Japan. I commanded the 678th Bomb Squadron, 444th Group. We were part of the 58th Wing during 1943,1944, and 1945. Most of our later missions were firebombing Japan, operating out of Tinian Island. After the war, I commanded the 98th Bomb Wing during the Korean action, stationed at Yokota, Japan. I commanded the 100th Bomb Wing, equipped with B-47s, in 1958, at Pease AFB, Portsmouth, New Hampshire, and the 321st Bomb Wing (B-47) at McCoy AFB during 1959 and 1960. After that, I commanded an air division consisting of a Wing of B-47s, a Wing of KC 97 Tankers, and an Atlas ICBM Squadron at Plattsburgh, N.Y., 1960-1962. In between commands, I was assigned for two tours at the Pentagon, and a tour at SAC Headquarters as Director of Plans. I consider myself fortunate to have been assigned to flying units for much of my 30 years of service.

Col. Donald S. Dunlap, USAF-Ret.
Flying Cadet Class of 1935B

When Japan occupied Kiska Island in 1942, the tiny 11th Air Force had the job of sending its handful of fighters and a few B-17s on a round-trip of more than 500 miles to stop construction of a runway and buildings. True, it's a tiny island resting between the Bering Sea and the Pacific Ocean, but it belonged to Uncle Sam. Naval intelligence believed it could become a naval base and staging area for Japanese attacks on mainland Alaska. If so, it could seriously hamper General MacArthur's efforts in the South Pacific.

Short-ranged fighters of the P-40 and P-39 class could barely fly there and back, let alone do combat with Zero fighters. P-38s improved the situation later. B-17s had adequate range but the frequent low-cloud cover and intense anti-aircraft fire prevented accurate bombing. As a flight-leader of B-17s I decided to try a new method of attack similar to the hedgehopper. We went in a few hundred feet off the surface, behind a ridge of hills that prevented detection from the Japanese main base. Once in position, we flew single-file through the draw of a box canyon, joined up and dropped our incendiaries and demolition bomb load on the seaplane hangars and center of the main buildings from 100 feet altitude. We

A B-17 taxis into maintenance area for badly needed inspection. Oil streams from the outboard engine and the left tire is saturated. Mechanics had difficult times keeping their birds in top condition because of the demands for flying missions, In the Aleutians, Don Dunlap, 36th Bomb Sq. and Flying Cadet graduate of class 1935B, utilized B-17 as fighter to make low level attacks on Japanese hangar and planes on Kiska Island.

then did an abrupt 90-degree turn to the right in formation and flew due west across the narrow neck of land in back of Kiska Harbor. We stayed low through the valley and out to sea. I pulled up into a gentle turn traversing a wide arc back across the north end of the island. I wanted confirmation of the hit. It was good. Most of their planes were afire and a smoke ball was rising over the target. I waggled my wings and we headed for home. Mission completed and all crews safe.

Col. John W. Weltman, USAF Ret.
Flying Cadet Class of 1939A

I was graduated in the class of 39A. On December 1, 1941, I was at Fort Wright, New York, to pick up my wife and return to Selfridge Field. I led the 27th Pursuit Squadron over the North Atlantic to England and later to Africa. In early 1943, I was made Group Commander of the 82nd Group. The Flying Cadets moved up in a hurry, and in July 1943, I made full Colonel. At the beginning of the Korean conflict I commanded the 51st Fighter Wing.

Maj. Gen. David M. Jones, USAF Ret.
Flying Cadet Class of 1938B

My military service started in 1936 when I entered active duty as 2nd Lieutenant in the 8th U.S. Cavalry at Fort Bliss, Texas. I liked horses, but airplanes fit my spirit more and in 1937 I enlisted in the army air corps as a Flying Cadet. My best dreams couldn't create the adventures that were ahead. My first impression of Randolph Field has never changed: it's pure beauty. Those of us lucky enough to become officers and military pilots look back fondly on the training and lifelong friendships that enriched our lives and outlook. In 1942, I volunteered for a highly classified mission led by a great pilot, Jimmy Doolittle. The B-25 medium bomber was selected for the mission. We met Colonel Doolittle, who briefed us that it would be a dangerous mission; one for volunteers only. At Eglin Field we practiced short-field takeoffs under the watchful eyes of a navy pilot. We concluded it would be a carrier mission. After our training flights, we flew to Alameda, California, where our planes were loaded on the navy aircraft carrier *Hornet*. Not until the second day at sea was it announced that Tokyo would be our target. The plan called for a takeoff 400 miles out from Japan. We were spotted 800 miles from the target and made our takeoffs for the first time from the pitching deck of a carrier. The B-25 performed perfectly. After sighting Japan's coast, I selected secondary targets, due to poor visibility. The first was a large fuel storage, which the bombardier hit setting off a huge fire and smoke. The next target—a power plant—was knocked flat. Then a large, flat-roofed manufacturing building was hit with the incendiary bomb, causing huge flames to shoot up followed by explosions. The last bomb was dropped on a tall office building, but only a portion of it was hit. Daylight was fading and I turned southward, heading for the southern tip of Japan. We arrived 50 minutes ahead of our ETA and set course for China across the China Sea. With a good tailwind, I stayed VFR underneath some stormy weather. As we made landfall in China, I went on instruments. Expected signals from navigation aids were not coming in. The navigator, using dead reckoning fixes, set a course for Chusien radio beacon. I could still see the terrain. We couldn't receive the radio beacon signal and fuel was low. I fired a flare and could see rocky hills. I decided we had better jump. I told the crew to get ready. With the controls set, I followed the crew. I pulled the ripcord, hitting the ground almost immediately, tumbling down the slope in the dark. I grabbed a tree to break the fall and clung to it for dear life. I was cold, tired, wet, and exhausted. I awakened at dawn, took off my shoes and wiped my feet with the chute. My kit had a pair of clean socks, which I put on, then started slowly down the rocky slope. As I reached the small valley below, I came face to face with some Chinese farmers. I drew a picture of a train and they led me to the railroad station. I met up with Colonel Doolittle and completed a wrap-up of the Tokyo raid.

Back in the States, we were given our choice of new duty assignments. I picked the 12th Air Force commanded by Maj. Gen. Jimmy Doolittle. I admired him as a leader. My new duty with the 319th Bomb Group would take me to North Africa flying B-26 Martin Marauders, a fast but temperamental plane. On November 8, the Group departed England for La

Cenia, an airport five miles south of Oran, Algeria, with P-38s flying escort. Operation Torch was launched that morning. It was a significant effort: 120 transports, supported by fighting ships, landed 107,000 troops along the North African Coast. On December 4, our target was Bizerte, Tunisia. A Luftwaffe fighter base was nearby and heavy flak was reported in the area. I had a crew of seven, including my co-pilot, Sam Agee. Bizerte rests on a little bay of the Mediterranean Sea. I briefed my pilots to fly low to the target for surprise and to confuse their warning system. Just before reaching the target area, I pulled up sharply to 2000 feet and selected my target. We swept over the target but just before bombs away, the flak hit us hard. The right engine was hit, causing the plane to yaw badly. I held full left rudder to stay on target and yelled to drop the bombs. Agee slumped forward and appeared to be hit. My trim control, airspeed, and throttle controls were shot out. Losing airspeed, I shoved the nose down for better control. The beach was too rough to land on. I was at 1000 feet, losing altitude, and no place to land. Just ahead I saw two small hills close together. I guided the plane toward them, hoping to sheer off the wings. As I started between, I cut the switches. The wings were shorn off and we went sliding along on the belly. The fuselage held together and came to a stop. We got Sam out. He was OK. The bombardier was badly injured. We rigged a flap from a wing as a stretcher and started hiking toward the coast. A platoon of Germans stopped us with bayoneted rifles. I stopped and said, "Good morning, gentlemen, can you direct us to a hospital?" No response. Their commander indicated—with his rifle— for us to move. We did. At the Luftwaffe fighter base, the injured men were taken to a hospital. I never saw them again. I was bunked in with the Luftwaffe pilots and slept handcuffed to the bed. I was banged up and sore. I was soon transferred to Stalag Lust III, a German POW camp deep in Germany, and remained there until the end of the war. I helped dig a tunnel to escape but was transferred to another compound. Royal Air Force officers used the tunnel, but those who did escape were caught. With few exceptions their treatment was barbaric. After the war, I commanded the 47th Bomb Wing in 1952, and moved it to England. I returned in 1955 and served in many interesting and demanding capacities of the United States Air Force until 1964. I then became Deputy Associate Administrator for the Manned Space Flight at the National Aeronautics and Space Administration. Until my retirement, I served in command or staff capacities in support of the Apollo missions and the launch of America's first orbiting space laboratory.

USAFA

B-26 Marauders were hot, tough air machines engaging the enemy over North Africa, the European theater, and the Aleutians. Davy Jones, Flying Cadet class of 1938, flying in 12th Air Force under command of Gen. Jimmy Doolittle, led the 319th bomb group for attack on Bizerte, Tunisia. He flew into heavy antiaircraft flack that knocked out his right engine. With heavy foot and leg on the left rudder he held the course to bombs away over the target. He and copilot Sam Agee, Flying Cadet class of 1938, crash-landed the stricken plane and were captured.

James Webb, Former U.S. Secretary of the Navy

B-29s conducted almost daily raids against Japan. Among the young airmen, there was an abiding sense of purpose: If their efforts did not bring Japan to its knees, a long and bloody ground campaign would ensue.

It is difficult for Sweeney [pilot of the aircraft to drop an A-bomb on Japan] and others to comprehend the allegations by some historians that Japan would have surrendered without this effort, embodied in the recent controversy over the Smithsonian Institution's drastically scaled-back atomic bomb exhibit. In its original form, the exhibit downplayed the casualty estimates for a U.S. invasion given to President Truman prior to his decision to drop the bomb, provided more narrative space to anti-Asian racism in the U.S. than to the attack on Pearl Harbor, included only six sentences on Japan's nearly 10 years of aggression in Asia prior to the U.S. entry in the war, and showed 49 photos of suffering Japanese and three of Americans.

When asked about the exhibit, Sweeney may have spoken for a multitude who have had to endure the moral ambiguity of virtually every battlefield: "I don't need some '60s-type professor poisoning the minds of our kids about how terrible America was. Did any of these historians have the strength to make the decision that Truman had to make?"

By the time Sweeney took off to drop the second atomic bomb, we'd been fighting for more than three years to push back a Japanese military expansion that had conquered Korea, most of China, Southeast Asia and Pacific Oceania. Island by island, cave by cave, America and its allies had paid a heavy price to reverse this aggression.

And despite contemporary argument to the contrary, those who would be invading Japan if the war continued had no doubt that casualties would be immense. As Bruce Lee notes in his book *Marching Orders,* President Truman had been briefed to the effect that an invasion would mean 600,000 U.S. casualties in the first 30 days alone.

To preclude such slaughter, the U.S. military in early 1945 began a massive bombing campaign to break Japan's spirit and force an end to the war. Firebombs were dropped on predominantly civilian targets. "They'd run 16,000 pounds of napalm per plane," recalled Sweeney. "Hundreds of planes a night, for months on end. By August there was no reason to put the atomic bomb on Tokyo, Osaka or Nagoya. They were already reduced to rubble."

American leaders and citizens alike were strongly behind such bombings. But even after the first atomic bomb was dropped, Japan did not surrender. Just the day before Sweeney's flight, a strong faction in the military, led by Japan's War Minister. Gen. Korechika Anami, still wanted to fight one more great battle on Japan's main islands, regardless of cost.

Sweeney recounted that by the time they departed on the Nagasaki mission, he and his crew had been through nearly a year of rigorous, highly secret training. The 509th Composite Group—commanded by Col. Paul W. Tibbets, who piloted the first atomic bomb mission—was organized outside normal military chains of command, reporting only to the highest authorities. The mission was so classified that crew members were forbidden even to talk to each other about it. Upon arriving on Tinian, they were instructed to tell other airmen they were merely developing a new block-buster conventional bomb.

On the morning of Aug. 9, Sweeney took off from Tinian, banking over the island of Saipan, where some of the bloodiest fighting of the war had taken place. Because of bad weather, the mission's three planes flew over Iwo Jima, where more Marines had died than would perish in the entire Korean war. If the mission were aborted or they ran out fuel, they would be diverted to Okinawa, where the bloodiest battle of the Pacific had been waged. The dead there had included 150,000 civilians—more than the number of military deaths on both sides.

The mission became treacherous for Sweeney and his crew. Weather forced them from Kokura, their principal target, to Nagasaki, a secondary one. Once the bomb was dropped, fuel was so low that Sweeney canceled a damage-assessment turn over the city and headed for Okinawa, at the same time preparing to ditch in the sea. When Sweeney landed on Okinawa, he and his crew had been flying for 12 hours. "I was exhausted, physically and mentally." he recalled.

After the war, Sweeney combined running a business with a career in the Air National Guard. He rose to the rank major general before retiring in 1976. Sweeney has made few public statements regarding the atomic bomb missions, mostly due to his deference to Paul Tibbets. But as he looks back a half-century to the conflict that shaped both him and the world in which we live, those last few days of the war still rankle.

"People should spend more time talking about the Russians, who after a week of war moved in and took the spoil," said Sweeney, pointing out that Russia has yet to return the Kurile Islands to Japanese sovereignty. "We left whatever spoils the Japanese wanted and shipped more to them. We saved five times as many lives as we took, and then we rebuilt their country[1].

Gen. Horace M. Wade USAF-Ret.
Flying Cadet Class of 1938C

I received advanced training in bombers at Kelly in 1938, flying the B-4, B-7, and B-18. My first assignment from flying school was to the 7th Bomb Group, Hamilton Field, California. On December 7, 1941, we were poised for departure to the Philippines in new B-17Es. Instead, we flew four days on anti-sub patrol, then ordered to Davis-Monthan Field to pick up an LB-30 and proceed to the Philippines. I arrived in Java on January 12, 1942, where the 7th Bomb Group combined with the 19th Bomb Group in a joint effort to defend the Netherlands East Indies. When the fall of Java became imminent I received orders to fly British Sir Archibald Wavell and his staff from Java to India. While in India I joined the 7th Bomb Group when it was reorganized and in July 1942 was transferred with the 9th Squadron, 7th Group to the Middle East.

I was assigned to the Halverson Project flying B-24 missions against the Germans. The routine was to fly a mission, miss or claim hits on the target, take some flack or fighter hits, return to base and fly another bombing mission. In May 1943, I was reassigned to the States and to the

---

[1] Reprinted with permission from Parade, copyright 1995

USAF

B-24 crew waits for skipper. These made the first strikes in the European theater with Col. Harry Halverson's 23 aircraft. The Halverson group was the forerunner of the 9th Air Force. Horace Wade, Flying Cadet class of 1938, flew B-24s against the Germans.

War Department General Staff in 1944. In 1947 I was assigned to the Air Staff, then to SAC (Strategic Air Command) in 1948 to command a Bomber Wing, later an air division, and then a numbered Air Force. In 1966, I was reassigned to Air Staff as Deputy Chief of Staff, then to Commander in Chief, USAFE in 1968, followed by assignment to SHAPE (Supreme Headquarters Allied Powers Europe) as Chief of Staff. I retired from active duty as Vice Chief of Staff, USAF, November 1, 1973.

Col. Jack L. Randolph, USAF-Ret.
Flying Cadet Class of 1932A

I enlisted in the United States Army, 6th US Engineers, in 1930. My interest was in flying and I transferred to the Air Corps as a Flying Cadet in July 1931. I completed the course, graduating from Advanced Stage, Kelly Field, in June 1932. I was rated as Airplane Pilot and Airplane Observer and commissioned as 2nd Lieutenant, Air Corps Reserve. In 1936 I was commissioned in the regular army of the United States.

In 1944, I was assigned to the 15th Air Force in Italy, 463rd Bomb Group (H) as Deputy Group Commander. Subsequently, I was reassigned as Group Commander of the 449th Bomb Group (H). On June 26, I was briefed to lead a B-24 strategic mission. The target was the aircraft factory at Schewechat, Austria. We encountered intense anti-aircraft fire going in, over the target, and flying out. We received direct hits during the initial run, knocking out some instruments and our fuel lines. Fires burned in the nose and tail turrets. One gunner was killed and the other seriously wounded. The entire plane was heavily damaged from AA fire. It was essential that our plane hold its position for maximum concentration by the group over the target. Once clear of the heavy ground fire, I reformed the group while my crew worked to control damage and keep the plane flying. With their outstanding assistance, we cleared the area, eventually landing safely on an emergency strip. Intelligence photos later revealed heavy damage to the factory. On August 27, my group received a briefing to destroy a vital railroad bridge in northern Italy at Ferrara, approximately 25 miles northeast of Bologna. Prior to the initial run, we encountered heavy AA fire causing severe damage to my plane. As lead plane, I managed to hold my position, bringing the entire concentration of our bombs onto the target for maximum effect. Although my controls were damaged, it was possible to maintain controlled flight and lead the group away from the area. I landed the damaged plane safely at our base. Results of the raid revealed heavy damage to the railroad bridge. At the conclusion of my tour, I had flown 48 sorties for a total of 248 operational flight hours. Prior to my retirement in August 1961, I graduated from the Armed Forces Staff College and also the Industrial College of the Armed Forces.

Olin K. Haley
Civil Aeronautics Inspector, USA
Flying Cadet Class of 1932B

Upon completion of studies at North Georgia College, I found myself looking for a job and profession. The depression was just starting and jobs were scarce. Being interested in aviation, I applied for training in the Army Air Corps. I completed the primary course at Brooks and was sent to Randolph Field for basic, then to Kelly Field. My class graduated in 1932. I was assigned to the 33rd Pursuit Squadron, Langley Field. The military medically retired me with a burned retina. In March 1934, I met Bill Croswell, chief pilot for Curtiss-Wright, who checked me out in the Curtis-Wright seaplane in Colombia, South America. I remained with the Colombian Air Force as instructor until October 1937. I had hoped to fly with one of the airlines but my medical discharge for burned retina disqualified me. After returning to the States, I instructed pilots at the Park Air College at the Alabama Institute of Aeronautics during 1940 and 1941. I joined the Civil Aeronautics Administration (CAA) in 1941 as training assistant Aeronautic Inspector in the Western Region. Following the attack on Pearl Harbor, I was transferred to Reno, Nevada, to set up the CAA office there. Later, I received orders from Washington to go to Mexico and set up a commercial pilot training program. I remained there for five years as special assistant to the American Embassy, however, still assigned to the CAA. Upon conclusion of my duty, I returned to Fort Worth as Supervising Inspector in the district office. I remained there for 15 years, with a final 12 years at New Orleans as Supervising Inspector. After 33 years of service: one as Flying Cadet; one in the 33rd Pursuit Squadron; and the rest as a Civil Aeronautics Inspector, I retired. Regrets? Not really, I remained in aviation, my first love. Just wish I hadn't looked into the sun.

Lt. Gen. James V. Edmundson, USAF Ret.
Flying Cadet Class of 1938A

"Six churning and four burning" was a term used to report the operating B-36. This huge, long-range bomber was designed to fight across the

The B-29, left, is dwarfed by the B-36 Peacekeeper, which was conceived as a long-range bomber. Lt. Gen. Jim Edmundson, Flying Cadet class of 1938, recalls leading a group to test America's defenses.

Atlantic just in case the Germans took away England as our operating base. There was a distinct possibility that German submarines could cut off surface contact between America and Europe. Fortunately, this concern disappeared with the German surrender. With the advent of the Cold War, it was clear that the only way to attack the Soviet Union was with long air legs. The B-36 could do this. There were many models, but I flew the D and F with six Pratt and Whitney four-bank radial engines, and four jet engines hung in twin pods near the wingtips. Demands for operating excellence came from my boss, General LeMay.

One of the many missions to test our competence and readiness was an assignment named Upshot-Knothole. At 4:00 A.M. I launched in the lead plane with 14 others following, climbed to altitude, and headed for Davis Monthan AFB in Tucson. I received a block clearance from the Federal Aviation Administration air traffic control and established a bomber stream with each plane tracking the one ahead from half a mile behind and 100 feet above. On arrival, I checked in with the tower for clearance to land and closed our flight plan. Our landing pattern was at three-minute intervals. As each B-36 reached 500 feet, the wing flaps were retracted, landing gear sucked up, power applied, and a course set for Mexico at 500 feet altitude. We maintained radio silence. As far as the FAA knew we were on the ground. (SAC had a trusted tower agent on duty in the tower to make sure that facility didn't pass on that we had not landed.). We flew about 300 miles into Mexico to avoid Air Defense Command, then headed west until we reached a point 500 miles at sea where we took a northern heading. We were flying in a bomber stream at 1000 feet. At 10:00 that evening we reached a position off the coast of Vancouver Island. We then lit up the jets, turned southeast toward the United States, and began a maximum climb to 40,000 feet. We assumed a spread formation, with radar station keeping, remained under radio silence and turned off our running lights. Air Defense Command radar screens picked us up and identified us as Russians, but the Strategic Air Command had stationed one of their members who announced: "These are B-36s, see what you can do about it." When we hit our pre-initial point, each B-36 went after its assigned target. We "hit" Seattle, Bremerton, Renton, Tacoma, Portland and others. After a theoretical "bombs away," I went on the radio with instructions to turn on the running lights, and called FAA for a descent clearance back to Fairchild. We had hit all our assigned targets without intercept. Air Defense Command was very upset but General LeMay had learned the capability of one of his units to attack. The standard in-flight status report was: "Six churning and four burning." It indicated everything was going well on the B-36. Only the B-36s pilots could make such a report.

Author's note: The following article by Lt. Gen. James V. Edmundson was excerpted from the Air Force Association magazine July 1994:

> John Correll has never been better. He hit a three-bagger in the April issue, and that's pretty good batting in anybody's league. His editorial, Hawkish Moves, Dovish Means, blew the whistle on a whole bevy of "do-gooders" who are doing their best to send our military forces to the landfill. These are the same individuals who will yell the loudest when they want the military to do a job someday and the capability isn't there.

The decision that launched the Enola Gay [to drop the A-bomb on Japan] is a scholarly examination of the options available to President Truman to end the war quickly and save lives. During that time, I commanded a B-29 group on Tinian and, like General LeMay, I believed the war was won. We were just waiting for the Japanese to admit it. Paul Tibbets and I were flying-school classmates, and, when he arrived on Tinian with his 509th Group, I visited him several times, but none of us knew what he was up to until he'd done it. There is no question that the use of the bomb persuaded the Japanese to admit defeat months before they otherwise would have, sparing tens of thousands of lives, both Japanese and Americans. We were all proud of our President for having the courage to make a tough call, and of Paul and his outfit for doing their part in such a professional manner. The "bleeding hearts," who have belabored us since with the message that it was immoral to drop the bomb and that those who did it were monsters, are presenting a dishonest and distorted story. Mr. Correll's article about the distortion of history at the Smithsonian's National Air and Space Museum is a masterpiece. As an American who was stationed at Hickam Field, Hawaii, on December 7, 1941; who fought at such places as Midway, Tulagi, and Guadalcanal; who was returning from a strike on the Kidari Naval Arsenal on August 14, 1945, when the unconditional surrender was announced; and who led the formation of 500 B-29s that passed in review while the surrender was signed on the deck of USS *Missouri* on September 2, 1945, I deeply resent an agency of my government telling the American people that the war aims of the Japanese were more noble than those for which so many of my friends died. I don't really blame the Secretary of the Smithsonian Institution for promoting anti-American exhibits. After all, he is the product of his environment, and typical of some of the educated idiots who crawl out from under the wet rock of academia from time to time. The real blame rests on those responsible for placing him in a position where he could do so much damage. A big thank you to John Correll for bringing it out into the open.

Brig. Gen. Paul W. Tibbets, USAF-Ret.
Flying Cadet Class of 1938A

Author's note: The following excerpt is taken from *The Tibbets Story* by Paul Tibbets relative to his experience as a Flying Cadet at Randolph Field:

> For those who have had no experience with the old "tail draggers" as they were called, let me explain what a landing was like in those days. The idea was to make a three-point landing in which the two wheels and the rear skid touch the ground at the same instant.

Such a landing required judgment and coordination. To achieve one, you chop the throttle and aim for the spot on the field where you intend to land, maintaining a good, safe gliding speed during descent.

Near the ground, you pull back on the control stick. This slows the airplane. Ideally you reach what is called the stall speed, at which the airplane refuses to fly, when you are only a foot or less above the ground, whereupon the plane settles gently on the surface.

Two things can go wrong. If you fail to reach stall speed, you can fly the airplane into the ground. If you stall prematurely and run out of air speed while 10 feet or more above the surface, you drop suddenly to a hard and sometimes disastrous landing.

I developed the haunting fear that either of these miscalculations would wreck the frail airplane and wash me out of the air cadet program. George Slater (instructor) sensed this and decided one day to cure me of my timidity. As I came around for a landing, and started to ease back on the control stick for what would certainly be a mushy landing, the stick suddenly jumped out of my hand and the instructor's voice came through the gosport to my earphones.

"I'll show you that you can't hurt this damned thing," he shouted. With that he jammed the throttle all the way open and pushed the stick forward. The two wheels smacked into the ground with such force that I expected the whole airplane to collapse in a mass of broken struts and torn fabric with the hot engine ending up in my lap.

Instead the plane took a mighty bounce. We leaped up higher than the top of the hangar. My heart flew right up into my throat. At the top of the bounce, Slater didn't let the plane stall out. He simply gave it power and we started around the pattern again. I learned my lesson. The PT-3 was more rugged than I had thought. My next two landings were so successful that when we rolled to a stop after the second, the instructor climbed out of the cockpit.

"'Now, we'll see if you've really got it,' he said, waving me on for my first solo attempt in a military airplane."

Col. Victor L. Anderson, USAF-Ret.
Flying Cadet Class 1934B

During the Depression I had the flying bug. My chances of learning to fly were slim to zero. By luck I heard the Army Air Corps wanted Flying Cadets to train at its military flying center, Randolph Field. The course required a year to complete and graduates won their wings and a reserve commission as 2nd lieutenant. It looked like a real opportunity to get into aviation. I applied and passed the tests. My first flying was on the primary stage in small training planes, then I graduated to basic stage and flew much larger ones. After completing my training at Randolph Field, I was transferred to Kelly Field for the advanced stage and that's why I'm relating these facts.

It's a strange feeling. One minute I'm sitting in the cockpit, the next I'm sitting alone in the sky. It happened this way. I'm flying a P-12 pursuit (fighter) training plane at Kelly Field, Texas. My instructor has the lead plane in the formation and I'm flying the number three position on his left wing. The P-12, a single-seater, is an excellent trainer to fly, very responsive on controls for acrobatics and maneuvering.

We are flying at 3000 feet altitude. As he starts a turn to the left, my engine sputters warning me of low fuel. I reach down to switch on reserve fuel and fail to notice my sleeve catch the latch pin, unlocking my safety belt. The lead plane is increasing the turn and is almost in front of me. I quickly correct my position using left rudder and pushing the stick forward creating a negative "G" force. With my safety belt unlocked I shoot out of the cockpit into space. For a second I wonder what happened. Then I start falling. I quickly feel for the rip cord and pull it. For a moment I experience panic as the 'chute takes a few seconds to feed out. I feel a jerk and look up to see the billowing canopy above me. I hit the ground safely and my instructor lands his plane nearby to see if I'm OK. I assure him I am—just a little sheepish.

Col. William F Stewart, USAF Ret.
Flying Cadet Class of 1938B

I was graduated from Kelly Field with the class of June 1938. During the war I was assigned as Division Air Advisor, 101st Airborne Division. On the eve of the Normandy invasion I received a call from Brig. Gen. Maxwell D. Taylor, our commander, advising me to expect Gen. Dwight Eisenhower for a visit that evening. I was to act as escort in place of General Taylor who would be making the "jump" into enemy territory the next morning. General Eisenhower had indicated he wished to pay a visit to some of the troops who would be making the first jump. He arrived with his British aide and his driver, Kay Sommersby. They got out of the car and I started to introduce myself, but General "Ike" stopped me by

saying, "Hello, Colonel Stewart, I understand you will escort us tonight."
I saluted, saying that would be my privilege. He introduced me to his aide
and driver Sommersby. She was a British soldier and very pleasant. She
had the General's schedule and our first stop was at headquarters where
he stopped to visit with General Taylor. They spoke for a few minutes and
shook hands. When General "Ike" got back in the car he told his aide to
see that General Taylor received his second star immediately. The next
stop was Ramsbury where the 435th Troop Carrier Group was stationed.
On our way there General Eisenhower asked me where my home was
and where I had gone to school. I informed him I was from Kansas and
had gone to the University of Kansas. He said his brother Milton was the
school president and seemed pleased that we had that mutual contact. I
was aware that the General must have felt a great deal of stress as only a
few hours separated us from the initial Normandy landing, but he gave
no indication. He seemed at ease and very upbeat in attitude. There were
numerous newsmen and photographers trailing behind as we made our
stop at Ramsbury. General "Ike" stepped out of the car, saluted, and met
with the unit commander, and some of his staff officers and paratroopers.
The newspeople crowded around and were busy taking pictures and writing. I stood back with the aide and Kay Sommersby as General
Eisenhower spoke with the troops. He spoke with force so all the men
could hear and assured them of victory. He said it was a dangerous undertaking and every man had to look to his safety and that of his fellow
soldier, but they would be victorious. He then stepped back and saluted
all the troops and they returned it with gusto. Kay Sommersby had the
door open for the General. We got in and took off for the next stop at
Membury, where the 436th Troop Carrier group was stationed. When we
arrived it was necessary to climb up over a rice field to a bluff where the
men were assembled. Everything was high security and as we reached
the top, I saw a two-foot roll of barbed wire in place. I motioned to the
aide to come over and help me stand on the roll so the General could get
across to the men. With our weight the wire sagged down enough to step
over. General "Ike" spoke to the troops in an intense and down-to-earth
man-to-man manner. He said it's a tough mission for tough men and they
were trained to win. He reminded them that they were the pivot point for
those to follow and stick to the mission plan. On the way back, the
weather was overcast and I mentioned the difficulty in flying close formation and the added problem of long columns of C-47s taking off in the
dark and getting into position. General "Ike" looked at me and com-

mented, "The weather is as good as it's going to get." I had spent five memorable hours with the one man who carried on his shoulders the responsibility of his men, his country, and indeed the world, just hours before the battle would commence.

8

Quo Vadis

I N A FOREWORD to the book *The Next War,* written by Casper Weinberger, Margaret Thatcher, former Prime Minister of Great Britain, writes: *The only why of securing peace and freedom is to ensure that the peaceful, democratic states—at the core of which are still the United States and her allies—have military superiority over the aggressive troublemakers..*

With the cooling of the Cold War and the warming of Russia's interest in democracy, the United States and Russia seem to be headed in a non-nuclear direction. While Russia's dismantling of lethal weapons appears reluctant and lacking of real determination, a more worrisome problem has been her penchant for selling military hardware to China and small nations that covet the wealth of the United States. Military weakness invites boldness from such countries. Iraq is a good example. Several nations have access to powerful weapons. Efforts by pacifists, those with an anti-defense bias, or misguided critics of military readiness, form a ready-made center for propaganda and they use it. How much of our vital technology has been damaged through theft or destruction is unknown.

When technology is permitted to become dormant through a lack of funding, and the nation's security is dependent on that growing technology, the results can be compared to the French Maginot Line. Built before WWII, it was heavily relied upon by the French government to withstand attack on the eastern front of France. It failed to stop the German attack. Whether it could have been effective is unknown. Nothing had been done to update or improve it for years after construction, so it was bypassed. It is classified as wasted technology. We might be as guilty with our Strategic Defense Initiative (SDI), given the reluctance to fund it properly.

Defense technology cannot be stopped within its development unless a new and better technology is developed.

Since the beginning of the 20th Century, when the United States was concluding the Spanish-American War, we have been engaged in WWI, WWII, the Korean War, the Viet Nam War, and the Gulf War. We have been close to involvement in wars over missiles placed in Cuba, the Bay of Pigs, a skirmish over development of a strategic runway on the Island of Grenada, and assistance to England in its tussle over the Falkland Islands. The United States has sent Marines to numerous locations for announced short tours, which have turned into extended involvement. Our naval forces have been used to provide air threat for various problems, such as Taiwan and China, where we are committed to protect Taiwan. These "hot-spots" have the capability of expanding into real confrontations, critical to our reduced military units. Some have already resulted in death or injury to our troops, as in Africa. Others are ticking away.

With this military activity occurring during the 20th Century, leaders who are taking us into the 21st Century have seemingly learned nothing. Downsizing has reduced our forces to a shadow of their former military capability. It is doubtful that the two-hemispheric defense forces could be mustered, should they be needed to meet aggressive forces having missile and atomic weapons capabilities. Following the attack on Pearl Harbor, those responsible for the safety of our nation learned the difficult dilemma of arming ourselves to prevent further inroads from the attacker. In this re-spect the United States had no ability to prevent enemy-landing parties on Hawaii, had the Japanese chosen to do so, leading to its capture and becoming an enemy base. This would have presented a long-term effort of re-acquisition, with domination of the South Pacific by the Japanese. Probably, the battle of the Coral Sea would not have happened, leaving Japan to control Australia from New Guinea and Port Moresby. In addi-tion, only a few older military planes represented the air strength in Alaska. It would have been relatively easy to attack and control the naval base on Kodiak Island. The air bases at Anchorage and Fairbanks could have been bombed easily by carrier-based planes, rendering them useless for defense. Probably, in the most grievous mistake committed by the Japanese, the Japanese planners omitted these options. It is difficult to comprehend why such an armada would have been sent so far without a plan to support landing troops either at Pearl Harbor or Midway Island. Whatever the reason, the United States lucked out of a long and difficult effort to regain control of the Pacific Ocean area. Still, more than four and a half years were required to create a huge military and naval presence to ultimately end the war with Japan in September 1945. Many needless deaths occurred in our air force, our army, our Marines, and our navy due to the protracted effort required to subdue this small island community that is Japan.

Have we learned anything from that experience or the combination of military confrontations since? The record speaks loud and clear: downsizing following each buildup. Caspar Weinberger, former U.S. Defense Secretary, in his book *The Next War*, lists these salient points: the navy will have only 346 ships in 1999, the lowest number since 1938. The military strength will be cut by 33 percent in 1999. The air force is being reduced from 34 fighter wings required to maintain combat strength for the 10 wings utilized during Desert Storm, downward to 21 wings. The question is, of course, where will replacement pilots come from? With the malaise that exists today concerning their future, talented pilots are looking elsewhere. During the 1930s, pilots were procured from the volunteer Flying Cadets who, in 1941, provided the nucleus of officer/pilot personnel around which the air force could build its new squadrons, groups and wings for combat during WWII. There is, however, no longer a Flying Cadet replacement program.

Seeking pilots from the Air Force Academy might be wishful thinking. Lead time to train an F-22 or B-2 pilot might require years due to restrictions placed on qualifications by squadron commanders. When funds become limited, so does availability of the airplane for flight hours. When the B-17 was first delivered to squadrons, it was mandatory to spend 50 or more co-pilot hours before checking out as pilot could be considered. Many requirements of test questions concerning the functioning and operation of the various systems had to be answered. If they weren't correct, more time would be required in study. During the early years of WWII, after attending a multi-engine school, pilots could check out with less than 10 hours co-pilot time. It was not unusual for more experienced pilots to read the flight manuals, make a few landings with the instructor, and be cleared as first pilot.

Of greater concern for today's pilot is the huge investment made in the airplane. The cost was $50,000 each for the P-51, one of the most effective fighters during WWII. Today, the cost has skyrocketed into the multimillions—much more for the B-2 bomber and F-22 fighter. Of course, the fighters and bombers of today far exceed the combat capability of older planes, with the caveat that any new weapon will, in time, meet the response of an adequate defense. The atomic bomb might be the exception.

Pilots in today's air force can only look to an ever-increasing use of public funds for domestic programs. During 1937, some of the newer pilots of the Air Corps were advised to seek other means to build flying time, the fund for fuel was depleted. To maintain their flying careers, some resigned to join the airlines. There is the possibility that the same thing can happen once more as funds are removed from the military budget. One concern is the gradual elimination of Senators and Representatives who have had military service and understand the necessity of maintaining adequate military strength. Gutting the military budget is not new, and there are few constituents demanding explanations. However in today's world, more than the United States is involved. As the most powerful nation, we are looked to for the maintenance of stability in the world. Without it, smaller nations can only look on helplessly when their markets collapse and credit is destroyed. Or worse, small countries might be occupied and looted, as many were by the Japanese in WWII.

The time to stop this activity is before it begins. Can this be done? Yes, but only when the mistakes of the past are not repeated. Recalling events of the 20th Century makes it crystal clear that almost every mistake of the past is repeated: we engage ourselves in a war, spend huge sums of money to equip and train soldiers while the pathetic force we have is trying to hold the fort against superior forces. In the process they are killed, mauled, and taken prisoner to be starved and reduced to humble begging for food and water. If there is any doubt of this, refresh the memory with the Bataan Death March that occurred in the Philippine Islands in 1942. A numerically stronger force of Japanese soldiers attacked, destroyed, or captured the pitiful remnants of sick, starving American soldiers. Soldiers whose leaders in Washington had placed in harms way.

Did it happen again? Yes, five years later when the decision was made to save the south Koreans from the communists in the North, aided and abetted by China. A small American force was again committed to war. Air force support was not available as the fighter planes of WWII had been chopped up and sold for scrap aluminum. This time, the Air National Guard was called upon to commit its weekend warriors and trainer P-51s to battle the North Korean and the Chinese pilots who were equipped with Mig jet fighters made by Russia. The inferior American planes held their ground until the F-84 jet was ready. As in the Philippines, the price was high in lives, paid for by outgunned pilots flying old P-51s.

The question arises as to whether the United States can always count on being able to use its giant resources while mobilizing. It's very doubtful. Wars are no longer fought with rifles and cannons and transports moving personnel and equipment through the air and on the oceans. Ballistic missiles and weapons of mass destruction have reduced distances and time for defense preparations, making it impractical to mobilize and even reach the battlefields. The ability of mass destruction might preclude wars beyond the threat and the action phase.

The military defense created by Ronald Reagan, plus the very competent and elite military force of professionals, displayed its capabilities and effectiveness during the Gulf War. Coupled with the towel thrown in by the Russians, Americans reacted at first with pride and pleasure. It was a testament to the training, organization of troops, and air power. Then, the inverse reaction set in. The man most responsible, who carefully managed the preparation, action, and finale, plus the cost allocations, was dismissed from office. Since then the politicians have wasted little time in carving out huge hunks of the defense budget. And, if the predictions are correct, more and more will be cut.

The populace, however, probably concluded that with the end of the cold war such an elite force was not needed. Once this idea was conveyed to the politicians, a field day was in the making. But, mistakes were made that might become costly. The Gulf War was almost a perfect paper-exercise. The enemy officers were bound by a leader who made stupid decisions, shot off his mouth too much, and allowed the enemy to bring in all its forces without retaliation. He sent his army into combat without air support and seemed determined to fly planes out of the country. He also permitted practically all the enemy air support to be located near the battlefield where it could continually harass his own forces. All in all, the exercise was a good field test and valuable lessons were learned, but it's not likely it would happen again. It required years of dedicated planning and training of an elite volunteer organization, from private to general, razor sharp, equipped with modern equipment, and led by tough, competent leaders to reach readiness for the Gulf War. Air power was available in depth, assuring air superiority and scoring major hits on selected targets at will.

That force no longer exists. It was as though the American people watched, applauded as they would a July Fourth celebration, then turned their backs to engage in the more mundane tasks of making money and taking vacations. Next, the downsizers appeared. Military and naval facilities were closed and reduced, air power was drastically cut, with reserves used as replacements. Resignations and disappointment decimated the all-volunteer force of proud men and women over broken promises of military careers. As strength was cut the caliber of volunteers dropped. No longer are the enlistees the elite of American youth. The effort to utilize the services for social experimenting has been damaging to all military and naval services. Civilian leaders have stood mute as these experiments have been carried out, afraid of media backlash. In addition, the leadership from Congress has been quiet over the continued use of special Marine forces as world United Nations' peacekeepers. This has drastically reduced their efficiency as a front-line fighting force. The result has been an inability to secure top volunteer replacements through recruitment.

World-wide responsibilities

Pentagon funds have been used to pay for United Nations' peacekeeping functions in Haiti, Bosnia, Iraq, and Somalia. This is totally outside the military budget requirement for national defense. Also, environmental expenses are being charged to military preparedness. With the end of the cold war and collapse of communism in Russia, nuclear weapons were thought to be of no major concern. Yet, the Russian arsenal of nuclear weapons is still usable and pointed at America. With the fluidity of policy and weakness of Russia's intransigent government, our leaders are ignoring the risk that exists. There are others just as deadly and destructive: biological and chemical devices capable of mass destruction in selected areas bringing to a total halt all activities; terrorism, concentrated in domestic air and ground transportation systems, without limitations; existing global conflicts in former Yugoslavia; the Middle East and Persian Gulf; the Korean peninsula, and disputed China Sea territories. Rogue governments such as Iran, Syria, Iraq and Libya are backers of extreme terrorists, and seeking development or purchase of nuclear devices. China is considered to be the world's leading exporter of technology for weapons of mass destruction, including nuclear missiles. Russia, with its internal problems and need of funds, cannot be dismissed as a supplier. India, in constant dispute with Pakistan, exploded a nuclear device and continues its long-range ballistic missile program. It must be remembered that what exists today in the arsenals of the world powers, large and small, drastically changes without announcements. Unfortunately, this also holds true for the terrorists, and there is no moral or conscience-judgment restraint that governs their decisions or determination.

Before striking, terrorists need the weapon and assurance of success. They depend on secrecy and absolute control. It is, therefore, essential that terrorists be known throughout world agencies, their activities monitored, and plans crippled by informants, thus preventing their success.

Nations depend on their security forces, working together, to ferret out these warped terrorist extremists whose purpose is to use disorder as a political weapon. An unexpected event that will work to favor terrorist activities is the new lease given to Panama Ports Company, a Chinese Company that has been granted a 25-year lease on the ports of Cristobal and Balboa, plus an option for 25 more years. These ports, at opposite ends of the Canal, control traffic through the docks. While all elements of the lease have not been made public, it does specify piloting services, tugs and other boats required for canal passage. Other companies, such as Bechtel International, were refused the right to bid on both Cristabal and Balboa ports. Also permitted is the transfer of the rights to piers and facilities to an unspecified third party.

The Panama Canal Treaty was promoted by then President Jimmy Carter in 1977. It was negotiated with a protective clause, which provided for the Panama Canal Commission to control the roads and other parts of the Canal for security purposes important to the United States. Some measures of the lease appear to be in conflict with those arrangements and have not been explained. As the lease stands, it provides a monopoly over canal shipping. U.S. Ambassador William Hughes states he received a copy of the lease, after it was signed. Action to be taken by the administration has not been announced concerning security measures, and assurance that the canal would be open, as before, to traffic sailing on the high seas. The lease is scheduled to be activated in 1999.

Of concern is the Panama Ports Company, a trade name for Hutchinson Wampoa of Hong Kong. It is owned by Li-Ka-Shing who has business ties to Beijing. In 1999, the Port Authority will be replaced. Security of the Canal has existed under its control. Appointment authority will then rest in the hands of the Panama president. There is no assurance that appointments won't be political or nepotistic in practice, with no requirements for security of the Canal, or use of it. Selective control of maritime traffic passing through the Canal, for political or purposes contrary to the security of the United States, is possible. There is nothing that will prevent establishment of a foreign military presence in the Panama Zone, disguised as a security force. The Panama Canal has long been identified as a potential target for terrorists' activities. For those unfamiliar with it, the Canal provides for transition between the Pacific Ocean and the Atlantic Ocean. As such, its usage bears heavily on the financial impact on shipping companies moving cargo and passengers through it. There is no mention of transition for U.S. Navy transfers.

Another area of concern is the Middle East and the oil-rich countries of Iran, Saudi Arabia, Iraq, and Kuwait. The major shipping lanes through the Persian Gulf, Red Sea, Mediterranean, Caspian Sea, and the Sea of Oman, are vital to the movement of oil to the Atlantic Ocean, reaching all parts of the Globe. The Gulf War was about a "bully" country taking the oil of a smaller one. No other commodity would have produced the resultant gathering of arms for war. The Gulf War was a field exercise in logistics, moving personnel and war arms to a battlefield under the auspices of the United Nations. It succeeded under the most favorable of conditions. It denied a stupid bully the right to his unlawful acquisition of property. The property was a big pile of sand of no value, but beneath it rests huge reservoirs of oil. Fortunately, few lives were lost. It represents, however, the lengths to which human beings will go to protect a product that is vital to a quality of life we have provided.

For many years the Saudi government has been friendly to the United States. However, health and age limit the present ruler. The new King might not be as friendly to the United States as in the past. In that event, the United States would no longer retain its position of influence in the Middle East. Iran and Iraq are not friendly to the United States. It is known that Iran has acquired highly sophisticated weapons of destruction from China and Russia. More will be added. The Gulf War, pursued with honorable intentions, created tensions among the Arab countries and Persian Iran. Many view it as an intrusion by Christian forces. They are well aware that the military forces used no longer exist.

Executive personnel at the top level of government should have a military background. Important decisions of a military nature should be accurate. Our sparse military units are spread around the world, some in dangerous locations. They are in danger wherever they might be posted, because adequate backup does not exist. To obtain the best persons available, military promises were made—and broken. Efforts to socialize the military and naval units have resulted in an internal confusion, creating distrust and derision in the ranks. In addition, charges taken against highly skilled personnel in matters of social gender problems—having no relation to military fitness or qualifications—provide for zero replacement of the skills of those careers cut short. There is no gain in simply assigning the assistant as replacement. Invaluable expertise in military experience is lost, as are huge amount of funds and years required for training. It requires extreme caution.

Our lack of defense should not return us to the position of pre-Pearl Harbor. The dependence on sophisticated weapons must be proven and reliable to protect us from attack. Long ago, this nation relied on the "two-ocean" theory of protection. Pearl Harbor proved that theory weak then, and it would be even weaker today. Too many countries and privateers have the weaponry capability to seriously undermine the essentials for this country to safely protect its citizens. That must be underwritten by the sworn obligation of its leaders. It was forgotten before World War II, causing great damage to its installations at Pearl Harbor. The United States could be pushed to defend itself today against such weapons. In Russia alone, the number of nuclear bombs with transport capability in the wrong hands, could destroy our viability of life. We have nothing but promises to destroy those nuclear weapons, and there is no assurance who will control Russia tomorrow. We have an unenforceable agreement that might not be honored. Unlike Pearl Harbor, any attack must be repulsed and the enemy destroyed by defenses.

Where will America go?

Quo Vadis asks: Whither Goest Thou? The 1700 Flying Cadets, who volunteered their lives to their country, learned to fly in old crates and dedicated themselves beyond duty—to honor! Their quest to fight and win, at all costs, is over. To the new volunteers, whomever they might be in the 21st Century, the gauntlet is passed. Former Flying Cadets of Randolph Field never failed the task. In 1934, flying outdated military planes with no communications system and no deicing equipment, they flew the airmail through the night during the worst of winter storms and delivered it—on time—for morning distribution. For the first time the Air Corps was given command of its own destiny, and tasted the sweetness of success. Within a short time, it would fight the enemy all over the globe: the South Pacific, the Philippines, Aleutians, Europe, North Africa, China, Ploesti, Tinian, and Japan, Wherever the enemy appeared, the fighters and bombers were there, always leaving their calling card with the imprint from their country—*freedom will survive!*

In a flight toward the future, Gen. Ron Fogleman, USAF-Ret., poses the question: *Where are the air power advocates to lead us away from frivolous argument toward honest, truthful debate? What is so different today from the 1920s and 1930s when the birth of modern air power was midwived by courageous pioneers? In fact, there is an eerie similarity. Though we may not need a new Billy Mitchell, destined to die a martyr's death while labeled a zealot, we do need new torch-hearers to cast light on the single most important fact of any warfare debate—air power, properly used, is dominant, decisive and indispensable in war. And if you don't believe it, try fighting without it.*

Information is, and always will be, the essential ingredient for defense or actual warfare. Preventing its loss to spies or eavesdropping can be the catalyst for winning. During activity there must be an ability to counter the enemy with exploitation, deception, and disruption of the information systems. During these periods we must simultaneously prevent leakage of our own systems. Information, at its best, should be analyzed and activated for commanders quickly and decisively, otherwise the advantage is lost. The ability to furnish an accurate and integrated layout of the battlefield, revealing possible targets of opportunity, friendly forces, and possible enemy threats, is invaluable for decisions within a planned order of surveillance and precision-strike platforms. Such technology is assurance for victory.

In a speech, Lt. Gen. David L. Vesely, headquarters USAF, reported that the military is in the process of transitioning to space as the high frontier. He said the stunning successes of Desert Storm in areas of navigation, weather, surveillance, missile warning, and communications, illustrate the capabilities that space offers to the military services. Information is now capable of being transmitted from space into aircraft cockpits. He advised that space is already linked to military operations on land, sea and air. Operations that now focus on air, land and sea will eventually migrate into space. It charts a course that will take the military beyond this transitional period into the future where dramatic changes wrought by technology will be the norm. Most importantly, this nation's devotion to air and space power will continue to provide the strategic perspective and rapid response the nation will need as it enters the 21st Century.

It would appear we should no longer think in terms of air power, but instead think in terms of Space Power, as in United States Space Force.

9

Medal of Honor: Flying Cadets of World War II

MEDAL OF HONOR

CARSWELL, JR. HORACE SEAVER

Major, United States Army Air Corps, South China Sea, night of 26 October 1944. *Citation:* After taking the enemy force of 12 ships escorted by at least 2 destroyers by surprise, he made one bombing run at 600 feet, scoring a near miss on one warship and escaping without drawing fire. He circled and, fully realizing that the convoy was thoroughly alerted and would meet his next attack with a barrage of antiaircraft fire, began a second low-level run which culminated in two direct hits on a large tanker. A hail of steel fired from Japanese guns riddled the bomber, knocking out two engines, damaging a third, crippling the hydraulic system, puncturing one gasoline tank, ripping uncounted holes in the aircraft, and wounding the copilot, but by magnificent display of flying skill, Major Carswell controlled the airplane's plunge toward the sea and carefully forced it into a halting climb in the direction of the China shore. On reaching land, where it would have been possible to abandon the staggering bomber, one of the crew discovered that his parachute had been ripped by flak and rendered useless. The pilot, hoping to cross mountainous terrain and reach a base, continued onward until the third engine failed. He ordered the crew to bail out while he struggled to maintain altitude and, refusing to save himself, chose to remain with his comrade, and attempted a crash landing. He died when the airplane struck a mountainside and burned. With consummate gallantry and intrepidity,

Major Carswell gave his life in a supreme effort to save all members of his crew. His sacrifice, far beyond that required of him, was in keeping with the traditional bravery of America's war heroes.

MEDAL OF HONOR

GOTT, DONALD JOSEPH

First Lieutenant, United States Army Air Corps, Saarbrüken, Germany 9 November, 1944. *Citation:* A B-17 aircraft piloted by Lieutenant Gott was seriously damaged beyond control and on fire; dangerous flames from the number 4 engine were leaping back as far as the tail assembly. Flares in the cockpit were ignited and a fire raged therein which was further increased by free flowing fluid from damaged hydraulic lines. The interphone system was rendered useless. In addition to those serious mechanical difficulties the engineer was wounded in the leg and the radio operator's arm was severed below the elbow. Suffering from intense pain, despite the application of a tourniquet, the radio operator fell unconscious. Faced with the imminent explosion of his aircraft and death to his entire crew, mere seconds before bombs away on the target, Lieutenant Gott and his co-pilot conferred. Something had to be done immediately to save the life of the wounded radio operator. The lack of a static line and the thought that his unconscious body striking the ground in unknown territory would not bring immediate medical attention forced a quick decision. Lieutenant Gott and his co-pilot decided to fly the flaming aircraft to friendly territory and then attempt to crash land. Bombs were released on the target and the crippled aircraft proceeded alone to Allied controlled territory. When that had been reached Lieutenant Gott had the co-pilot personally inform all crew members to bail out. The co-pilot chose to remain with Lieutenant Gott in order to assist in landing the bomber. With only one normally functioning engine, and with danger of explosion much greater, the aircraft banked into an open field, and when it was at an altitude of 100 feet it exploded, crashed, exploded again, and then disintegrated. All three crew members were instantly killed. Lieutenant Gott's loyalty to the crew, his determination to accomplish the task set forth to him, and his deed of knowingly performing what may have been his last service to his country was an example of valor at its highest.

MEDAL OF HONOR

BONG, RICHARD IRA

Major, United States Army Air Corps, Southwest Pacific Area from 10 October to 15 November, 1944. *Citation:* Though assigned to duty as gunnery instructor and neither required nor expected to perform combat duty, Major Bong voluntarily and at his own urgent request engaged in repeated combat missions, including unusual hazardous sorties over Balikpapan, Borneo, and in the Leyte area of the Philippines. His aggressiveness and daring resulted in his shooting down eight enemy airplanes during this period.

Lockheed

Swastikas on the side of this P-38 shows it achieved 12 German victories. The P-38 enabled Richard Bong to destroy 40 Japanese Zeros, earning him a Medal of Honor, and a place in American air history.

MEDAL OF HONOR

KEARBY, NEEL EARNEST

Colonel, United States Army Air Corps, Wewak, New Guinea, 11 October, 1943. *Citation:* For conspicuous gallantry and intrepidity above and beyond the call of duty in action with the enemy. Colonel Kearby volunteered to lead a flight of our fighters to reconnoiter the strongly defended enemy base at Wewak. Having observed enemy installations and reinforcements at 4 airfields, and secured important tactical information, he saw an enemy fighter below him, made a diving attack and shot it down in flames. The small formation then sighted approximately 12 enemy bombers accompanied by 36 fighters. Although his mission had been completed, his fuel was running low, and the numerical odds were 12 to 1, he gave the signal to attack. Diving into the midst of the enemy airplanes he shot down 3 in quick succession. Observing one of his comrades with two enemy fighters in pursuit he destroyed both enemy aircraft. The enemy broke off in large numbers to make a multiple attack on his airplane but despite his peril he made one more pass before seeking cloud protection. Coming into the clear he called his flight together and led them to a friendly base. Colonel Kearby brought down 6 enemy aircraft in this action, undertaken with superb daring after his mission was completed.

MEDAL OF HONOR

KNIGHT, RAYMOND LARRY

First Lieutenant, United States Army Air Corps, Po Valley, Italy, 24 and 25 April, 1945. *Citation:* Lieutenant Knight piloted a fighter-bomber aircraft in a series of low-level strafing missions, destroying 14 grounded enemy aircraft and leading attacks which wrecked 10 others during a critical period of the Allied drive in northern Italy. On the morning of 24 April, 1945, he volunteered to lead two other aircraft against the strongly defended enemy airdrome at Ghedi. Ordering his fellow pilots to remain aloft, he skimmed the ground through a deadly curtain of antiaircraft fire to reconnoiter the field, locating eight German aircraft hidden beneath heavy camouflage. He rejoined his flight, briefed them by radio, and then led them with consummate skill through the hail of enemy fire in a low-level attack, destroying five aircraft while his flight accounted for two others. Returning to his base, he volunteered to lead three other aircraft in reconnaissance of Bergamo airfield, an enemy base near Ghedi and one known to be equally well defended. Again ordering his flight to remain out of range of antiaircraft fire. Lieutenant Knight flew through an exceptionally intense barrage, which heavily damaged his Thunderbolt, to observe the field at minimum altitude. He discovered a squadron of enemy aircraft under heavy camouflage and led his flight to the assault. Returning alone after this strafing, he made 10 deliberate passes against the field, despite being hit twice more by antiaircraft fire, destroying six fully loaded enemy twin-engine aircraft and a fighter airplane. He then returned to his base in his seriously damaged airplane. Early the next morning when he again attacked Bergamo, he sighted an enemy aircraft on the runway. Again he led three other American pilots in a blistering low level sweep through vicious antiaircraft fire that damaged his airplane so severely that it was virtually nonflyable. Three of the few remaining twin-engine aircraft at that base were destroyed. Realizing the critical need for aircraft in his unit, he declined to parachute to safety and unhesitatingly attempted to return the shattered airplane to his home field. With great skill and strength, he flew homeward until caught by treacherous air conditions in the Apennine Mountains, where he crashed and was killed. The gallant action of Lieutenant Knight eliminated the German aircraft which were poised to wreak havoc on Allied forces pressing to establish the first firm bridgehead across the Po River. His fearless daring and voluntary self-sacrifice averted possible heavy casualties among ground forces and the resultant slowing of the drive which culminated in the collapse of German resistance in Italy.

MEDAL OF HONOR

JERSTAD, JOHN LOUIS

Major, United Army Air Corps, Ploesti Raid, Rumania, 1 August, 1943. *Citation:* For conspicuous gallantry and intrepidity above and beyond the call of duty. Serving as lead pilot in his Group in a daring low level attack against enemy oil refineries and installations of Ploesti, Rumania, and although he had completed more than his share of missions and was no longer connected with this Group, so high was his conception of duty that he volunteered to lead the formation in the correct belief that his participation would contribute materially to success in this attack. Major Jerstad led the formation into the attack with full realization of the extreme hazards involved and despite withering fire from heavy and light antiaircraft guns. Three miles from the target his airplane was hit, badly damaged, and set on fire. Ignoring the fact he was flying over a field suitable for a forced landing, he kept on the course. After the bombs of his aircraft were released on the target, the fire in his ship became so intense as to make further progress impossible and he crashed into the target area. By his voluntary acceptance of a mission he knew was extremely hazardous, and his assumption of an intrepid course of action at the risk of life over and above the call of duty, Major Jerstad set an example of heroism which will be an inspiration to the armed forces of the United States.

MEDAL OF HONOR

HUGHES, LLOYD HERBERT

Second Lieutenant, United States Army Air Corps, Ploesti Raid, Rumania, 1 August, 1943. *Citation:* For conspicuous gallantry in action and intrepidity at the risk of his life and beyond the call of duty. On that date, Lieutenant Hughes served in the capacity of pilot of a heavy bombardment aircraft participating in a long and hazardous minimum altitude attack against the Axis oil refineries of Ploesti, Rumania, launched from the northern shores of Africa. Flying in the last formation to attack the target, he arrived in the target area after previous flights had thoroughly alerted the enemy defenses. Approaching the target through intense and accurate antiaircraft fire and dense balloon barrages at dangerously low altitudes, his airplane received several direct hits from both large and small caliber antiaircraft guns which seriously damaged his aircraft causing sheets of escaping gasoline to stream from the bomb bay and from the left wing. This damage was inflicted at a time prior to reaching the target when Lieutenant Hughes could have made a forced landing in any of the grain fields readily available at that time. The target area was blazing with burning oil tanks and damaged refinery installation from which flames leaped above the bombing level of the formation. With full knowledge of the consequence of entering this blazing inferno when his airplane was profusely leaking gasoline in two separate locations, Lieutenant Hughes, motivated only by his high conception of duty which called for the destruction of his assigned target at any cost, did not elect to turn back from the attack. Instead, rather than jeopardize the formation and the success of the attack, he unhesitatingly entered the blazing area and dropped his bomb load with great precision. After successfully bombing the objective, his aircraft emerged from the conflagration with the left wing aflame. Only then did he attempt a forced landing, but because of the advanced state of the fire enveloping his aircraft, the airplane crashed and was consumed. By Lieutenant Hughes heroic decision to complete his mission regardless of the consequences, in utter disregard for his own life, and by his gallant and valorous execution of this decision, he rendered a service to our country in the defeat of our enemies which will be everlastingly outstanding in the annals of our nation's history.

MEDAL OF HONOR

SHOMO, WILLIAM ARTHUR

Major, United States Army Air Corps, Luzon, Philippine Islands, 11 January, 1945. *Citation*: For conspicuous gallantry and intrepidity at the risk of his life above and beyond the call of duty over Luzon. Major Shomo was lead pilot of a flight of two fighter planes charged with an armed photographic and strafing mission against the Aparri and Laoag airdromes. While enroute to the objective he observed an enemy twin-engine bomber, protected by twelve fighters, flying about two thousand five hundred feet above him and in the opposite direction. Although the odds were thirteen to two, Major Shomo immediately ordered an attack. Accompanied by his wingman he closed on the enemy formation in a climbing turn and scored hits on the leading plane of the third element, which exploded in mid-air. Major Shomo then attacked the second element from the left side of the formation and shot another fighter down in flames. When the enemy formed for counterattack Major Shomo moved to the other side of the formation and hit a third fighter which exploded and fell. Diving below the bomber he put a burst into its under side and it crashed and burned. Pulling up from this pass he encountered a fifth plane firing head on and destroyed it. He next dived upon the first element and shot down the lead plane, then diving to three hundred feet in pursuit of another fighter he caught it with his initial burst and it crashed in flames. During this action his wingman had shot down three planes, while the three remaining enemy fighters had fled into a cloudbank and escaped. Major Shomo's extraordinary gallantry and intrepidity in attacking such a far superior force and destroying seven aircraft in one action is unparalleled in the Southwest Pacific Area.

MEDAL OF HONOR

LAWLEY, JR., ROBERT WILLIAM

First Lieutenant United States Army Air Forces. Continental Europe, 20 February, 1944. *Citation:* For conspicuous gallantry and intrepidity in action above and beyond the call of duty, while serving as a pilot of a B-17 aircraft on a heavy bombardment mission over enemy occupied Continental Europe. Coming off the target he was attacked by approximately twenty enemy fighters, shot out of formation and his plane severely crippled. Eight crew members were wounded, the co-pilot was killed by a 20mm shell. One engine was on fire, the controls shot away and Lieutenant Lawley seriously and painfully wounded about the face. Forcing the co-pilot's body off the controls, he brought the plane out of a steep dive, flying with his left hand only. Blood covered the instruments and windshield and visibility was impossible. With a full bomb load the plane was difficult to maneuver and bombs could not be released because the racks were frozen. After the order to bail out had been given, one of the waist gunners informed the pilot that two crew members were so severely wounded that it would be impossible for them to bail out. With the fire in the engine spreading, the danger of an explosion was imminent. Because of the helpless condition of his wounded crew members Lieutenant Lawley elected to remain with the ship and bring them to safety if it was humanly possible, giving the other crew members the option of bailing out. Enemy fighters again attacked but by using masterful evasion action he managed to lose them. One engine again caught on fire and was extinguished by skillful flying. Lieutenant Lawley remained at his post, refusing first aid until he collapsed from sheer exhaustion caused by loss of blood, shock and the energy he had expended in keeping control of his plane. He was revived by the bombardier and again took over the controls. Coming over the English coast one engine ran out of gasoline and had to be feathered. Another engine started to burn and continued to do so until a successful crash landing was made on a small fighter base. Through his heroism and exceptional flying skill, Lieutenant Lawley rendered outstanding, distinguished and valorous service to our nation.

MEDAL OF HONOR

MATHIS, JACK WARREN

First Lieutenant, United States Army Air Corps. Vegesack, Germany, 18 March, 1943. *Citation:* For conspicuous gallantry and intrepidity above and beyond the call of duty in action with the enemy. Lieutenant Mathis, as leading bombardier of his squadron, flying through intense and accurate antiaircraft fire, was just starting his bomb run, upon which the entire squadron depended for accurate bombing, when he was hit by the enemy antiaircraft fire. His right arm was shattered above the elbow, a large wound was torn in his side and abdomen, and he was knocked from his bomb sight to the rear of the bombardier's compartment. Realizing that the success of the mission depended on him, Lieutenant Mathis, by sheer determination and will power, though mortally wounded, dragged himself back to his sight, released his bombs, then died at his post of duty. As a result of this action the planes of the 303d Bombardment Squadron placed their bombs directly upon the assigned target for a perfect attack against the enemy. Lieutenant Mathis' undaunted bravery has been a great inspiration to the officers and men of his unit.

MEDAL OF HONOR

McGUIRE, JR., THOMAS BUCHANAN

Major, United States Army Air Corps. Luzon, Philippine Islands, 25 and 26, December 1944. *Citation:* For conspicuous gallantry and intrepidity over and beyond the call of duty. Major McGuire led a squadron of fifteen P-38s as top cover for heavy bombers striking Mabalacat Airdrome, where his formation was attacked by twenty aggressive Japanese fighters. In the ensuing action he repeatedly flew to the aid of embattled comrades, driving off enemy assaults, while himself under attack and at times outnumbered three to one and, even after his guns jammed, continuing the fight by forcing a hostile plane into his wingman's line of fire. Before he started back to base, he had shot down three Zeros. The next day he again volunteered to lead escort fighters on a mission to strongly defend Clark Field. During the resultant engagement he again exposed himself to attacks so that he might rescue a crippled bomber. In rapid succession he shot down one aircraft, parried the attack of four enemy fighters, one of which he shot down, single-handedly engaged three more Japanese, destroying one, and then shot down still another, his thirty-eighth victory in aerial combat. On 7 January, 1945, while leading a voluntary fighter sweep over Los Negros Island, he risked an extremely hazardous maneuver at low altitude in an attempt to save a fellow flyer from attack, crashed and was reported missing in action. With gallant initiative, deep and unselfish concern for the safety of others, and heroic determination to destroy the enemy at all costs, Major McGuire set an inspiring example in keeping with the highest traditions of the military service.

MEDAL OF HONOR

METZGER, JR., WILLIAM EDWARD

Second Lieutenant, United States Army Air Corps, Saarbrücken, Germany, 9 November, 1944. *Citation:* While serving as co-pilot on a B-17 aircraft on a bombing run upon the marshaling yards serious damage resulted from antiaircraft fire. Three of the aircraft's engines were damaged beyond control and on fire; dangerous flames from the fourth engine were leaping back as far as the tail assembly. Flares in the cockpit were ignited and a fire raged therein which was further increased by free flowing fluid from damaged hydraulic lines. The interphone system was rendered useless. In addition to these serious mechanical difficulties the engineer was wounded in the leg and the radio operator's arm was severed below the elbow. Suffering from intense pain, despite the application of a tourniquet the radio operator fell unconscious. Faced with the imminent explosion of his aircraft and death to his entire crew, mere seconds before bombs away on the target, Lieutenant Metzger and his pilot conferred. Something had to be done immediately to save the life of the wounded radio operator. The lack of a static line and the thought that his unconscious body striking the ground in unknown territory would not bring immediate attention forced a quick decision. Lieutenant Metzger and his pilot decided to fly the flaming aircraft to friendly territory and then attempt to crash land. Bombs were released on the target and the crippled aircraft proceeded alone to Allied controlled territory. When that had been reached Lieutenant Metzger personally informed all crew members to bail out upon the suggestion of the pilot. Lieutenant Metzger chose to remain with the pilot for the crash landing in order to assist him in this emergency. With only one normally functioning engine and with the danger of explosion much greater, the aircraft banked into a open field, and when it was at an altitude of 100 feet it exploded, crashed, exploded again, and then disintegrated. All three crew members were instantly killed. Lieutenant Metzger's loyalty to the crew, his determination to accomplish the task set forth to him, and his deed of knowingly performing what may have been his last service to his country were an example of valor at its highest.

MEDAL OF HONOR

BAKER, ADDISON EARL

Colonel, United States Army Air Group (H), Ploesti Raid, Rumania, 1 August, 1943. *Citation:* For conspicuous gallantry and intrepidity above and beyond the call of duty in action with the enemy on 1 August, 1943. On this date, he led his command, the 93d Bombardment Group on a daring low level attack against enemy oil refineries and installations at Ploesti, Rumania. Approaching the target his aircraft was hit by a large caliber antiaircraft shell, seriously damaged, and set on fire. Ignoring the fact he was flying over terrain suitable for safe landing he refused to jeopardize the mission by breaking up the lead formation and continued unswervingly to lead his group to the target upon which he dropped his bombs with devastating effect. Only then did he leave formation, but his valiant attempts to gain sufficient altitude for the crew to escape by parachute were unavailing and his aircraft crashed in flames after his successful efforts to avoid other planes in formation. By extraordinary flying skill, gallant leadership, and intrepidity, Colonel Baker rendered outstanding, distinguished, and valorous service to our Nation.

MEDAL OF HONOR

CHELI, RALPH

Major, United States Army Air Corps, Wewak, New Guinea, on 18 August, 1943. *Citation:* While Major Cheli was leading his squadron in a dive to attack the heavily defended Dagua Airdrome, intercepting enemy aircraft centered their fire on his plane, causing it to burst into flames while still two miles from the objective. His speed would have enabled him to gain necessary altitude to parachute to safety, but this action would have resulted in his formation becoming disorganized and exposed to the enemy. Although a crash was inevitable, he courageously elected to continue leading the attack in his blazing plane. From a minimum altitude, the squadron made a devastating bombing and strafing attack on the target. The mission completed, Major Cheli instructed his wingman to lead the formation, and crashed into the sea.

MEDAL OF HONOR

KANE, JOHN RILEY

Colonel, United States Army, Air Corps, 9th Air Force, Ploesti Raid, Rumania, 1 August, 1943. *Citation:* For conspicuous gallantry in action and intrepidity at the risk of his life above and beyond the call of duty on 1 August 1943. On this date he led the third element of heavy bombardment in a mass low-level bombing attack against the vitally important enemy target of the Ploesti oil refineries. En route to the target, which necessitated a round-trip of over 2,400 miles, Colonel Kane's element became separated from the leading portion of the massed formation in avoiding dense and dangerous cumulous cloud conditions over mountainous terrain. Rather than turn back from such a vital mission he elected to proceed to his target. Upon arrival at the target area it was discovered that another group had apparently missed its target and had previously attacked and damaged the target assigned to Colonel Kane's element. Despite the thoroughly warned defenses, the intensive antiaircraft fire, enemy fighter airplanes, extreme hazards on a low-level attack of exploding delayed action bombs from the previous element, of oil fires and explosions and dense smoke over the target area, Colonel Kane elected to lead his formation into the attack. By his gallant courage, brilliant leadership, and superior flying skill, he and the formation under his command successfully attacked this vast refinery so essential to our enemies' war effort. Through his conspicuous gallantry in this most hazardous action against the enemy, and by his intrepidity at the risk of his life above and beyond the call of duty, Colonel Kane personally contributed vitally to the success of this daring mission and thereby rendered most distinguished service in the furtherance of the defeat of our enemies.

MEDAL OF HONOR

WILKINS, RAYMOND HARRELL

Major, United States Army Air Force, Rabaul, New Britain, 2 November, 1943. *Citation:* For conspicuous gallantry and intrepidity above and beyond the call of duty in action with the enemy near Rabaul. Leading his squadron in an attack on shipping in Simpson Harbor, during which intense antiaircraft fire was expected, Major Wilkins briefed his squadron so that his airplane would be in the position of greatest risk. His squadron was the last of three in the group to enter the target area. Smoke from the bombs dropped by preceding aircraft necessitated a last second revision of tactics on his part, which still enabled his squadron to strike vital shipping targets but forced it to approach through concentrated fire, and increased the danger of Major Wilkins' left flank position. His airplane was hit almost immediately, the right wing damaged, and control rendered extremely difficult. Although he could have withdrawn, he held fast and led his squadron into the attack. He strafed a group of small harbor vessels and then, at low level attacked an enemy destroyer. His thousand pound bomb struck squarely amidship, causing the vessel to explode. Although antiaircraft fire from this vessel had seriously damaged his left vertical stabilizer he refused to deviate from the course. From below mast-head height he attacked a transport of some nine thousand tons, scoring a hit which engulfed the ship in flames. Bombs expended, he began to withdraw his squadron. A heavy cruiser barred the path. Unhesitatingly, to neutralize the cruiser's guns and attract their fire, he went in for a strafing run. His damaged stabilizer was completely shot off. To avoid swerving into his wing planes he had to turn so as to expose the belly and full wing surfaces of his plane to the enemy fire; it caught and crumpled his left wing. Now past control, the bomber crashed into the sea. In this fierce engagement, Major Wilkins destroyed two enemy vessels, and his heroic self-sacrifice made possible the safe withdrawal of the remaining planes of his squadron.

MEDAL OF HONOR

ZEAMER, JR., JAY

Major, United States Army Air Corps, 16 June, 1943, Buka, Soloman Islands. *Citation:* For conspicuous gallantry and intrepidity in action above and beyond the call of duty, Major Zeamer volunteered as pilot of a bomber on an important photographic mapping mission covering the formidable defended area in the vicinity of Buka. While photographing the Buka airdrome, his crew observed about twenty enemy fighters on the field, many of them taking off. Despite the certainty of a dangerous attack by this strong force, Major Zeamer proceeded with his mapping run, even after the enemy attack began. In the ensuing engagement, Major Zeamer sustained gunshot wounds in both arms and legs, one leg being broken. Despite his injuries, he maneuvered the damaged plane so skillfully that his gunners were able to fight off the enemy during a running fight lasting forty minutes, and to destroy at least five hostile planes, of which Major Zeamer himself shot down one. Although weak from loss of blood, he refused medical aid until the enemy had broken combat. He then turned over the controls but continued to exercise command and, despite lapses into unconsciousness, to direct the flight to a base five hundred and eighty miles away. In this voluntary action, Major Zeamer, with superb skill, resolution and courage, accomplished a mission of great value.

MEDAL OF HONOR

TRUEMPER, WALTER EDWARD

First Lieutenant, United States Army Air Force, Europe, 20 February, 1944. *Citation:* For conspicuous gallantry and intrepidity at risk of his own life above and beyond the call of duty in action against the enemy in connection with a bombing mission. The aircraft on which Lieutenant Truemper was serving as navigator was attacked by a squadron of enemy fighters with the result that the co-pilot was killed outright, the pilot wounded and rendered unconscious, the radio operator wounded, and the airplane severely damaged. Nevertheless, Lieutenant Truemper and other members of the crew managed to right the airplane and fly it back to the home station, where they contacted the control tower and reported the situation. Lieutenant Truemper and the engineer volunteered to attempt to land the airplane. Other members of the crew were ordered to jump, leaving Lieutenant Truemper and the engineer aboard. After observing the distressed aircraft from another airplane, Lieutenant Truemper's commanding officer decided the damaged airplane could not be landed by the inexperienced crew and ordered them to abandon it and parachute to safety. Demonstrating unsurpassed courage and heroism, Lieutenant Truemper and the engineer replied that the pilot was still alive but could not be moved and they would not desert him. They were then told to attempt a landing. After two unsuccessful efforts their airplane crashed into a open field in a third attempt to land. Lieutenant Truemper, the engineer, and the wounded pilot were killed.

MEDAL OF HONOR

PEASE, JR., HARL

Captain, United States Army Air Force. Rabaul, New Britain, 6 and 7th August, 1942. *Citation:* For conspicuous gallantry and intrepidity above and beyond the call of duty in action near Rabaul. When one engine of the bombardment airplane of which he was pilot failed during a bombing mission over New Guinea, Captain Pease was forced to return to a base in Australia. Knowing that all available airplanes of his group were to participate the next day in an attack on an enemy held airdrome near Rabaul, New Britain, although he was not scheduled to take part in this mission, Captain Pease selected the most serviceable airplane at this base and prepared it for combat, knowing that it had been found and declared unserviceable for combat missions. With the members of his combat crew, who volunteered to accompany him, he rejoined his squadron at Port Moresby, New Guinea, at 1:00 A.M. on August 7 after having flown almost continuously since early the preceding morning. With only three hours' rest, he joined with his squadron for the attack. Throughout the long flight to Rabaul, he managed by skillful flying of his serviceable airplane to maintain his position in the group. When the formation was intercepted by about thirty enemy fighter planes before reaching the target, Captain Pease, on the wing which bore the brunt of the hostile attack, by gallant action and the accurate shooting of his crew, succeeded in destroying several Zeros before dropping his bombs on the hostile base as planned, this in spite of continuous enemy attacks. The fight with the enemy pursuit lasted 25 minutes until the group dived into cloud cover. After leaving the target Captain Pease's airplane fell behind the balance of the group due to unknown difficulties as a result of the combat, and was unable to reach this cover before the enemy pursuit succeeded in igniting one of his bomb-bay tanks. It is believed that Captain Pease's airplane and crew were subsequently shot down in flames as they did not return to their base. In voluntarily performing this mission Captain Pease contributed materially to the success of the group, and displayed high devotion to duty, valor, and complete contempt for personal danger. His undaunted bravery has been a great inspiration to the officers and men of his unit.

MEDAL OF HONOR

MICHAEL, EDWARD STANLEY

First Lieutenant, 0742443, Army Air Forces, United States Army. Germany, 11 April, 1944. *Citation:* For conspicuous gallantry and intrepidity above and beyond the call of duty while serving as Pilot of a B-17 aircraft on a heavy bombardment mission. The Group in which Lieutenant Michael was flying was attacked by a swarm of fighters. His plane was singled out and the fighters pressed their attacks home recklessly, completely disregarding the Allied fighter escort and their own intense flak. His plane was riddled from nose to tail with exploding cannon shells and knocked out of formation, with a large number of fighters following it down, blasting it with cannon fire as it descended. A cannon shell exploded in the cockpit, wounded the Co-Pilot, wrecked the instruments and blew out the side window. Lieutenant Michael was seriously and painfully wounded in the right thigh. Hydraulic fluid filmed over the windshield making visibility impossible and smoke filled the cockpit. The controls failed to respond and 3,000 feet were lost before he succeeded in leveling off. The Radio Operator informed him that the whole bomb bay was in flames, as a result of the explosion of three cannon shells, which had ignited the incendiaries. With a full load of incendiaries in the bomb bay and a considerable gas load in the tanks, the danger of fire enveloping the plane and the tanks exploding seemed imminent. When the emergency release lever failed to function Lieutenant Michael at once gave the order to bail out and seven of the crew left the ship. Seeing the

Bombardier firing the Navigator's gun at the enemy planes, Lieutenant Michael ordered him to bail out as the plane was liable to explode at any minute. When the Bombardier looked for his parachute he found that it had been riddled with 20 millimeter fragments and was useless. Lieutenant Michael, seeing the ruined parachute, realized that if the plane was abandoned, the Bombardier would perish, and decided that the only chance would be a crash landing. Completely disregarding his own painful and profusely bleeding wounds but thinking only of the safety of the remaining crew members, he gallantly evaded the enemy, using violent evasive action despite the battered condition of his plane. After the plane had been under sustained enemy attack for forty-five minutes, Lieutenant Michael finally lost the persistent fighters in a cloud bank. Upon emerging an accurate barrage of flak caused him to come down to tree top level where flak towers poured a continuous rain of fire on the plane. He continued into France, realizing that at any moment a crash landing might have to be attempted but trying to get as far as possible to increase the escape possibilities if a safe landing could be achieved. Lieutenant Michael flew the plane until he became exhausted from the loss of blood, which had formed on the floor in pools and he lost consciousness. The Co-Pilot succeeded in reaching England and sighted a RAF field near the coast. Lieutenant Michael finally regained consciousness and insisted upon taking over the controls to land the plane. The undercarriage was useless, the bomb bay doors were jammed open, the hydraulic system and altimeter were shot out. In addition, there was no airspeed indicator, the ball turret was jammed with the guns pointed downward and the flaps would not respond. Despite these apparently insurmountable obstacles he landed the plane without mishap.

MEDAL OF HONOR

PUCKET, DONALD DALE

First Lieutenant, United States Army Air Forces. Ploesti Rumania, 9 July, 1944. *Citation:* As pilot of a B-24 bomber, he took part in a highly effective strike against vital oil installations. Just after bombs away the plane received heavy and direct hits from antiaircraft fire. One crew member was instantly killed and six others severely wounded. The airplane was badly damaged: two engines were knocked out, the control cables cut, the oxygen system on fire, and the bomb bay flooded with gas and hydraulic fluid. Regaining control of his crippled plane, Lieutenant Pucket turned its direction over to the co-pilot. He calmed the crew, administered first aid and surveyed the damage. Finding the bomb bay doors jammed, he used the hand crank to open them to allow the gas to escape. He jettisoned all guns and equipment, but the plane continued to lose altitude rapidly. Realizing that it would be impossible to reach friendly territory, he ordered that the aircraft be abandoned. When three of the crew were found to be suffering from such crippling wounds and shock that they were unable to comply with his order, he urged the others to jump. Ignoring their entreaties to follow, he refused to abandon his badly wounded crew and was last seen fighting to regain control of the airplane. A few moments later the flaming airplane crashed on a mountainside. Lieutenant Pucket, unhesitatingly and with supreme sacrifice, gave his life in his courageous attempt to save the lives of three others.

MEDAL OF HONOR

LINDSEY, DARRELL ROBINS

Captain, United States Army Air Corps. L'Isle Adam railroad bridge over the Seine, France, 20 August, 1944. *Citation:* Captain Lindsey led a formation of thirty B-26 medium bombers in a hazardous mission to destroy the strategic enemy held bridge in occupied France. With most of the bridges over the Seine destroyed, the heavily fortified L'Isle Adam bridge was of inestimable value to the enemy in moving troops, supplies, and equipment to Paris. Captain Lindsey was fully aware of the fierce resistance that would be encountered. Shortly after reaching enemy territory the formation was buffeted with heavy and accurate antiaircraft fire. By skilled evasive action Captain Lindsey was able to elude much of the enemy, but just before entering the bombing run his B-26 was peppered with holes. During the bombing run the enemy fire was even more intense, and Captain Lindsey's right engine received a direct hit and burst into flames. Despite the fact that his ship was hurled out of the formation by the violence of the collision, Captain Lindsey brilliantly maneuvered back into the lead position without disrupting the flight. Fully aware that the gasoline tanks might explode at any moment, he gallantly elected to continue the perilous bombing run. With fire streaming from his right engine and his right wing half enveloped in flames, he led his formation over the target upon which the bombs were dropped with telling effect. Immediately after the objective was attacked, Captain Lindsey gave the order for the crew to parachute from the doomed aircraft. With magnificent coolness and superb pilotage, and without regard for his own life, he held the swiftly descending airplane in a steady glide until the members of the crew could jump to safety. With the right wing completely enveloped in flames, and an explosion imminent, Captain Lindsey still remained unperturbed. The last man to leave the stricken plane was the bombardier, who offered to lower the wheels so that Captain Lindsey might escape from the nose. Realizing that this might throw the aircraft into an uncontrollable spin and jeopardize the bombardier's chances to escape, Captain Lindsey refused the offer. Immediately after the bombardier had bailed out, and before Captain Lindsey was able to follow, the right gasoline tank exploded. The aircraft, sheathed in fire, went into a steep dive and was seen to explode as it crashed. All who are living today from this plane owe their lives to the fact that Captain Lindsey remained cool and showed supreme courage in this emergency.

Appendix

Graduates of Randolph Field and Kelly Field

Graduates June, 1932

Aring, Wilbur W.
Baker, Carl F.
Beck, Stephen A.
Beldon, Lloyd I.
Bell, Jasper N.
Bird, A.J. Jr.
Bogardus, Wm. I.
Bonnell, Wm. F.
Borchers, Adrian
Bordelon, Henry O.
Borgers, Eldor W.
Brady, Robert W.
Brannon, Wm. F.
Brashear, Maurice P.
Brockliss, Cedric J.
Bruce, James I.
Cahill, Martin B.
Cassady, George S.
Cazier, Frank W.
Christner, John W.
Churchill, Randolph E.
Clark, Glenn C.
Clark, Wm. L.
Combest, Wm. L.

Cooper, Robert E. Jr.
Corrigan, Emmett, Jr.
Coursey, Harry
Cox, Dudley S.
Cox, Homer M.
Culler, Harry H.
Davis, Wm. E.
Demler, Marvin C.
Ditzen, Wm. G.
Doherty, John C.
Duckworth, Hubert B.
Eaker, Carl H.
Earle, Lloyd W.
Flower, Scott Jr.
Fouche, John S. Jr.
Freyer, Fredrick R.
Gates, Thomas L.
George, Clifton V.
Glasgow, Marvin C.
Govini, George L.
Haarman, Donald W.
Haley, Olin K.
Hamilton, Edward N.
Hanspeter, Paul J.

Harris, Clyde C. Jr.
Henderson, Richard W.
Hill, Robert L.
Hoffman, Cecil R.
Horvath, Lewis, Jr.
Hughes, Lewis R.
Hunt, Jack S.
Hunt, Wilburn, R.
Hurst, Don L.
Jackson, Edmund, L.
Jarmon, Robert L.
Jobson, Theron S.
Kane, John R.
Keenan, Gregory F.
Krug, Lester E.
Lancaster, David B.
Lovelace, Wm. F.
Mackelean, Howard W.
Mathews, James M.
Moody, Howard A.
Moore, Ralph J.
Mosman, Ormand J.
Murchison, George, M.
Neal, Jesse
Nelson, David R.
Nuckols, Wm. P.

Oglesby, Walter A.
O'Hara, Byron G.
Parrish, Noel F.
Payne, Samuel V.
Philip, Donald E.
Purser, Brittain H.
Qualm, Joseph R.
Randolph, Jack L.
Reynolds, Roger M.
Richardson, Harold G.
Searles, Nathan F.
Shockley, Moir L.
Smith, Elton
Spake, John P.
Sprunger, Noble O.
Stevers, Fred D.
Swift, Harry W.
Trimble, Wm. L.
Unruh, Marion D.
Ward, Roy P.
Wassell, Ralph L.
Weller, Richard C.
Wooley, Paul S.
Workman, James T.
Zealazo, Steve L.

Graduates November 1932

Amorous, William W.
Bogen, William
Caldera, Joseph D.
Cunningham, Charles
Claassen, Clayton B.
Collier, Claire B.
Cooper, Marcus P.
Corley, Quinn M.
Cowing, Charles A.
Crutcher, Harry Jr.
Dahl, Harold, E.
Darnell, Cecil

Dittrich, Charles M. Jr.
Doole, George A. Jr.
Ducrest, James R.
Eisenmann, Samuel B. Jr.
Fator, Jepththa W.
Ford, Vincent
Furlow, James W.
Gavin, Edward M.
Geblin, John Jr.
Gephart, Laurel J.
Halversen, Lars J.
Harmon, Harold D.

Harris, Lester S.
Hutchinson, Donald R.
Johnson, Earl D.
Joyce, Edwin A.
Kelley, Joseph J.
Kleinoeder, Leodard F.
Kolb, Julius A.
Lovvorn, Ancel L.
Lesesne, Charles H. Jr.
Manchester, Horace H. Jr.
Miller, Clark L.
Moyers, Frank N.
Muhlheisen, Dolf E.
Oppenheim, Russell I.
Pettigrew, Bruce C.

Plummer, Everett C.
Renshaw, Harry N.
Rogers, Craven C.
Rutherford, Stuart Z.
Shedd, Morris H.
Sindo, William J.
Skaer, Arthur H. Jr.
Stophlet, Richard P.
Stouff, Charles W.
Sweetser, Luther W. Jr.
Tibbs, Orville E.
Vavrina, Richard F.
Wackwitz, Donald N.
Wood, Clyde H. Jr.
Woodward, Raymond C.

Graduates March, 1933

Algert, Thomas S.
Allen, Keith N.
Allison, Wayne, N.
Ambrose, William M.
Arnold, Bob
Arrington, Robert M.
Backus, Edward N.
Barkley, David M.
Barry, John H.
Bissell, Harry H. Jr.
Bardeno, John W.
Brewster, Pete
Brown, William M.
Busch, Frank E.
Byerly, Jean R.
Cannon, Robin C.
Coln, William A. Jr.
Cook, John E.
Diggs, George C.
Dilley, Murray B. Jr.
Diltz, Henry C.
Dittman, Clarence P.
Dunlap, Duncan H.

Erickson, Allen L.
Fly, George L.
Foster, Joshua H. Jr.
Frutchey, Watson M.
Gardner, Kenneth F.
George, John F. Jr.
Glasser, Maurice E.
Goodbar, James M.
Gorman, Edmund T.
Grabill, Wilson F.
Gray, Ernest W.
Haid, Arthur A.
Hooten, William B.
Hopwood, Lloyd F.
Houston, James H.C.
Huffman, Clifford L.
Kennedy, Edward D.
Kiehle, Edward G.
Kitchens, Cyrus W. Jr.
Kriloff, Leo
Langhen, Thomas F.
Logan, Arthur L.
McAllister, John L.

McCray, W. K. Jr.
McDonald, Doyle
McHenry, Charles M.
Messer, Cleopas J.
Miller, Wilton B.
Moomaw, Chester C.
Neal, John O.
Neely, Harold L.
Newland, Millard R.
O'Connell, John J.
Payne, William K.
Price, James H.
Rainey, LeRoy A.
Reid, William M.
Richmond, William F.
Ritland, Osmond J.
Roberts, James J.
Rohl, Elden A.
Root, Berton
Sanders, William I.

Schaerdel, William W.
Schmid, Herman A.
Sherman, Dallas B.
Shields, Donald C.
Simons, Richard W.
Smith, Donald K.
Speaker, Norman W.
Springer, Charles R.
Stevens, Fred J. Jr.
Stewart, Malcolm F.
Strickland, Robert F.
Thompson, Jerome P.
Tindall, Edward F.
Viar, Paul
Way John A.
White, Edwin D. Jr.
Wild, Wilcox
Williams, Lester R.
Wolf, Edmund, C.
Wood, Thurman A.

Graduates July, 1933

Aigeltinger, Howard O.
Allee, Edward S.
Altenburg, William M.
Arthur, William T.
Avery, Edwin D.
Barton, Joe E.
Bateman, Martin A.
Bear, Henry S.
Bidwell, Lloyd H.
Booker, Richard C. W.
Boushay, Homer A. Jr.
Bradenberger, Clyde P.
Brown, Willard V.
Cheney, Howard A.
Connally, James T.
Crain, George K.
Crouch, Joel L.
Crumley, Newton H.

Davidson, John F.
Darrow, Don O.
Davis, Herman S.
Davis, Walter E.
Diehl, Donald B.
Dietz, Harold L.
Donlin, John P.
Dorsey, Edwin R.
Dunlap, Samuel C.
Eastham, James Y.
Edgar, William S.
Ellis, Dross
Endress, Albert V.
Eskridge, Ladson O. Jr.
Evans, Frank H.
Flaherty, Charles E.
Fulwider, Lawrence S.
Gaughen, Thomas J.

Gentry, Jay L.
Gibbon, Elwyn H.
Gibson, John H.
Goyette, Cyril A.
Gregory, Hal W. Jr.
Grenier, Jean D.
Gunn, Harold A.
Hale, Elkins H.
Hamilton, Charles L.
Harcos, Kermit A.
Heacock, Lowell E.
Hollstein, Charles P.
Holtermann, Eyvind
Hooks, Daniel E.
Hoyt, Stanley G.
Hudnell, William T.
Jones, Harold L.
Klein, Philip B.
Kruse, Roger H.
Lambie, John S. Jr.
Lay, Beirne Jr.
League, James B. Jr.
Love, Sterling T.
McDermott, George F.
MacIntyre, George H.
Manhart, Charles D.
Mock, Jeff O.

Moore, Joseph C.
Noland, Ray A.
Paul, Franklin K
Pippinger, Daniel W.
Pocock, William S.
Pope, Francis
Portman, Herman C. Jr.
Ricks, Lewis P.
Rogers, Charles D.
Schofield, Thomas J.
Schriever, Bernhard, A.
Schwartz, Elmer P.
Senter, Edward G.
Siebanaler, Frank J.
Smith, Carlton P.
Smith, Hamilton IV
Strickler, John F. Jr.
Stroud, James E.
Treher, John D.
Warren, Edwin A.
Wells, Raymond W.
Wickland, Daniel W.
Williams, James W.
Wittan, Edgar M.
Wynne, Andrew M.
Young, Raymond A. Jr.
Youngerman, George W. III

Graduates October, 1933

Allen, Robert H.
Anderson, J. E.
Bain, W. G. Jr.
Baldwin, B. R.
Barnes, W. B.
Bohl, J. P.
Coddington, L. G.
Denham, W. M.
Dennison, J. W. Jr.
Dunahoo, R. A.
Elliot, W. S.

Fahey, S. L.
Fairchild, K. C.
Fischer, C. M.
Freeman, S. D.
Gaster, C. J.
Griffin, R. E.
Griggs, M. J.
Hand, S. D.
Harrell, B. S.
Hausafus, E. T.
Hayden, J. H. Jr.

Hoxie, H. L.
Hurst, H. R.
Inman, W. B.
Irvine, J. S.
Kinkel, R. S.
Laird, R E.
Miller, F. H. Jr.
Mitchell, C. C. Jr.
Mitchell, W. D. Jr.
Nelson, O. M.
Peeler, C. E.
Powers, D. J.

Read, R. N.
Reid, R. L.
Rivard, F. L.
Roberts, J. E.
Schuster, O. J. Jr.
Smith, F. J.
Terry, A. L.
Warner, G. E.
Williams. H. S. Jr.
Winstead, J. T. Jr.
Woodruff, J. E.
Wood, O. L.

Graduates March, 1934

Altman, Dale E.
Ashman, Robert
Bennett, T. Allan
Bryant, Alexande
Bullock, Cady R.
Burton, Alexander T.
Caldwell, Neil M.
Capp, William C.
Carter, James T.
Clark, William H.
Clement, Browne
Cook, Frank R.
Dolezal, Glen M.
Eades, William
Ecklund, S. H.
Eisenhart, Donald W.
Evans, Archie J.
Fischer, John F.
Gray, Fredrick C. Jr.
Hatcher, William A. Jr.
Hay, James B.
Hilger, John A.
Hinton, J. W.
Holladay, Wendell G
James, Weldon M.
Keese, William B.

Kester, Edson E.
Kugel, Richard C.
Lerche, Andrew O.
Luedecke, Alvin R.
McDermont, Verne A.
McKinney, James E.
McMahon, George R.
Martin, Leslie E.
Moore, Horace G.
Moser, Glenn C.
Motley, Clifford
Mueller, Robert H.
Mundell, Lewis L.
Olmstead, Fay W.
Palmer, Albert L.
Pannis, William W.
Penland, Hugh S.
Peterson, Clair A.
Pierce, Arthur J.
Pierce, George E.
Proper, Lewis W.
Rendle, Irvine A.
Rodieck, Ralph W.
Root, Edgar W.
Sanford, George S.
Schoellkoph, Jacob F. IV

Shafer, George H.
Shoemaker, George E.
Simmons, James O.
Spicer, Henry R.
Stewart, John P.
St. Germain, Don P.
Stone, Frank C.

Timper, Norman E.
Todd, Paul E.
Turner, John H.
Virgin, Edward W.
Von Weller, Phil J.
Walker, Victor H.
Wilson, Paul B.

Graduates, July 1934

Allen, Brooke E.
Anderson, Victor L.
Black, Richard T.
Boutz, William R.
Burks, Jesse B.
Carney, Boatner R.C
Carson, James W.
Cochran, James C.
Coddington, Nathan H.
Cote, Roderick O.
Cunningham, Jordon J.
Cunningham, Tom J.
Drake, Francis R.
Duke, Paul D.
Fernald, Frank S.
Firsht, Peter
Gardner, Robert A.
Gilkes, Clarence W.
Gist, William H. Jr.
Graf, Henry B.
Gresham, Robert A.
Harding, William W.
Hargis, George R. III
Hatcher, George A.
Hird, Robert C. H.
Holtoner, J. Stanley
James, Elliot L. Jr.
Kennedy, Preston A.
Koch, George P.
Kreps, Kenneth R.
Lampl, Milton A.

Lumsden, J. Frank
McCune, Elton L.
Marks, William M. Jr.
Martin, Robert K.
Melden, Theodore, M. Jr.
Minnis, Gilmore V.
Mitchell, Willis W.
Nye, Glenn C.
Olsen, Robert F.
Paige, Potter B.
Payne, Jack
Poor, Richard L.
Reedy, James R.
Richards, Silas R.
Robertson, William R. Jr.
Rockwood, Ralph C.
Samuels, Nelson T.
Sangster, Alexander F
Schneider, Joe G.
Schwartz, William H. Jr.
Scherer, Robert M.
Selser, James C. Jr.
Smith, James A.
Staley, Poyntell C. Jr.
Templeton, John L.
Van Deventer, Robert G.
Williams, Douglas E.
Williams, Ernest F.
Williamson, Robert L.
Worden, Robert F.

Graduates October, 1934

Brock, Horace
Callish, Norman L.
Cheatwood, John L.
Clausen, Radcliffe C.
Coleman, Garrett S.
Councill, William H.
Desmond, David G.
Eichelberger, David M.
Estes, Harney Jr.
Fieldler, Charles W.
Finch, Richard O.
Fisher, Charles E.
Ford, Oliver E. Jr.
Hale, Joseph E. Jr.
Jeter, Charles H.
Johnson, Fred C.

Keppler, Arthur M.
Knieriem, Herbert E.
Lawing, Oscar K
Lester, Wendell P.
Luna, Harry P.
Martha, Harry D.
Mason, Ben A. Jr.
Miller, William A.
Nightingale, Frank, N.
Ogden, Donald G.
Ogle, John N.
Streater, Robert C.
Tinker, Frank G.
Volin, Herbert R.
Zimmerman, Raymond P.

Graduates March, 1935

Amspaugh, Paul E.
Barrow, David O. Jr.
Bartley, Thomas M. Jr.
Bennett, Frank J.
Bolton, Tom
Breck, George F. Jr.
Brewer, George S.
Brown, Stetson M.
Buchanan, Chester F. M.
Buchanan, George S.
Chennault, John S.
Cherymisin, Gerald L.
Coats, Leo B.
Cochrane, Carlos J.
Cornett, John B.
Darrell, Willie M.
Du Frane, John L. Jr.
Edwinson, Clarence T.
Elkins, Marshall A.
Eubanks, Anthony G.

Fernald, William I.
Fridge, Charles O.
Garrison, Walter J. Jr.
Greenback, Lawrence W.
Guilmartin, John F.
Haynes, Frank V.
Higgs, Frank L.
Hubbard, Boyd, Jr.
Jarrell, William W. Jr.
Jeffus, John H.
Jones, Arthur V. Jr.
Kuhn, David B.
Lawrence, Baskin R. Jr.
McClellan, Robert B.
McGehee, James C.
MacDuff, Francis H.
Marvin, William S.
Montgomery, John B.
Moomaw, Lorris W.
Moore, Thomas E.

Olmstead, Lawrence R. Jr.
Peterson, Norman L.
Powell, Lucion N.
Rankin, William Q.Q.
Reed, Podge M.
Rogers, Authur H.
Rouse, Frank E.
Schnanbeck, Raymond V.
Scott, Frank B.

Smith, Jess A.
Snell, Arthur Y.
Thomas, Joseph A.
Walker, Lloyd A. Jr.
Walsh, Tracy R.
West, Frederick W. Jr.
Williams, Ansel S. Jr.
Wilson, Joseph H.

Graduates July, 1935

Adair, Claude B.
Allen, Lawrence T.
Barrett, Thomas
Bates, Earl E.
Berry, Jack W.
Branch, Irving L.
Brendle, Frank W.
Brush, Robert P.
Campbell, Blaine B.
David, William B.
Davis, Willam E. Jr.
Dunlap, Donald S.
Feaganes, Joseph F.
Fisher, William P.
Freeman, Moultre P.
Graham, John W.
Hale, Sam H.
Haugen, Victor R.
Hazlett, George W.
Hoover, Herbert H.
Hudgens, Cedric E.
Junger, Mathias F.
Lawver, Kenneth W.
Long, Frederick C.
McElwain, Douglas S.
McKesson, Elmer E.
Markey, Harry W.
Marks, Jack S.

Massion, John, W.
Morgan, Herbert Jr.
Nelson, Hilmer C.
Olson, Abraham D.
Pearson, Benjamin J.
Pender, Preston P.
Petersen, Alton T.
Philpot, James A.
Polhamus, Robert G.
Ragsdale, William P. Jr.
Raines, Charles T.
Rambo, Wilkie A.
Reed, Robert R.
Reeder, William K.
Rodgers, John N.
Schmid, Clarence L.
Schumacher, Richard P.
Scott, Emil S.
Stewart, Allan J. Jr.
Smith, Argyle L.
Smith, Charles E.
Smith, Douglas W.
Strother, Donald R.
Terrill, Thomas S.
Thomas, Lawrence M.
Travis, James L.
Whisenand, James F.
Wilbur, Walter F.

Williamson, Paul B.
Wilson, Monty D.
Womble, Robert B Jr.

Wood, Don M.
Ziller, John C.

Graduates October 1935

Allen, James W.
Bockman, Charles E. Jr.
Chapman, James W.
Cochran, Franklin M.
Coulter, Theron
Crank, Howell G.
Crowell, Frank O.
Ellis, James O.
Hall, Robert W.
Hedlund, Evart W.
Herlick, Conrad J.
Kight, Richard T.
Kleine, Bingham T.
Lazarus, Willard W.
Le Penske, Edward A.
Love, Robert C.
McKissack, Thomas L.

Mackiln, Raleigh H.
Malcolm, Marion
Moser, William J.
Nichols, Howard F.
Paul, Robert C.
Quick, Quentin T.
Randall, John L.
Reid, Edward L.
Remington, Peter H.
Reynolds, John M.
Shepard, Horace A.
Snyder, Graves H.
Thayer, Merrill E.
West, Herbert M. Jr.
Wilson, Cy
Zidiales, Stanley A.

Graduates March, 1936

Ames, Kenneth G.
Atkinson, Robert S.
Bailey, Dalene E.
Bras, Glenn E.
Brown, Nelson T.
Bruce, Bertrand B.
Camp, William D.
Campbell, Arch G.
Cavenah, Kenneth A.
Cecil, Chester W. Jr
Creer, Wham E.
Donicht, Harry L.
Eakin, John H.
Finn, Ryder W.

Flolo, Russell L.
Gibson, Kenneth H.
Harcos, Bela A.
Hardy, John S.
Hawes, Edwin H.
Hayes, William L. Jr.
Helfert, Howard W.
Johnson, Lowell F.
Johnston, Robert L.
Kellogg, Ralph M.
Kramer, Charles E.
Lancaster, Charles E. Jr.
Lessig, Cecil P.
Longacre, Clarence K.

Marion, Charles E.
Olinger, Robert L.
Pariss, Wolcott
Rethorst, William
Reynolds, Elbert D.
Roberts, Roder M.
Reuter, Chris H. W.
Ryder, Robert W.
Sexton, Robert C.
Sherman, Willard E.

Stevens, Kermit D.
Sutherland, Russell T.
Wackwitz, Ernest F. Jr.
Walker, Audria R.
Walker, David H.
Warren, Beverly H.
Whitt, John D.
Willoughhy, Earl
Wood, Robert C.
Young, Harry B.

Graduates July, 1936

Baumler, Albert J.
Beardsley, Melville W.
Bicking, Charles W.
Bledsoe, James L.
Boyer, Jimmy V.
Bronson, Howard F. Jr.
Buller, Howard L.
Burke, Kevin
Catlin, Ralph W.
Chapman, Charles T. Jr.
Converse, Lawrence. F.
Cullerton, Edward F.
Curry, William L.
Dane, Paul H.
Eyre, Lloyd
Faulkner, Ted S.
Fausel, Robert W.
Ferguson, James
Griffith, Willard
Grove, Robert L.
Hampton, Thomas K.
Hardy, Robert F.
Haws, Jesse W.
Jones, James M.
Ketcham, Edward W.

McClosky, Richard D.
Mears, Frank H.
Michael, Bruce E.
Miller, William W.
Moore, Andrew D.
Navitt, William R.
Osborn, Ray W.
Osher, Norman C.
Pechuls, John A.
Peterson, Homer F.
Powers, Robert B.
Reynolds, John N.
Ridings, Donald E.
Russell, Clyde R.
Saehlenou, Hadley V.
Sandegren, Thomas E.
Schaetzel, George E.
Schultz, Herbert D. Jr.
Sluder, Chester L.
Strieber, Edward M.
Thomas, Jack
Trembly, Wonderful A.
Warner, Jo K.
Whitfield, Hervey, H.
Zehrung, Paul W.

Graduates October 1936

Adkinson, Bourne
Anderson Arthur R.
Anderson, George R.
Anderson, James W. Jr.
Averill, James C.
Barrett, Henry G.
Boyd, Robert
Bradshaw, John O.
Childre, Cecil H.
Coffield, Michael, J.
Couch, Alexander P.
Ferris, John M.
Funk, Ben I.
Gardner, Raymond H. Jr.
Gray, Howard W.
Howe, Charles J.
Huish, Fredrick O.
Keith, Troy
Kennedy, William J.

Kent, Billy W.
Kllgore, John R.
Kunze, Royce J.
Learned, Park R. Jr.
Leber, Harry P.
McIntyre, Patrick W.
Nelson, Charles K.
Ogden, Alban B. Jr.
Ohlke, Howard W.
Orth, Robert C.
Pharr, Marion N.
Ranney, George F.
Rohrbough, Leonard M.
Schmitt, Arthur W. Jr.
Scott, Churchill L.
Stetson, Lorling F. Jr.
Thompson, Milton E.
Todd, Jack F.
Wangeman, Herbert O.

Graduates February 1937

Blyer, Julian M.
Box, Clyde
Brogger, Jacob J.
Cochran, Philip G.
Dalton, Lloyd H. Jr.
Dillingham, Walter H.
Dubose, James R.
Eubank, William E.
Harvey, Sterling G.
Helton, Elbert
Hillery, Edward G.
Hoffeditz, Aaron H.
Hunker, Joseph F.
McDonald, Donald W.
Margrave, Thomas E.

McNown, William K.
Myers, Thornton K.
Nau, Wallace E.
Patterson, Steele R.
Perry, Norris
Phelps, James W.
Schoch, Jack L.
Snavely, Eugene H.
Tate, David A.
Theobald, Robert A.
Thorne, Henry G. Jr.
Triffy, Sam P.
Watson, Harold E.
Young, Earl B.
Zemke, Hubert

Graduates June 1937

Alison, John R.
Aynesworth, Horace D.
Baker, Ancil D.
Bastin, Henley V.
Bayse, William E.
Blakey, George A.
Bradley, Follett, Jr.
Brown, Thomas D.
Butner, Thomas L.
Bywater, Murray A.
Carr, George R.
Chickering, Edwin S.
Clancy, Charles A.
Cobb, Raymond L.
Countway, Lewis
Crowder, Murray A.
Culbertson, Allman T.
Curtice, Raymond L.
Davis, Waymond A.
Fallows, Ronald F.
Fiegel, Leland E.
Freeman, Julien W.
Godman, Henry C.
Greening, C. Ross
Hardeman, Milton L.
Hudson, Guy L.

Kauffman, Donald H.
Kegelman, Charles C.
Kellond, Arthur W.
Lorenz, Richard F.
McKay, Homer M.
Marshall, John R.
Means, Howard M.
Montgomery, Guilford R.
Moore, Frederick L.
Morris, Joseph A.
Payne, John H.
Rau, Harold J.
Reed, James O.
Robinson, George L.
Russell, Barton K.
Sewart, Harold Y.
Sprague, Wilbur B. Jr.
Stark, William B.
Stunkard, McClellan F. Jr.
Suiter, Theodore A.
Thomas, Morris E.
Thompson, Frank K.
Tokaz, Adolph E.
Viccellio, Henry
Watson, Ansley
Wilson, Delmar E.

Graduates October 1937

Agan, Arthur C. Jr.
Baker, James B.
Barrett, Everett R.
Black, Francis J.
Bleasdale, Jack W.
Caldwell, Robert M.
Calloway, Richard D.
Carlson, Arthur C. Jr.
Carr, Richard P.
Daniel, William A.

Dyess, William E.
Elder, William E.
Ewing, William G.
Field, Charles W.
Fletcher, Eugene B.
Gallagher, Francis B.
Grogan, Charles E.
Harper, Bryan B.
Hatch, Edwin H.
Heath, Victor M.

The Air Corps Training Center

requests the honor of your presence

at the Graduation Exercises

Kelly Field, Texas, October 5, 1937

Aerial Review   Exercises

9:30 A.M.   Post Theater 10:45 A.M.

Heflin, Clifford J.
Hinton, Coleman
Hughes, Jack W.
Lowery, Herman F.
Maddux, Sam, Jr.
McNickle, Marvin L.
Miller, Warren M.
Miller, Wilbur G.
Mills, Frederick W.
Olmsted, Charles T.
Paul, Joseph H.
Pelham, Morris
Peterson, Arman
Randall, Clifford
Rindom, Frank O. Jr.

Rogers, Floyd W.
Schoephoester, Melvin W.
Sutterlin, Frederick J.
Tacon, Avelin P.
Taylor, J. Francis, Jr.
Torrey, Alfred J.
Truitt, Homer M.
Tyler, Kermit A.
Voorhees, Burton K.
Warren, Roy E.
Wilhelm, Don L. Jr.
Wurzback, Clemens K.
Young, Charles H.
Younkin, William L.

Graduates March, 1938

Ames, Richard A.
Anderson, Dale L.
Armstrong, Hal B. Jr.
Atkinson, Gwen B.
Bailey, J. C.
Beverly, Ernest H.
Bowen, John C.
Brannon, Dale D.
Breathitt, James III
Calloway, Richard D.
Clark, William C.
Coupland, Don
Cowles, Ned A.
Dick, Richard D.
Edmundson, James V.
Emmens, Robert G
Feallock, William J. II
French, Donald J.
Garman, Ralph S.
Greene, George B. Jr.
Haskett, James W.
Hays, McDonald, H.
Heintz, Adam J.

Kearby, Neel E.
Keeffe, Harold M.
Kofahl, Harold E.
Konopacki, Hubert J.
Korges, Woodrow W.
Kummrow, Robert A.
McClure, Hamilton
McNickle, Melvin F.
McPherson, Clarence E.
MacNicol, George M.
Marcy, Joseph C.
Marks, Magnus B.
Martin, Kenneth R.
Mason, Robert J.
Maupin, Robert N.
Miller, Frank
Pardee, Elliot T.
Parker, Frank C. Jr.
Proxmire, Theodore S. Jr.
Pusey, Ralph L.
Ranck, Nathan H.
Reedy, Alan D.
Richardson Wayne K.

THE AIR CORPS ADVANCED FLYING SCHOOL
Kelly Field, Texas
Class No. 38-B
March - June, 1938

Rison, Whitmell T.
Sturgis, Claude C. Jr.
Taylor, Ray D.
Tibbets, Paul W. Jr.
Tobler, Jesse A.
Wanamaker, Martin E.

Wasem, Clinton C.
Watt, James R.
West, Graham W.
Waltz, Eugene C.
Zipp, Marvin S.

Graduates July, 1938

Adams, Louis Charles, Jr.
Ambrose, Joseph
Arnold, Patrick R.
Arnold, Richard, Jr.
Ashkins, Milton H.
Bacot, Henry P.
Bagby, Robert C.
Billings, Herman
Bowen, John E.
Bowie, William A.
Brenner, Francis E.
Bridges, John D.
Carr, John K.
Chalmers, Doublas
Champagne, Wilbur A.
Chick, Lewis W. Jr.
Chilton, Robert C.
Crimmins, Fred T. JR.
Cummings, William J.
Drafts, Lucius G.
Droz, Paul C.
Dunham, Earl H.
Fulcher, Richard P.
Griffin, James H.
Gurnett, Thomas E.
Hammers, Harold E.
Hampton, Edgar W.
Hebert, Alvin E.
Herder, Ralph F.
Higbee, Charles E.
Hoevet, Dean C.
Hormell, Earle, L.

James, Frank B.
Jones, David M.
Keating, Ernest W.
Kerwin, John J.
Krummes, Robert M.
Kurtz, Frank A.
LaBaw, Ralph G.
Lewis, David L.
Loe, Roy M.
Loveless, John R.
Lunde, Oswald W.
Lydon, Leonard C.
McCauley, Vernon
McNeese, George M.
MacNaughton, Franklin H.
Marett, Samuel H.
Martin, Charles H.
Meyers, Gilbert L.
Miller, Edwin B. Jr.
Moore, Joseph H.
Northcutt, Robert E.
Overing, Glendon P.
Philbrick, Richard W.
Polifka, Karl, L.
Pollard, John W.
Purinton, William R.
Putnam, Claude E. Jr.
Putnam, Walter B.
Ramage, Edwin M.
Randolph, John P.
Reed, Eliott H.
Rush, Richard F.

Sakowski, Peter C.
Scoggins, James E. Jr.
Shipley, Howard J.
Shoemaker, Francis D.
Skiles, Duane H.
Smith, Coalie F.
Stagner, Jack
Stewart, Robert R.
Stewart, William F.
Stinzi, Vernon L.
Stockdale, Charles H.
Strickland, John W.

Swenson, Raymond T.
Taylor, Broadus B.
Taylor, William E.
Wagner, Boyd D.
Wallace, David W.
Walseth, Marvin E.
Ward, Donald T.
Watkins, Harvey J.
Wells, Cecil L.
Wenrick, Stanley T.
Woolams, Jack
Yancy, William R.

Graduates October, 1938

Adams, Jack
Arnold, Walter E.
Bacon, Thomas P.
Baxter, Forrest H.
Bohnaker, William J.
Bullis, Harry J.
Bylander, Richard M.
Carlton, John N.
Casey, Edward R.
Cleveland, William H.
Cole, Perry S.
Courtney, Harold D.
DeShazo, Robert V.
Eidson, Harry T.
Eisenhart, Charles M.
Feeney, Francis R.
Fitzgerald, Maurice J.
Flack, Rudolph E.
Fountain, Willard A.
Gilbert, Huntington K.
Greasley, Philip H.
Green, Edwin S.
Hamilton, McHenry
Healy, John P.
Heinlein, Oscar A.
Holcombe, Elton E.

Hopper, Rowland W.
Howery, Allen M.
Hubbard, Glenn E.
Hubbard, Ronald D.
Kime, Duane L.
Kluever, Arnold F. A.
Knoree, Frederick J.
Knox, John M.
Lawrence, Reesor M.
Lindsay, James R.
Longino, Houston W.
Madre, John D.
Manierre, Ernest R.
Mason, Joe L.
McEntire, William E.
McGinity, Frank J.
McGowan, Leland S.
McKechnie, Robert R.
Moffett, Christopher O.
Nisbett, Charles A.
North, Charles L.
O'Brien, Frank E.
Osborn, John W.
Pinkston, Gladwyn E.
Prichard, William J.
Proctor, John P.

Quinn, Robert S.
Roberts, John A.
Robinson, Gerald G.
Rockey, Guy H.
Salzarulo, Raymond P.
Schwartz, Paul
Sharp, Frank D.
Shilling, Eriksen E.
Slayden, Van H.
Sparks, Walter W.
Starkey, James F.
Stefen, LeRoy L.
Stuart, Robert H.
Sullivan, John L.

Sullivan, William A.
Taylor, Ozburn E.
Thurman, Wayne E.
Toliver, Raymond F.
Tuell, Joseph C.
Wade, Horace M.
Walker, Arthur J.
Ward, Brewster
Welborn, Kenneth M.
Westbrook, Sam W.
Wintermute, Ira F.
Wiper, Samuel B.
Young, Sig R.
Yurkanis, Paul J.

Graduates March 1939

Armstrong, George H.
Aylesworth, Theodore R.
Babb, Harold T.
Banks, Wilson H.
Barksdale, Ralph A.
Barksdale, William S.
Barnett, James A.
Barrow, Leonard J.
Baseler, Robert L.
Beightol, Willis E.
Berry James D.
Birchard, Glen R.
Bloszies, Raymond F.
Bogan, Charles W.
Bond, Charlie R.
Bourgoin, Raoul J.
Breckenridge, John P.
Brewer, Paul M.
Brownewell, John L.
Bruce, James R.
Busch, Chester C.
Busse, Raymond J.
Camp, Marshall P.
Carmack, John E.

Carter, Roy M.
Cellini, Oliver G.
Chaffin, Harold N.
Chiles, Clarence S.
Clark, Eugene L.
Compton, Keith Karl
Coyle, Lawrence W.
Crabtree, Martin P.
Crouch, Robert E.
DeBolt, Arthur R.
Dechaene, Andre J.
DeRussy, John H.
Dick, Newton R.
Doerr, John J.
Dougherty, John E.
Dunn, Frank L.
Edwards, Albert H.
Ellison, Holden F.
Evans, John S.
Faulkner, Cecil L.
Fendrich, Charles N.
Fletcher, Thomas J.
Ford, Ernest G.
Galusha, Harry L.

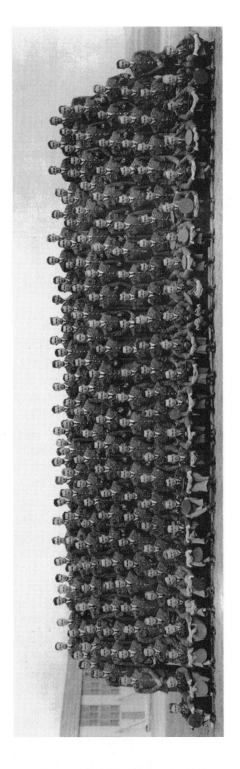

Garrett, Skidmore N.
Gayle, Charles A.
Giannatti, James
Gillum, Virgil M.
Gilmore, Jean D.
Gimble, Sidney B.
Glober, George E.
Gould, Campbell H.
Grambo, Frederick C.
Gray, Leon W.
Gustafson, Roy W.
Gutru, George H.
Hall, Byron E.
Hardy, Otha B.
Harman, Harold M.
Heber, Malcolm M.
Henry, John B.
Hindson, William S.
Holbrook, Thomas H.
Holsteen, Theodore F.
Holt, Harry J.
Howard, James Alva
Hubbard, William E.
Humfeld, Harold E.
Jackson, J. Garrett
Jarek, Frank W.
Jenkins, Harry A.
Jenkins, Jack S.
Johnson, James A.
Keiser, Donald M.
King, Henry P.
Lane, William
Lanford, William A.
Lewis, Dwight F.
Looke, Cecil J.
McCauley, Clarence V.
McClure, Byron E.
McKee, Seth J.
McNay, Joe K.
McNeal, Thomas C.
Manson, Hugh B.

Marcum, Jake M.
Marshall, Charles S.
Mathewson, Philip L.
Mayden, James D.
Momyer, William W.
Moore, Archibald W.
Moore, Paul L. G.
Morgan, Maurice A.
Morrissey, Robert L.
Mueller, Robert B.
Murrell, Carrell T.
Neely, Clarence A.
Newman, Neil A.
Oliver, Ralph L.
O'Neill, Brian
Opeil, Charles M.
Parker, Kingsbury E.
Peffer, David M.
Philbrick, Frederick N.
Potter, Philip O.
Price, Bruce B.
Randall, Heman W.
Riddle, Kyle L.
Romberg, Edgar A.
Rouse, John A.
Rowland, Robert R.
Rudell, Raymond F.
Saunders, Jack W.
Schofield, Parker F.
Schriever, Gerhard J.
Schroeck, Franklin E.
Schwind, Burton E.
Setchell, James F.
Sheffield, Charles P.
Skow, Delmer N.
Smelser, Harold C.
Smith, Joseph C.
Smith, Thomas C.
Smith, Weldon H.
Sneed, Charles R.
Spencer, Truman A.

Spurgeon, Raymond R.
Stinson, William E.
Storm, Leonard B.
Strickland, Eugene L.
Summers, Thomas B.
Swanson, William H.
Teats, Edward C.
Terry, David D.
Thornbrough, George W.
Tinker, Clarence L.
Tucker, Theodore W.
Turner, Sullins P.
Van Auken, Robert D.
Van Der Zee, John J.

Veatch, Bernard W.
Von Tungeln, Herbert A.
Waller, William III
Weltman, John W.
Whiteman, Harold J.
Willsie, Harold
Wilmot, Woodrow B.
Wilson, Harold F.
Wiltjer, Clarence P.
Wood, Curtis E.
Worley, Earl W.
Wrigglesworth, William J.
Wright, Adolf M.
Yarbrough, Eugene T.

Graduates July 1939

Alder, Glen M.
Allan, Charles O. Jr.
Anthis, Rollen H.
Ballard, Norman L.
Barham, James C.
Barnick, Roland J.
Barthelmess, Karl T.
Beard, Robert W.
Beyeler, Arnold W.
Boaz, William N.
Bowen, William J.
Bowen, William S.
Boyd, William E.
Bratton, Leslie R.
Brown, Paul D.
Carlson, Francis B.
Carpenter, Randall H.
Carter, John H.
Cate, Albert M.
Chandler, Charles G. Jr.
Clark, Donald L.
Cole, Nester E.
Conway, Ralph F.
Cook, Bailey C.

Cory, Albert
Cox, Ray L.
Cranston, George E.
Cunningham, Joseph A.
Dahberg, Charles W.
Danley, James R.
Darling, Henry B. Jr.
Davis, Allyn T.
Dech, Keith W.
DeVine, John I. Jr.
Durant, Francis H.
Durant, Leo F. Jr.
Emrick, Paul S.
Evanoff, Alexander G.
Evans, Robert C.
Exum, Wyatt P.
Ezzard, Richard F.
Fawcett, Ralph M.
Fisch, Ted B.
Folts, John L.
Franks, Perry L.
Gilbert, William F. Jr.
Gilchrist, William D.
Gordon, Michael J.

Gorman, Paul J.
Green, Franklyn T.
Gregory, Charles E.
Greiger, Harvey E.
Grossetta, Anthony V.
Habberstad, Edward C.
Hahn, Delbert H.
Harker, Ward W.
Hester, John E.
Higgins, Edward W. Jr.
Hornsby, Thomas W.
Hubbard, Harry V.
Hubbard, Thomas H.
Itz, Milford F.
Jackson, Thomas W.
Jeffrey, Thomas S. Jr.
Jones, James D.
Kelly, Joseph A.
Kittel, Robert S.
Kuhl, Philip J.
Laborde, Frederick N.
Lawrence, Samuel E. Jr.
Lichter, Carl J.
Loomis, Donald E.
Luker, James W.
McCafferty, Guy F.
McMillan, George B.
McNelly, Fred W.
MacDonald, Charles H.
MacPhee, Angus C. B.
Maney, John R.
Martin, Maurice L.
Matthews, Robert L.
Meng, Lewis B.
Milne, Jack G.
Morse, Raymond S.
Motyl, James D.
Munzenmayer, Wilmer W.
Myer, Glen A.
Newton, Dorr E. Jr.
Norris, Robert P.

Northamer, Kenneth W.
Ort, Rudolph K.
Pancake, Frank R.
Parker, Frank R. Jr.
Pike, Harry M.
Preston, Joseph J.
Ragland, Richard M.
Rector, Walter S.
Reed, William B
Reeve, Ralph A.
Rehmann, Orville H.
Riley, Harris D.
Rogers, George W.
Rosasco, Henry P.
Rozwenc, George S.
Ryan, Claire E.
Salmela, Oliver R.
Sams, Burton K.
Savoie, William F.
Schurter, Orie O.
Seymour, Rudolph R.
Simpson, John G.
Slocumb, Charles D. Jr.
Smith, Pinkham
Spieth, Harry E. Jr.
Sprankle, Kenneth W.
Stewart, Everett W.
Tarrant, Yancey S.
Tarter, Jerome
Terhune, Charles H. Jr.
Tokarz, Clemence P.
Van de Lester, John R.
Vosper, Stanley R.
Watkins, Tarleton H.
Wheeler, Ansel J.
Wheless, Hewitt T.
Whitaker, Narce
Wilkins, John C.
Williams, Adriel N.
Wood, Paul D.

Graduates October, 1939

Ainsworth, W. L.
Albin, George L.
Alexander, Donald M.
Anderson, George F.
Askew, Richard
Barnes, James H.
Bassett, Charles E.
Batchelor, Jack F.
Bennett, Donald K.
Bennink, Donald T.
Bowen, Ferrell L.
Burhus, John L.
Carragher, Francis D.
Caton, Curtis E.
Chitty, Charles D. Jr.
Clinkscales, Theodore R.
Close, Winton R.
Cofield, Curtis H.
Crow, Roger M.
Davis, Richard M.
Dittrich, Robert L
Doyle, Raymond W.
Ellis, Herbert S.
Ehret, Roland C.
Evans, John R.
Evans, Robert W.
Ford, John W.
Genovese, Joseph R.
Hall, Floyd D.
Hanes, Horace A.
Hawley, John R.
Hendrix, James M.
Herbes, Edward A.
Hoffman, Fredrick G.
Hubbard, Edward F.
Huffman, Ward G.
Jensen, Walter A.
Johnson, Vernon C.
Kidd, John L

Kinnard, Clayborne H.
Lackey, John H. Jr.
Lang, W. Howard
Lee, James L.
Leffingwell, Charles E.
Leidy, Charles A.
Lien, James O.
Lindberg, Allen
Lynnton, Keith X.
Martin, Bertram C.
McConnel, Landon E.
McCorkle, John
McElroy, Stephen D.
Merrit, Ralph L.
Moffat, William H.
Moore, Alvin N.
Moore, Malcomb A.
Musselwhite, William B.
Myers, Edward P.
Neal, Robert
Newton, Preston C.
Nowak, Albert C.
Ola, George J.
Oviatt, Karl E.
Passage, John T.
Piollet, Victor E.
Pomroy, Don A. Jr.
Porter, Stuart M.
Postlewaite, R Dean
Rains, Lawrence F.
Reed, James F.
Renshaw, Downer
Richardson, John L.
Roberts, Albert J.
Robinson, Charles G.
Ruggles, John H.
Sanders, Richard C.
Sapp, Russell H. V.
Schauer, Paul C.

Seeburger, Francis L
Selby, David C.
Shea, James H.
Sonnkalb, Charles D.
Stanton, Robert L.
Stenglein, Joseph
Stone, Rolle E.
Strathern, William E.
Strong, W.D.
Sullivan, Frank E.
Tedder, Irby V.
Thompson, Joe C.
Vereen, Lindsay, H.

Walmsley, William W.
Waltanski, Theddeus L.
Warren, Clarence N. Jr.
Watkins, Howard E.
Wertenbaker, George L., Jr.
Wheeler, Warren S.
Wilson, Keith S.
Wilson, William D.
Wood, Frank L.
Wood, George A.
Woolery, Edward R.
Wray, Robert S.

Suggested Reading

Arnold, Henry H. *GlobalMission*. New York: Harper & Bros. 1949.

Berger, Carl, ed. *The United States Air Force in Southeast Asia, 1961-1973: An Illustrated Account*, Office of Air Force History, 1984.

Coffey, Thomas M. *Hap*. New York: Viking Press, 1982. *Iron Eagle, The Turbulent Life of General Curtis LeMay*, New York: Crown Publishers, 1986.

Copp, Dewitt S. *A Few Great Captains*. New York: Doubleday & Co. 1982.

Cooling, B.F. *Air Superiority*. Center for Air Force History, 1991.

Glines, C.V. *From the Wright Brothers to the Astronauts: The Memoirs of Major General Benjamin D Foulois*. New York: McGraw-Hill, 1968.

Hansell, Heywood S. *The Air Plan That Defeated Hitler*. Atlanta: Hansell, 1972.

Mason, Herbert Molloy, Jr. *The United States Air Force. A Turbulent History*, Mason/Charter, New York, 1976.

Mitchell, William. *Memoirs of World War I: From Start to Finish of Our Greatest War*. New York: Random House, 1960.

Shiner, John F. *Foulois and the U.S. Army Air Corps, 1931-1935*.

Washington D.C: Office of Air Force History, 1983.

Weinberger, Caspar & Peter Schweizer. *The Next War*: Regenery Publishing, Washington, D.C. 1996.